Democratic Theorizing
from the Margins

Democratic Theorizing
from the Margins

MARLA BRETTSCHNEIDER

TEMPLE UNIVERSITY PRESS
Philadelphia

Temple University Press, Philadelphia 19122
Copyright © 2002 by Temple University

Cloth edition published 2002
Paper edition published 2007
Printed in the United States of America

♾ The paper used in this publication meets the requirements of the
American National Standard for Information Sciences—Permanence
of Paper for Printed Library Materials, ANSI Z39.48-1984

Library of Congress Cataloging-in-Publication Data

Brettschneider, Marla.
    Democratic theorizing from the margins / Marla Brettschneider.
      p. cm.
    Includes bibliographical references and index.
    ISBN 1-59213-654-0 (pbk: alk. paper)
    ISBN 978-1-592-13654-4 (pbk: alk. paper)
      1. Democracy—United States. 2. Minorities—United States—
Political activity. 3. Women in politics—United States. 4. Marginality,
Social—United States. I. Title.

JK1726 .B74 2002
306.2'0973—dc21   2001041448

This book is dedicated to my sisters,
Beth and Nina Brettschneider—
the people with whom I have learned
some of the most profound life-lessons
of equality across difference.

Contents

Acknowledgments

A BOOK is always a joint effort. I would like to thank Lori Marso and Pat Moynagh for their ongoing love and support with this work and so much more. Sandell Morse offered good writing tips and Laurie Zimmerman made time at a crazy point in her life to read an early draft of the manuscript. Judith Grant and Dennis Fischman gave me much-needed critical feedback that has greatly improved this book. Many still anonymous readers contributed tremendously to the development of this work and I am grateful to each of them. H. Mark Roelofs and Bertell Ollman continue to influence my thinking; you will again see much of yourselves in these pages.

Many thanks to my student assistants Raymond Jenkins, Jeremy Lamson, Matthew Tattar, and particularly Caroline Leyva, Cynthia Burns, and Paloma Bauer De La Isla. I am grateful to the wonderful students in the classes over the years in which I taught, tested, and revised many of the ideas in this book. When we study together minds edge open, hearts wrestle, the laughter helps, and theory and action join hands. The presenters, discussants, and attendees at the academic and other conferences where I presented arguments from this work also helped this to be a better book. From a deep place within me I want to thank the women and community of B'not Esh.

The Bloomsburg University Political Science Department and the Political Science Department, Women's Studies Program, and librarians at the University of New Hampshire supported me during the years I worked on this project. The University of New Hampshire College of Liberal Arts provided much-needed assistance toward the completion of this book, including a Summer Research Stipend; a grant from the Vice President for Research Discretionary Fund made it possible for me to take valuable time to write.

Doris Braendel and all those at Temple University Press and Graphic Composition have been wonderful to work with. I thank them for their vision and guidance in making this manuscript into a book.

Activists and average folk over the years have given me the content and helped me to clarify the yearnings readers will find in the following pages. May we keep beauty and kindness in the struggle, may we find peace through justice. With those fiery Jewish women: I want to dance with Emma Goldman in her revolution; I want bread *and* roses with Rose Schneiderman.

My family has been an important source of inspiration, fun, and support. My parents and grandmother help me keep my priorities in order. Dawn Rose, Paris (Peretz) Mayan, and Toni Louise (Tali Lilit) are my love and my joy. Dawn has lived through many years of this work in progress; her intellectual challenges move and sustain me. With the amazing guidance of my parents, my sisters—Beth and Nina—and I have been in a life-long process of loving, respecting, and enjoying each other as equals with the magnificent differences between us. I remember my great aunt Pauline (Epstein) Kaufman who died this day; may her memory be for a blessing.

This week, as I read through the page proofs, the Pentagon and the twin towers of the World Trade Center were demolished in violent attacks. So many lives lost. So many lives ruined. So many in mourning. Our media and senior politicians now seek to "root out" the "terrorists." I and many others seek to root out and challenge the very causes of what those in power demonize as terrorism. Central icons of the U.S. military-industrial complex have been hit. The U.S. president rallies for war. Anti-Arab and anti-Muslim hysteria soar. Average (U.S.) Americans are losing patience—yet again—with Jews, whom they see as the cause of it all. I grieve for the dead and for the loss, now and in the precarious times to come. We continue to work for peace. We continue to work for justice.

V.
New York City
September 2001
Erev Rosh Hashanah 5762

Democratic Theorizing
from the Margins

1   Introduction

TONY KUSHNER opens part two of his epic play, *Angels in America*, with a warning to us, the "pygmy children of a gigantic race," the historical inheritors of the West's grand theories:

> Alesksii Antedilluvianovich Prelapsarianov (the World's Oldest Living Bolshevik):
>
> The Great Question before us is: Are we doomed? The Great Question before us is: Will the Past release us? The Great Question before us is: Can we Change? In Time? And we all desire that Change will come.
>
> (Little pause)   (With sudden, violent passion)
>
> And *Theory*? How are we to proceed without *Theory*? What System of Thought have these Reformers to present to this mad swirling planetary disorganization, to the Inevident Welter of fact, event, phenomenon, calamity? Do they have, as we did, a beautiful Theory, as bold, as Grand, as comprehensive a construct. . . ? You can't imagine, when we first read the Classic Texts, when in the dark vexed night of our ignorance and terror the seed-words sprouted and shoved incomprehension aside. . . You who live in this Sour Little Age cannot imagine the grandeur of the prospect we gazed upon: like standing atop the highest peak in the mighty Caucasus, and viewing in one all-knowing glance the mountainous, granite order of creation. You cannot imagine it. I weep for you. (1993b, 13–14)

Yes, and we weep too. Such clarity, comprehensiveness. He asks us: "And what have you to offer now, children of this Theory? What have you to offer in its place?" We on the left will never again know such a theory. We will never have anything quite as grand. But we can know what it is like suddenly to see ourselves, we can know the power of naming our selves. We have Audre Lorde, Irena Klepfisz, Cornel West, Toni Morrison, Cherrie Moraga. For the first time in history we hear: Black, lesbian, Jewish, Chicana, poor, immigrant, slave, sick . . . poets all, and organizers, orators, prophetic voices . . . theorists.

Material from Tony Kushner, *Angels in America: A Gay Fantasia on National Themes (Part II: Perestroika)* (New York: Theatre Communications Group, 1993) appears by permission of the publisher.

1

The play's ancient, blind, and fragile figure continues:

Change? Yes, we must change, only show me the Theory, and I will be at
the barricades, show me the book of the next Beautiful Theory, and I
promise you these blind eyes will see again, just to read it, to devour that
text. Show me the words that will reorder the world, or else keep silent.
    If the snake sheds his skin before a new skin is ready, naked he will be
in the world, prey to the forces of chaos. Without his skin he will be dismantled, lose coherence and die. Have you, my little serpents, a new skin?
(1993b, 14)

Here is Alesksii Antedilluvianovich Prelapsarianov on stage. He and
his bold theory are withered and broken. How are we to respond to such
a display? How are we—inside the theatre as Kushner's audience and outside the theatre as Prelapsarianov's "little serpents"—to respond to such
a challenge? Kushner offers us a possible alternative to the Bolshevik's call
for order through a grand theory. True to *Angels in America*'s subtitle, "A
Gay Fantasia on American Themes," Kushner offers us phantasm. From
on high above the stage, with a crashing sound, an Angel appears to address a potentially new, "thirty-something" prophet. The Angel bellows:
    "The Great Work Begins: / The Messenger has arrived."
    She is speaking of Prior Walter. He is on stage lying in a bed. He's a
gay man living in New York City. Prior Walter has aids. He's annoyed
with the descending Angel. Prior's opening line, after the grand speech
by the Bolshevik, after the grand announcement by the Angel, consists
of two words:
    "Go away."
    Did you want him to say something else? What else could he say? At
the Christian millennium, he is sick and tired, alone and afraid. After
the death of grand theory, after the death of the telos, god, pure reason,
the dialectic of history, Prior Walter has been abandoned by his lover,
he has AIDS, and he has as little energy for a new prophet as he has to be
one himself. For us, Prior Walter's experience may be prophetic, but he
by himself does not have to be a prophet. This is not the "new skin" that
we need. Why? Because so many of us are in this together. Prior Walter
is not in struggle alone. We each can contribute to a new politics and to
a new political era. Because there are political *movements*, and there are
possibilities for *joint* action on a variety of scales.
    During the 1950s in the United States, Black men and women walked
together down Main Street, through their own towns run by white people

who mostly hated them. They insisted, "We will be treated with dignity." And then other women and gays and lesbians and other people of color marched through *their* towns and said, "See me and treat me with dignity." And young people said, "I will not kill." And together these groups saw that there were many connections between their oppressions and a system that drafted boys to die in an unjust war. These brave people may not have had a grand theory, but they had many compelling ideas: about freedom, and justice, and what democracy ought to stand for.[1]

Empowered with these ideas, marginalized groups in the United States began to act, to take action in historically unprecedented ways. More and more people were talking about "the movement," "true needs," "the people," and "participatory democracy." In the 1950s and 1960s, activists did not have a new set of "great works" to replace the ones Prelapsarianov had relied upon. Activists used vague reference points, searching for language, concepts, analytical frameworks, and strategies.[2] In the early stages of 1960s radicalism in Berkeley, a favorite slogan was even "the issue is not the issue" and in 1963 Betty Friedan had to name "the problem with no name." Melanie Kaye/Kantrowitz (1992, 198) reminds us, however, that in spite of the work of the sixties generation, today activists still often find it difficult to choose an appropriate and effective course of action because we are still at the beginning of a new kind of political movement in the making. She and Johnson Reagon (1983, 368) write about our insecurity, fear, and skepticism. They say that we are stumbling and we will continue to do so, but that we must take the next step and we will learn as we act.

Thus, Maria Lugones and Elizabeth Spelman, heirs of all these people who took to the streets, are able to say: "Have We Got a Theory for You!" In an article subtitled "Feminist Theory, Cultural Imperialism and the Demand for 'the Woman's Voice,' " one Hispanic and one white/Anglo woman build theory, even as they challenge it, through dialogue that is committed to honest attention to identity, power, and oppression. Here they tell us that "it matters what is said about us, who says it, and to whom it is said" (1983, 573). Aleksii Antedilluvianovich Prelapsarianov, we do not offer you a grand, all-encompassing theory . . . but we do have a theory for you. It is the people at work in ACT UP (AIDS Coalition to Unleash Power, an AIDS activist organization) or the Piedmont Peace Project (originally organized as a grassroots effort with African Americans and poor whites in South Carolina) who, even as they stumble, are giving us a theory.

In doing so, we might ask, are these activists out to obliterate the ideas and likes of Mr. Alesksii Antedilluvianovich Prelapsarianov? Although some might take Kushner's portrayal of the decaying soviet representative as a well-worn U.S. condemnation of socialism, it might better be understood as a constructive criticism of the Marxist/Leninist version of bolshevism. The theory I argue being developed in the streets by activists and grassroots organizations such as ACT UP is seen by them not as displacing Marx's ideas, exactly, but in many ways as much of a serious and much-needed critique as it is an enhancement.

It is a central assumption of this book that theory, the systematic analysis of ideas, is essential to coherent and effective political action. But despite the old Bolshevik's warning about the need for theory before action, the ideas and work of the 1960s political activists in the United States have created a new brand of theory. Diversity-based politics today stimulated by those on the margins of society is suggesting a relatively coherent form of new democratic thought. A renewed attention to diversity within the broader (U.S.) American arena has stimulated much work to reconceptualize difference. Activists, scholars, news commentators, and average citizens who may sit on a local school board are increasingly realizing that the common equation of difference with "other" has too often led to, and provided a justification for, oppression. We could say that at the root of the various moves toward what some have even termed multiculturalism[3] is the assumption of a celebration of our differences. Many of these politically salient differences are currently understood as created and nurtured through our various and intersecting communities of identification. Thus, the emergent democratic theory with which this work is concerned is a theory informed by diversity. This theory attends to issues of concern generated in the critical explorations, and in the shifting representations, of our diverse cultural identities.

Having said this, let me be clear: throughout this book I presume the importance of economic equality and issues of fair distribution. Without a fundamental transformation in the economic system no politics in this country can truly earn the right to be called democratic. By focusing on diversity politics I intend, however, to compensate for a previous omission of the political roles of difference and community-based identities in many earlier democratic and radical economic theories. Diversity politics is necessary to push us in our democratic pursuits, and it is necessary if we want to deeply challenge economic inequalities.

A radical democratic theory ought to be able to explain and to help make possible fundamental social change. Social transformation is not, however, a simple and straightforward matter. People do not just get a great idea, initiate change, oust the old paradigm, and slide into a new way of life. The fiasco that ensued during the 2000 U.S. presidential election had the nation and the world focused on the inadequacies of our electoral system. We saw for the first time in the major media that politics as usual does not even include a full, partisan-free counting of the votes cast by the bare majority of eligible voters who vote. We saw U.S. citizens in Haitian neighborhoods and numerous other minority precincts turned away from the polls. With concerted energy average citizens and elites struggled to amend the system. The flurry of activity, the numerous court cases, the constant media analysis, produced little in the way of meaningful discourse or structural change in a system plagued with inequality and discrimination. But even this is not the end of the story. Demonstrations at both the Democratic and Republican conventions were the largest we had seen in more than a generation. They gained strength and organizational momentum from the large protests of the World Trade Organization conference held earlier in Seattle. New groups and coalitions sprang up. Leftist third-party candidates such as Ralph Nader and Socialist Party candidate David McReynolds helped to revitalize activist energy. Votes cast for Nader, however, also made up more than the difference that ushered George W. Bush into the electoral college lead which made the confusion in Florida matter at all. Activists have learned not to expect linear developments. The question is how to continue to do our work and reevaluate our situations whatever the circumstances and whatever the setbacks.

On a less grandiose scale, if we pay careful attention we find that possibilities for change are created with surprising frequency. Sometimes, however, in what feels like the blink of an eye the most inspiring and radical call for action becomes a Madison Avenue marketing strategy to sell us more useless products. We need to recognize that change occurs on many levels simultaneously. Some changes will have a definitive role in the lives of ordinary people, lightening their burdens. Some of these changes can also create new problems; others can create new mechanisms for older oppressions. Even as capitalism often succeeds in commodifying newly rising voices from the very margins of society, I will argue that democratic theorists can utilize the insights and methodologies of

diversity-based politics in their vigilant critiques of oppression.[4] I wonder, however, if we can push things further. I wonder, how may diversity-
based theory resist and disrupt such potential commodification?

Part of the answer lies in the fact that this *theory* has an interestingly
reciprocal relation to activist *politics*. This new democratic theory may be
understood in the praxis tradition. Put most simply, praxis refers to theory informing and guiding action as it is created in the processes of, and
critical reflections on, action itself. This emergent political movement is
open-ended, to be tailored for specific needs as they arise. It is also struc-
tured, having both parameters and purpose. This book itself is an attempt
to keep the theoretical discussion connected to activist politics. It is also
an attempt to offer the tools of political theory to those involved in the
concrete workings of democratic practices. I hope that by offering these
tools this book can help keep the talk and the work of diversity politics
grounded in self-critical, radical aspirations for democracy. As Eloise
Buker writes, "Hollow abstractions are used to affirm such issues as
diversity, freedom, equality, and fairness without giving them sufficient
content to even make conversations about them meaningful" (1999, 5).
This book is intended to help us think clearly about the content of such
concerns, keeping our thinking about and our acting in diversity politics
meaningful.

Over forty years of grassroots activism, along with new research and
interpretation by women, people of color, those with disabilities, poor
and working-class folks, and various sexual minorities, have heightened
our critical awareness of issues related to identity. These concerns are by
no means new in Western political thought. Plato, for example, challenged his contemporaries with unorthodox ideas about women's capacities, considered foreigners to be less enlightened than Greeks, and felt
homosexual love between men to be the highest form of love. However,
since the social movements of the sixties, identity politics has become a
distinct method and theory of politics. This newer form of engagement
with identity issues in politics fundamentally transforms more traditional
approaches to identity. Diversity politics from the margins has yielded
new analyses of canonical, male, and privileged thinkers. In the process,
diversity politics has also uncovered the historical writings of some
women, nonwhites, workers, and gender/sexual boundary pushers.

What is most new in this post-1960s mode is that nondominant
groups are speaking for themselves. Previously, much of what we

learned about the lives and ideas of marginalized groups was told to us by members of dominant groups. The differences between the two show us clearly that who speaks matters. Scholars and activists from marginalized groups are now increasingly setting the terms of their inquiry. Over time new kinds of discussions are taking place, locating power and modes of resistance in more nuanced understandings of human relationship and political practices.[5]

Also new is that the point of marginalized groups speaking for themselves is to help set the terms of their own enfranchisement. Previously, when dominant groups called attention to nondominant groups, it often served to further solidify their status as "other" for the purpose of exclusion. At times open-minded citizens called for tolerance. Now democratic thought coming from the margins claims that toleration is not enough.[6] During periods of liberalization, the main model for reform aiming at inclusion presupposed that the "others" could and would assimilate to the hegemonic style, rather than allowing for reevaluation and change of the older, dominant fashions.[7] The pressure to assimilate remains strong, but the point of different forms of multiculturalism is to recognize and problematize such pressure as part of a movement of resistance and creativity. Those who have been disempowered are approaching their work in various arenas of political life with the goal of transforming those arenas as they gain access to them.

Although there is much written work on related trends of diversity, identity politics, and multiculturalism, scholars have not made a sufficient effort to bring this developing body of thought together. Despite differences among thinkers and practitioners, as well as the fact that this new mode is still emerging, we need to lay out (for theorists and other academics, students and activists) the basic parameters of an emergent form of diversity politics from the margins as democratic theory. If we have a clearer understanding of this new mode of democratic politics, then those working on diversity issues, whether in academia or on the streets, will be able to grasp its impact and direct their analyses and energies. Further, those working in the field often have trouble formulating coherent responses to critiques of a community-based politics of justice that challenges presumptions about the safety of distance, self-reliance, rational cost-benefit analysis, and neutrality. Even as activists still claim to be in need of a theory, too much of (U.S.) American democratic thought has gotten divorced from the concrete struggles that citizens face. This will not do. Democratic theory ought to serve democratic actors.

In articulating his vision of a Black identity politics as part of "a new progressive Black politics anchored in radical democracy" Michael Dyson (1995, 101) explains his project as seeking "to accent the emancipatory elements of political practice, signifying a broad emphasis on popular participation in the affairs of the citizenry." "For me," he writes, "radical democrats view issues of race, gender, sexuality, the environment, the workplace, and the like to be crucial spheres where the negotiation over identity, equality and emancipation takes place. My radical democratic principles commit me to a relentless quest for the sort of political behavior, economic arrangements, and social conditions that promote a full, productive life for the common citizenry" (1995, 197–98). Drawing on Dyson's vision, as a work in political theory, this book is intended to help us as citizens and/or members of a national community to utilize the lessons and methodologies of diversity more effectively as we work to overcome identity-based and intersecting oppressions. In the process, theory can help all those interested in exploring and establishing alternative social relations.

In this light, I found early on in my explorations that multiculturalism at its best asks us to acknowledge and explore our own identity and its constructed and multiple nature. What does it mean to say that I am a woman? How does the fact that I am Jewish change the practices through which I am gendered female? How does taking my class position, my sexuality, and my abilities seriously in politics highlight the ways that gendering some humans as female has changed over time? This is a politics that acknowledges certain cultural aspects of our lives together, and recognizes the group-based nature of contemporary social movements. In this way of understanding ourselves we see that no one has a single cultural form of identification, regardless of what individuals may prioritize at certain times. For example, one may benefit from male privilege in a sexist society, but be denied other access to privilege and social dignity due to the simultaneous workings of racism, classism, homophobia, anti-Semitism, and ableism. A person may choose to associate with a particular community as a grounding from which to innovate cultural forms and do politics even as that community will have diversity within it. Each of us has numerous points of reference in identity politics. Therefore, multiculturalism as a theory and practice is as much about acknowledging and working from the multiplicity of our communities in national politics as it is about multiplicity within communities. It is also, therefore, concerned with intersections across communities as well as the simultaneous and mutual constitution of various communal identities. In the following chapters I will explore more specifically what such a vision offers. For now, we can say that doing well what some call multicultural politics necessitates critically engaging in cultural forms and doing the politics of even one identity community in a multiply situated manner.

An historical example might best serve to demonstrate this point. AIM, a post-1960s movement of Native Americans, strove to reclaim native lands and to end harsh conditions on reservations, to secure tribal fishing rights, to protect tribal forms of spirituality, and to end general stereotyping and discrimination against Native Americans. Working with other First Peoples in the United States, "American Indians" worked to publicize and end forced sterilization of Native women and the horrific practice of stealing Native babies to put them on the illegal "white" adoption circuit. In these efforts, AIM and other groups engaged in activist politics by and on behalf of First Peoples in the territories governed by the United States. From the outside, U.S. government officials often saw "Native Americans" as a singular group with a specific laundry list of interests. Inside the movement, however, activists came from many different tribes. Respecting and working with tribal differences was also therefore important for the movement. Engagement with AIM or other such groups was often the first time many activists had worked with members of different tribes, or worked on behalf of a "Native American" collectivity at all. Further, historical differences between full-bloods and half-bloods and between different genders also played a significant part in what AIM did and did not accomplish. As AIM women came into contact with non-Native women activists and feminists, new political ideas and methods, tensions and insights emerged in both the broader Anglo-feminist movement as well as within Native American political movement. There are times when one's Apache identity is most important, times when being a half-blood most consciously affects your struggles for enfranchisement, times when being a woman in overlapping —though differently—sexist societies takes center stage. Multiculturalism as a coherent democratic theory can help us learn that we do not have to leave parts of ourselves at the door when engaging in activist, identity-informed politics. As we hone our skills as theorists of diversity, we can more fluently engage with shifting and multiple communities and political movements as members of multiple and shifting groups ourselves.

If multiculturalism is also often referred to as identity politics, then we must remember that it is about identities and it is about politics. Multiculturalism brings our critical eye to examining what factors of human experience are considered politically salient in any given cultural and historical context. Why are certain aspects of identities *politically* important in our era and culture? How and why have the terms of what is salient changed and to what ends? Diversity-based democratic theory thus questions and seeks to articulate the ways that different aspects of our identities situate us differently in power relationships over time. Now, for us in the United States, it compels us to ask what we ought to expect of citizens and others from nondominant groups in a democratic polity, and what we ought to be able to expect from those in dominant groups in our particular social context. Fluency with lessons of diversity-based democratic theory can enable us to negotiate the ways in which we are often multiply situated with respect to power given the multiple aspects of our historically situated and politically salient identities. Through the processes involved in such negotiations, we see that much in multiculturalism—as an emergent political theory—is reinterpreting such long-held core concepts as citizenship, justice, public space, equality, and freedom. Through this new attention to diversity, activists and scholars are also reviving old debates about, for example, the motivation in, and point of, politics. In addition, we find that those exploring issues of difference are often pushing historic debates forward and introducing new terms such as "cyborgs," "needs," "minoritizing and majoritizing," and "mestiza."[8] In this book we look at what minority communities mean when employing such terms and what these concepts might have to offer a new democratic theory.

METHODOLOGICAL NOTES

In this book I propose to set out the basic parameters of an emerging diversity-based democratic theory. Methodologically, then, I am interested in articulating an alternative democratic theory from the views, contributions, and experiences of those historically on the margins of society as well as those with whom they stand in solidarity. What might it mean, though, to theorize democracy specifically from the margins? Generally I understand working from the margins to indicate a sensitivity to the views, concerns, and aspirations of those on the margins of society and attempts to attend to these.

Activists and scholars have been demonstrating how previous so-called democratic theories written by privileged men served to exclude women as a group and numerous minorities from public participation in social governance.[9] They have shown how those forms of political philosophizing served to justify and also to reinforce the concrete oppression of these groups. Drawing on their work, we see that once we can articulate that concrete political problems of marginalized groups in societies classified as democratic are internally related to the form, and role, of the theories prevalent in those "democracies," we can understand such theories as problematic and in need of attention. But what kind of attention is still needed? What are some alternative approaches available to us that might help us develop further critical perspectives on, and present challenges to, such theories so intimately connected to oppression?[10]

One way to approach this project is to say that if women and oppressed minorities have been left out, let us include them. Philosophically, let us get beyond definitions of women, peoples of color (including Jews in this case), and homosexuals that essentialize them, for example, as extra-passionate, or too interested, meaning also that they are irrational or not capable of cool discernment. In the public face of the United States in this new (Christian) millennium, we all know that women and racial/ethnic/religious/gender/sexual minorities are not essentially idiots, in Platonic terms, so these groups can be included among those fit for democratic frameworks historically defined. The problem with this view of inclusion is, of course, that it retains the historical model that is problematically raced and sexed. Although we might find many useful aspects of the historical definition, a solution of enfranchisement that extends the historical category, intact, to cover previously uncovered groups does not sufficiently challenge the original model. In fact, it "covers" too much; that is, it covers over the distinct experiences of those marginalized that may destabilize the historical category and suggest alternative characteristics we now may wish to incorporate into our view of democratic membership and participation. By positing that we can include women, for example, into a theory that has been patriarchal historically ensures the continuation of patriarchy, even if now in a new form.

A second approach is to work through critique. On the one hand I could offer a critique from within, showing that one theory or another contradicts itself and therefore fails to deliver on its promise of democracy. On the other hand, I could come from outside the traditional theories to write critically about how elite men have created women and certain minorities as outside their definitions of citizenship and enfranchised members of democratic polities. The goal in this case would be to explore these traditional theories further, but now naming them as patriarchal, classist, racist, homophobic, ableist, anti-Semitic. In this case I would come to understand these theories better but in such a way that I do not ultimately accept their promise of democracy. Instead, I expose the falsehoods or hypocrisies entailed in their promises. Doing so can be very helpful for developing an alternative democratic theory. I will, however, address a drawback of this approach below.

As a third option, or even along with the above, I could work to challenge the elitist theories by directly destabilizing some of their categories, such as common distinctions between public and private. Whereas it is characteristic of Western patriarchal theory to place women as a group and many minorities in a sphere it deems outside politics, I could demonstrate that the experience of marginalized minorities and of women as a group actually is, and has been, political because the process of privileged men's defining these experiences as nonpolitical is itself a political act. This clarification ought to be helpful for activists. In all, however, these three responses leave me dissatisfied.

In the exploration of a new mode of democratic theorizing that I attempt in this work, I do not want only to understand the canonical views, to further the critique of theories that result in and/or defend oppression, or to show that elite men's acting on women and marginalized subcommunities makes them political. These are worthy methods that I will utilize at times, but for the purposes of this book as a whole they do not define my project. As described, each of these approaches remains defined in terms of the ideas and actions of privileged men. Each of these responses takes elite men, their views and experiences, as primordial. I wish to explore an alternative because I understand the liberatory potential in the various versions of the multicultural project as rooted elsewhere: here, what is primordial is groups at the margins.

In order to "theorize from" this place I begin with a concern for women and members of other groups that face oppression. I begin with a sensitivity to our lives. I begin with a commitment—which emerges from our lives—to overcome these oppressions to the extent that we can as we go along, and in a way that remains sensitive to our experiences, needs, and aspirations.[11]

I want to hear from the lives and ideas of diverse communities to see what these might have to tell us about a different sort of politics. I look to the margins so that we may talk about a democracy that, as it becomes more inclusive, is also fundamentally transformed. I seek a method that will include new groups along with some of the distinct cultural and ideological contributions of the newly included. I work to draw on the myriad discerning practices employed by marginalized groups in their political activism in order to enhance the critical capacities of a democratic polity to sort through these different potential contributions. In this book I seek to theorize democracy in a way that does not perpetuate the primacy and exclusive legitimacy of elite male viewpoints, basically delegitimizing and covering over the views of "others." I am testing models of theorizing that work toward the incorporation not only of the other people, but their views (treated critically through the process of politics over time) as well.

CRITICAL QUESTIONS

There are many challenges to this form of democratic theory. Many commentators have criticized these new theories of democracy and the critical politics of identities which generated them. Challenges to identity politics come from Conservatives, Liberals, and moderns, postmoderns, socialists, and self-critical diversity theorists.[12] Some have asked whether, in a largely antagonistic world usually hostile to nondominant groups, we need a politics based on distance? Maybe the right to be left alone is all we can really ask of democratic politics, for a politics of aid has often created new forms of dependency for the poor and disenfranchised. How can we trust a politics that promises fulfillment through identity when the dominant groups retain disproportionate power to construct our identities? Does an attention to marginalized groups mean that *any* group claiming to be marginalized, such as white/Christian supremacists, gets designated votes in the political process? Aren't we better off, given the fact of inequality, calculating costs and benefits as if we were disembodied selves, making the best of neutrality? Has this new form of thinking generated its own exclusions?

These are significant questions. In the course of this book these different questions will be highlighted. One thing we might want to be careful about is that although we may critique certain practices, we may not always want to simply argue for their opposites. For example, we will ask: if majority rule has historically kept minorities disenfranchised, can a "minoritizing" strategy alone bring about justice? The people who came by boat to the shores of the United States under horrific conditions from Vietnam became a new minority population in this country. Given their history, the circumstances of their arrival, and the clusters of needs for their communities, these Vietnamese immigrants had much work to do in order to establish themselves in the United States. What happened when a vocal portion of U.S. citizens protested the arrival of these Vietnamese refugees, speaking on behalf of the national, majority, interest? Such a new, and small minority does not have a lot of protection in a system governed by majority rule. But would the Vietnamese, and in the long run the country as a whole, be better served with a system that allowed all minorities to make policy on their own behalf? Activists and new democratic theorists must continue to engage with such challenging questions as we develop political praxis and break old modes that history has shown to stifle movements for social justice.

On another note, how can a politics that celebrates diversity make critical claims across communities? Does a democratic politics need to allow space for antidemocratic activities, such as the myriad white/Christian supremacist Web sites on the Internet or demands from antigovernment militia groups? If attempts to justify an "ethnic cleansing" use appeals to diversity, we must examine how that is possible and enhance our capacities for judging in such cases. The point of talking about a more inclusive theory is not to lose the ability to set limits. It is also not necessarily about saying in advance which particular groups or individuals should be given priority in decision making. The point of developing fluency with this mode of theorizing is to be able to discern different contexts in which respect, recognition, and democratic discussions and practices may be possible and where they are not at any given point. My hope is that the discussion in the following pages will enable participants in the political process to sort through the multilayered aspects of concern in such questions. For now, however, I will attend to an overarching critique presented by others also fundamentally concerned with overcoming oppression, but who find this form of response not only lacking but explicitly problematic.[13]

The overriding concern with the kind of democratic thought I will be discussing in the following pages is that, although at times called identity politics, it is actually a flight from politics. Some community-based thinkers look to identity and community associations as a retreat from the public world of flux and deliberation. We find some political theorists critiquing the aggressive world of agonistic, or oppositional, politics and referring to communities as harmonious. They caution against the evils of Liberalism[14] and evoke mythic notions of "home," safe-havens, in their ideal of community. In this view, multiculturalism is seen by critics as either an historically outmoded form of politics,[15] or explicitly as a reactionary foundationalism that developed merely in reaction to the disorientation of modernity. What these critics mean is that ideas of concretely bounded "communities" belong on the trash heap of modernism. They hark back to an imaginary time of essentialist notions of identity and group membership that look cozy but are, instead, oppressive and exclusionary. In the critics' view, multiculturalism is either hopelessly incapable of dealing with the difficulties of (Christian) millennial politics, or dangerously seeking a quiet, firm patch of ground amidst the dizzying superhighway of contemporary culture and knowledge production.

One of the most important articulations of this view comes from Wendy Brown, who argues that "much feminist anti-postmodernism betrays a preference for extra-political terms and practices: for Truth (unchanging, incontestable) over politics (flux, contest, instability); for certainty and security (safety, immutability, privacy) over freedom (vulnerability, publicity); for discoveries (science) over decisions (judgements); for separable subjects armed with established rights and identities over unwieldy and shifting pluralities adjudicating for themselves and their future" (1995, 37). Brown offers a clear critique of identity politics as *ressentiment*, as a politics "drap[ing] itself in powerlessness or dispossession" (1995, 45). Insofar as Brown does not mean to suggest that *ressentiment* is the basis of all leftist politics today, but that we should attend to these problems where they are,[16] those who agree with her will find much of interest in this book.

We can, and must, point to individuals, parts of movements, manifestos, and specific moments in political life that fall into *ressentiment*. At times those who seek freedom may turn toward this (Brown takes the concept from Nietzsche) "politics of reproach, rancor, moralism, and guilt" (1995, 26). In the following pages, however, I also intend to present a different understanding of diversity-based democratic theory that is as much about critique, deconstruction, and opposition as it is about construction and creation. Here we find critical discussion of harm and injury as we also find politics made toward ideals generated within the communal lives of peoples in history. Many women and members of minority communities find their identities and communal attachments empowering sources of political energy and cultural production. Unlike some others, I do not eschew the term multiculturalism. The particular view of it to be presented here is one that is neither explicitly postmodern, nor simply reactionary modernism. I hope to articulate a vision of identity that is multiple, constructed, and changing, even as it has both coherent valence in politics and meaning in people's lives. I will discuss an alternative democratic theory emerging from the margins that does relentlessly critique various forms of power in its incarnations as "possessive," "zero-sum," and the "I know I have power when I can see that I have 'power-over' you" varieties. Rather than "rejecting" power altogether, however, we will see attempts to grapple head-on with it and claim power for liberatory purposes. Rather than balkanization and an a political framework of sentiment, I find in diversity-based politics a certain internal logic of multiplicity and cross-fertilization. Theorizing from that basis leads many to principles and ethics. Moreover, theorizing from that basis leads many back to the drawing board of action when an earlier "great idea" proved disastrous once implemented.

We must address *ressentiment* and a politics of victimization, simplistic notions of home and static conceptualizations. I also find that there is far more to a diversity-based democratic theory.[17] As I will argue in the following pages, I find that critique is intricately bound with inspiration. Even songs of lamentation—usually and simultaneously—serve to strengthen. Even art depicting oppression often helps to clarify our emotions and analytic capacities for proactive politics. Discrimination weighs down heavily on the spirit of those targeted, even as historical struggles enliven individuals and communities. Many on the margins clearly recognize that their struggles have helped shape what they find to be the richness of their cultures. We also do not want to miss the celebratory and creative aspects of community-based politics. A central reason many fight for the self-determination and dignity of their peoples is because their peoples—their histories, cultures, and ways of knowing—are deemed worth fighting for.

What we often hear from those in marginalized communities with strong ties to their peoples is that "home" is not necessarily a placid, tranquil place. Actually, it is not even the static, serene idea that gives "home" a feeling of refuge for many. Home is often just the place we do a certain kind of wrangling. Sometimes struggling with members of our own communities provides enhanced avenues toward empowerment in comparison to (even similar) work done in a national arena. The wrestling[18] we do "at home" in community can often provide us with the skills, encouragement, direction, and voice we need to be effective agents in relation to other community members as well as "outside" in broader spaces for what we hope will be a more democratic politics.

A democratic theory grounded in cultural diversity seeks out insights and alternatives from myriad groups and their experiences in history. There are alternatives to rational, bureaucratic modes of welfare reformism as a model for progressive politics. In this light, some have even pointed to "enchantment." Here, artists and theorists explicitly critique the mechanistic view of politics and life that modernism promotes and that informs the postmodern critique of "multiculturalism" as a singular endeavor which amounts simply to a politics of *ressentiment*.[19] As we will discuss in later chapters, I will position aspects of what is often called multiculturalism as a diversity-based democratic theory that frequently moves out of the modernist/postmodernist impasse in academic writings with respect to politics.[20]

This is not to claim that activists have discovered an escape from co-optation and commodification. To assume this is to assume there is some radical Archimedean point, a site outside the configuration of our social constructions that is pure democracy and mutual deliberation. New, radical democratic theory needs no such outside point to do its work. So, how do we go about pursuing democratic alternatives in the midst of a messy political reality? The role of political theory here is to help us clarify the ideas we use and work from in our political lives. The premise of this book is that, the clearer we can get about the basic parameters of the new form of diversity-based democratic theory, the better we will be able to work effectively in the face of the challenges described above. For example if we prioritize overcoming oppression in our understanding of politics, we find that we must vigilantly explore the multifaceted nature and networks of oppression, both historical and current. Diversity, as it has been foregrounded by grassroots activists and academics, can keep us attuned to the power of identity, of naming ourselves, of recognition and needs as politically important categories. Many progressives in the academy and on the streets are thus exploring new strategies and methods for democratic politics, and new places to push questions of social justice. In the process they are developing new understandings of citizenship and national membership as relationships with transformative power, responsibilities, and benefits. Out of such praxis they are creating new forms of democratic theory that must be tested continually. In setting out the basic concepts and debates arising in diversity-based politics, I hope that this book can help us organize our ideas, more effectively plan our engagements, and honestly grapple with the challenges and critiques as they arise.

CHAPTER OUTLINES

In order to present a concise and coherent account of this form of democratic thought as it is emerging in the United States, this book examines the questions of the who, what, when, where, why, and how of contemporary democratic theorizing from the margins.

Chapter 2. When: History

The next chapter will introduce this emergent democratic theory in terms of the history of new social movements and the development of political ideas so that readers have a clear sense of *when*, historically, this form of democratic theory arrives as a significant force. Looking to the shift from what some have referred to as the "old left to the new left," the theory is contextualized as emerging in a cross between developments within international Marxism and traditional (U.S.) American democratic thought, and differing in certain significant respects from the French postmodernism.

Chapter 3. Who: Identity

Chapter Three will examine identity as a category of political experience to clarify debates about *who* constitutes "the people" in this new way of thinking about democracy, touted as a system of governance by, for, and of "the people." New political views of identity will be explicated through a comparison with other philosophical approaches such as postmodernism, Marxism, and modernism more broadly.

Chapter 4. What: Recognition

"*What* is it that those involved in a politics of identity are after?" will be the central question of Chapter Four. When viewed from the margins, a primary goal of politics is understood to be overcoming oppression. An analysis of such a view leads to an examination of a politics of recognition and of other aspects of politics when the "goods" of democracy are not viewed as commodities, or products to be possessed and therefore distributed by a (perhaps even generous) central authority structure. This conceptual base leads theorists to redefine central concepts in Western democratic thought, such as freedom, justice, and equality.

Chapter 5. Why: Rethinking Universals and Particulars

In the fifth chapter I will address the *why* question: why do we engage in politics? Here I offer a critique of self-interest as a dominant understanding of political motivation in Western-style democracies. I address alternatives to this mode and make an argument for breaking down the rigid boundaries democratic thinkers find between selfish and altruistic motivations. As the debate has historically occurred under the auspices of citizenship, I look closely at democratic ideas about citizens, even as I seek a politics inclusive of all members of a democratic polity, citizens or not.

Chapter 6. Where: Multiple Publics

Moving to the *where* of this diversity-based democratic theory, Chapter Six will look to multiple and subaltern (alternative local and subnational) public spaces as the site(s) of this new politics. In addition, using insights from the field of geography, I examine democratic concerns for the relationships between these sites and among subgroups within new sites. Here we will need to challenge our understandings of community itself. Despite the growing ability to see the United States at large as a complex multicultured society, problematic assumptions of homogeneity still find their way into conceptions of the subcommunities constituting the larger mosaic. A more dialectical approach to theorizing community is thus necessary in the current debate as we rethink the possibilities of democratic public spaces.

Chapter 7. How: Minoritizing and Majoritizing

In Chapter Seven I look at the *how* question of this notion of democracy. We will look critically at the normative answer to this question in democratic thought: majoritarianism. By focusing on coalitions and alternatives to majoritarian democracy as the process of politics, I will examine what contributions to possible decision making and organizational structures marginalized groups have been making in democratic thinking.

2   When: History

INTRODUCTION

OVER TIME, the national project in the United States has included testing numerous approaches to dealing with the challenges that difference poses to democracies. Using violence and propaganda to wipe out diversity, promoting the values of assimilation, or sometimes glorifying images of multiplicity all have their intertwining genealogies in U.S. history. Another interesting way to analyze how popular currents have changed is to look at the politics of shifting the boundaries between what is an acceptable difference and what are unacceptable differences among the populace. The contention between those who seek to define the parameters of national variation narrowly and those who promote openness has characterized U.S. politics from its founding period. The struggles between those already considered within the national self-image and those still outside it constitute much of what may be understood as U.S. political history. The complicated roles played by those on the inside seeking to be more inclusive and those on the outside wanting the gates opened far enough to let only them enter are part of this history as well.

This is not a book about history. Situating current struggles historically, however, will help us to understand the contexts that shaped them. Even the most innovative and spontaneous activist politics are best seen as parts of a larger dynamic exchange across space and time. Multiculturalism emerges as it does in the United States due to the particular political landscape in which it was generated. The ideas associated with it that we will be looking at in this book are in conversation with numerous other political philosophies, and most directly with those specifically promoted, attacked, fashionable, and/or frightening

Early versions of the argument presented in this chapter were prepared for delivery at a meeting of the Pennsylvania Political Science Association in Gettysburg, April 1995.

21

at the historical moment of its development. I realize that no two people would characterize an historical account in the same way. Whether as participants and/or observers, we all have our own way of understanding the connections between and priorities among complex historical circumstances.

In this chapter I offer a specific framework in order to help clarify the intellectual history of contemporary diversity politics. In offering this framework I do not claim that it is the only way to make sense of a politics emerging with insights from the margins. I do hope, however, that my rendition will appropriately orient students newer to these phenomena as well as reground readers more familiar with these historical developments. In this chapter I will treat the emergence of diversity-based politics as a new form of democratic theory as the product of two simultaneous political developments. As an outgrowth of 1960s activist politics in the United States, it can be seen as stemming from the way that changes within the (U.S.) American democratic imagination of the time cross-fertilized with an (U.S.) American response to eruptions in international leftist politics. In this chapter we will, therefore, take a brief look at each of these developments, and how they intersect. First, let us note in what ways this new form of politics from those on the margins of society must be understood in the context of the shift in leftist modernism.

FROM THE OLD TO THE NEW LEFT

Contemporary diversity-based politics is often referred to as "the new left" in relation to what came increasingly to be called "the old left." Even given the broad range of ideas and organizations, what people generally mean when employing such terms is that the old left was largely a Marxist-based movement. In this instance, class was the privileged tool of analysis for thinkers and was the organizing framework for practitioners. The fundamental shift from old to new left that occurs in both thought and practice is that class and strictly economic interpretations lose their privileged place analytically and organizationally. It is not that class or economic analysis are not significant for the new left. Instead, class and economic critiques become important lenses among many with which to identify power and inegalitarian social structures. The 1960s is the pivotal decade, at which time a form of politics emerges that looks at race and ethnicity, sex/gender, sexuality, religion, ability, and other characteristics in addition to class in order to understand and struggle against exploitation. But why did this major shift occur in this way, and why in this particular decade? It is most common to note that the rise of the "new left" comes at the time to fill a vacuum left by the utter dissolution of what then begins to be called the "old left." Let us look at this shift a bit more closely.

The "Old Left" and Its Demise

Since the 1800s, leftist politics was mostly influenced by Marxist ideology which saw class struggle as the motive force in history, and the working class as that which held the future in its hands. Despite the scathing critique of modern bourgeois society and social relations, this was a bold and optimistic theory, appealing to a grand historical narrative in the philosophical language of universals. By mid-twentieth century, however, ideologies based on grand universals came crashing down from the heavens to earth. The Western world was emerging from a scary flirtation with the grandest regime of "truth" known thus far, the Nazi form of fascism. In addition, the left was also suffering from catastrophic disillusionment about the Soviet experiment in the wake of Stalin's purges. Finally, in the realm of U.S. politics, the crisis in grand theories for liberation, and of communist theory as a vanguard among them, was aided by the right-wing hysteria of the McCarthy period. Thus, in order to understand contemporary diversity politics as an inheritor of and a step beyond the older Marxist-based left, we need to see that the breakdown in the old left was caused by two developments, one from within and one from without.

The Breakdown from Within

In Western politics, the breakdown of the old left from within is largely a result of the crisis in confidence that resulted from the historical particularities of the socialist experiment in Russia. When the Russian revolution exploded, most progressives—whether card carrying communists or more mainstream U.S. supporters of free speech—were energized with the prospect, the potential, for fundamental social change.[1] But groups such as the anarchists had always significantly disagreed with communists on certain fundamental philosophical grounds; grounds that the revolution unfortunately showed were sound. Communists believed that with a workers' revolution from below there would be a provisional dictatorship of the proletariat. Through the inevitable course of history, the state itself would eventually wither away and the populace would be left with a direct and participatory democracy. Although Marx actually writes very little about this ultimate communist society, what he does envision looks very much like what anarchists were working to put into effect.

Anarchists, however, argued that movements must have their means more solidly related to their desired ends. In this case, such a maxim meant that anarchists believed that a democratic revolution cannot rely on a dictatorship of any kind, that power amassed from above will always be violent. In the early stages of the Russian revolution, and particularly among the soviets, or workers' councils, the differences between anarchists, socialists, and communists did not keep them from being mostly (in the grand scheme of intellectual and movement histories) supportive cousins.[2] But specific historical developments and Lenin's belief in a vanguard led the Russian experiment with mass democracy down a path of its own form of despotism and expansionism. While certainly under constant international pressure to fail, Soviet leaders made explicit choices of ruthless repression. Stalin's signing a nonaggression pact with Hitler in 1939, his internal purges, forced labor camps, and secret police led many progressives, anarchists, and even long-time communists to abandon the hope they had held in the soviets and in the socialist promise of the still new Soviet Union.

The Breakdown from Without

The left within the United States had also long been under attack from outside. In the 1940s the U.S. government revived the 1919–1920 Red scare.[3] Following the newly updated Espionage Act of 1940 (with its upgraded penalties), the Smith Act, for example, was originally passed toward the end of 1940 due to concerns with domestic Nazi infiltration. The act stated that it is a crime to believe, teach, or advocate overthrow of the federal government.[4] Instead of being used against its primary original target, fascism, the Smith Act quickly came to be a major weapon in the U.S. government's fight against communism in particular and the organized left more generally. In response to anti-imperialist agitation, by the end of the decade the Smith Act was also adapted to apply in the U.S. administration of Puerto Rico.[5] In 1947, in the same month the Truman Doctrine was announced as the U.S. approach to fighting our "enemies" abroad, Truman signed Executive Order 9835 to fight our "enemies" at home. This executive order allowed the government to investigate federal employees and dismiss them if there were "reasonable grounds for belief in disloyalty" and to establish a central index of all those brought under investigation since 1939. (The order was expanded in 1951 to cover a "reasonable doubt of loyalty.") From 1947 to 1956 the U.S. federal government fired approximately 2,700 workers on these grounds, while an estimated 12,000 resigned out of fear (Anderson 1995).

By 1950 Congress had passed the Internal Security Act, more commonly known as the McCarren Act, which required organizations and members—or those "under the influence"—of the Communist Party to register with the federal government. The McCarren Act also established the Subversive Activities Control Board to undertake the investigations and allowed for the establishment of concentration camps for "subversives."[6] The Immigration and Nationality Act, also known as the McCarren-Walter Immigration Act, passed two years later, streamlined previous limitations on immigration to still over thirty provisions through which to bar new immigrants, including: the insane, narcotic drug users, homosexuals, prostitutes, communists, subversives, and those opposed to organized government. Within another two years (1954), President Eisenhower had signed the Communist Control Act, which made the Communist Party illegal, without "rights, privileges and immunities." By the time the United States got into its war against communism in Korea, Senator McCarthy had begun his investigations into the political activities of average Americans, looking to rout out the specter of communism from our national midst.

McCarthy's notorious mechanism used during the Red scare was the committee formed in the national House of Representatives on "unAmerican activities." The HUAC was originally chaired by Congressman Martin Dies of Texas and was constituted to investigate Nazi, fascist, communist, and other organizations termed "unAmerican in character."[7] By the 1950s it was instead using the lesser term "subversive," stating that the purpose of its investigations was to frame legislation appropriate for the protection of the United States and its citizens. Using the Smith Act from the 1940s, the HUAC sent the leadership of the Communist Party U.S.A. to prison and indicted over one hundred people for being communists.

Also during this period, state and local governments began requiring loyalty pledges for all employees. Anderson writes that "during the Truman administration alone, the FBI conducted 25,000 full-scale investigations; 6.5 million Americans were checked for loyalty" (1995, 11). As even entry-level political science students will point out, the perversity of the United States becoming like the enemy it is protesting is all too obvious from this vantage point in history. U.S. leaders supposedly hated the collectivism of communism. They decried what they believed to be the loss of personal liberties and expression in the Soviet Union as ideologically the greatest affront to the "American way of life" (not to mention capitalism). And yet, these men turned the United States itself into a frightened land of conformity.[8] Ironically, on the level of movement politics, Horne (1986, 149) notes that the same issues that had been popular progressive causes of the 1930s and 1940s had become the radically subversive causes in the 1950s. As subversive, however, much of this activity was becoming illegal, and the risk of democratic participation was becoming too high for too many people. An aura of silence and fear infected progressive politics in the United States at the same time that news of atrocities in the Soviet Union was reaching even committed communists. The 1950s marks this turning point, as the left was dismantled as a mass movement and new forms of participation began to germinate.

Ties between the Old Left and the New Left

Although it is popular to discuss the shift from the old left to the new left as if it were a clear break, we need to be more careful. When looking at concrete developments of historical ideas and movements, the shifts are often not so clear. It is important to understand the shift from the old to the new left so that we may understand contemporary diversity politics. We do want to see the differences between the two modes of thinking in order to explain what is new about the more recent ideas and actions in this form of democratic participation. However, the two periods are actually quite intertwined through individuals, ideas, and organization in ways that must also be understood.

The civil rights movement, for example, was a significant part of what came to be called the new left. Although cast in popular history as a 1960s phenomenon, the civil rights movement actually has deep roots in the United States, gaining new ground in the 1940s and escalating further in the 1950s. As another example, in 1956, socialist and communist leaders were already holding meetings to discuss reviving the left, and the *National Guardian* published an article titled "The New Left: What Should It Look Like?" This was the first time the term the "new left" was used in print (Anderson 1995, 60). In January/February of 1960, the *New Left Review* was first published in Britain. In that first year of publication, C. Wright Mills wrote that people should look to the younger generation for the future of leftist politics. It was also leading figures of the old left such as C. W. Mills, Albert Camus, and Erich Fromm who are often said to have been primary intellectual influences on the Port Huron statement drafted by Tom Hayden for SDS (Students for a Democratic Society). The early student protests of 1960 at Berkeley were actually targeted against the HUAC, then developed into the Free Speech Movement, and later into the anti-war and other movements discussed below (Morgan 1991, 111–12; Viorst 1979, 173). Further, some might say that the beats of the 1950s gave a cultural and antiestablishment cast to progressive political movements that would come to characterize 1960s activism (Rothman and Lichter 1982, 8).

Having said all this, however, it will help us more to look to the communities of activists instrumental in the shift from the old left period to the new left. The main way to do so is to notice a little-discussed facet of the McCarthy period: minorities in the United States were targeted under the Red scare far beyond their percentages relative to the majority population. For example, U.S. homosexuals, Jews, Blacks, and Puerto Ricans, as well as indigenous people and Pacific Islanders in Hawaii, bore a disproportionate share of the burden of domestic repression during this period. The Red scare marked a period of intense repression of anyone presumed to be queer. In Hawaii, an older anti-Japanese racism converged after World War II with nonwhites there characterized as dangerous communist agitators. On the mainland, Blacks and Jews were disproportionately "screened" from numerous unions, the majority of federal employees questioned in the loyalty investigations were Black and/or Jewish, and nearly half of the communist leaders actually tried for violation of the Smith Act in 1947 were Jewish.[9] A race-conscious analysis of the period reveals that the Red scare was a particular avenue for vicious racism and anti-Semitism, which ended up protecting the Ku Klux Klan and domestic fascist activity. In a telling "coincidence" of 1950, W.E.B. Du Bois was ordered by the Department of Justice to register as a foreign agent on the same day that the Rosenbergs were indicted on charges of espionage.

Women and minorities have long been active politically in the United States, but before the 1960s rise of community- and identity-based social movements, much of gender and minority activity occurred through the labor movement. Minorities long marginalized in (U.S.) American political life not only had more need of radical movements working against injustice, they also had less reason to believe U.S. myths of a nation merrily pursuing its individual and collective freedom, equality, and happiness. The image of the United States as simply the great defender of democracy and all that is good, and communism as the harbinger of all that is despotic, understandably held less sway among marginalized minorities than among others more likely to participate in the benefits of the national myth.

As Horne writes about African Americans of the period, "Blacks had less cold war fever than whites, fewer supported the major policies of the period, i.e.: the Marshall Plan, Truman Doctrine, aid to Greece and Turkey, they were less concerned about communist parties in Western Europe and less hostile to the Soviet Union" (1986, 2). A much higher percentage of American Jews (32 percent) originally reported "warm feelings for the Soviet Union" than non-Jews (13 percent) in the United States.[10] In post–World War II Hawaii, the native Hawaiians, Japanese, and Filipina/o immigrants—many with ties to the Communist Party—formed the core of a strong and centralized labor movement. In fact, in the first labor strike after the war, in 1946 twenty-one thousand workers on sugar plantations in Hawaii went on strike. The majority of the workers were of Asian ancestry, and Bell writes that "Non-Caucasian ethnic groups tended to sympathize with the strikers and supported the strike with financial contributions" (1984, 140). Further and importantly, at least until the heat of the McCarthy period, this tendency of women and minorities to support "radical" and labor groups often cut across class lines. While the labor movement supported the emerging civil rights movement, until the devastation of the Red scare there were more dues paying Black members in the labor movement than there were in the NAACP. Progressives and radicals were among the founders of pre–cold war, relatively mainstream, communal civil rights organizations such as the Urban League, the American Jewish Congress, and the American Civil Liberties Union. It was socialist W.E.B. Du Bois who founded the NAACP, and Du Bois himself is mentioned by 1960s civil rights activists for his influence more than any other individual figure. Anticipating language that would become popular in the 1960s, Ralph Bunche (a figure central to the 1950s growing civil rights movement) referred to the influence of the 1930s and 1940s as that of a "cultural democracy movement" (Keppel 1995).

Among minority activists, the change from old left to new left was far more a subtle shifting than a radical break. Some point to the unusual situation of a disproportionately high representation of Jewish activists in the old left, while the majority of early new left founders of SDS were also Jewish.[11] It is reported that both the radical Jewish and Black students of the 1960s tended to come from liberal to radical homes (most from families that were at least against the anticommunist craze) and were basically supported—even if they often disagreed on tactics— in their work by parents and other family members. Studies of the generational politics of the civil rights movement also show that Black parents were most often proud of their kids at the sit-ins at Greensboro and other Southern towns. Given the importance of student movement to the new left, it is also significant that Jewish faculty were more supportive of student protests than were non-Jewish faculty. As Rothman and Lichter (1982, 82) describe it, those educated in the old left were there to give support to the young activists of the new left.

The measures taken by defenders of the status quo and more explicit reactionaries also linked the old and new left. In Hawaiian politics after World War II, party alignments were heavily affected by the overlap of labor and nonwhite ethnic groups in the Democratic Party, and anticommunist whites controlling the Republican Party. A primary point of contention in the debate over Hawaiian statehood was whether statehood could be the tool to break the communist leanings among the nonwhites in Hawaii, or whether the United States should first wipe out communist influences before granting statehood (Bell 1984). Moving to the U.S. South, anticommunist measures intended for international use were employed by white racists against newly rising civil rights activism (e.g., the Internal Security Act; Horne 1986, 227). This is because the new movements were definitively grounded within the structures of the old. Du Bois, the National Negro Congress, and other early civil rights groups connected U.S. policies abroad to domestic race issues. Du Bois's 1950 New York senate campaign theme was "Peace and Civil Rights," which also targeted a nascent antinuclear movement that likewise came under attack from the HUAC.[12] His partners on the American Labor Party ticket were far more diverse than those from the two mainstream parties, and this smaller third party was home to more women and Puerto Ricans than other official party outlets. Other well-known early civil rights voices also demonstrated this multiply oriented outlook that connected various social justice issues. For example, Lorraine Hansberry, famous as a civil rights leader by her twenties for her prize-winning play *A Raisin in the Sun*, was also a communist, a peace activist, and a vocal supporter of both women's and homosexual rights.

Given the multi-layered platform of (U.S.) socialist activism in the 1950s—which targeted not only labor and economic exploitation, but also women's issues, peace and antinuclear policies, anti-Semitism and antiracism—government officials sought to break the bonds between the movements. Extreme pressure was placed on minority and civil rights organizations to join in the anticommunist campaign. Threats of increased racism and anti-Semitism were made if minorities did not distinguish themselves from communist influence, and do so publicly. Fearing existing prejudice and its rise, over time most of these groups acquiesced in varying degrees. They came to sever economic issues from civil rights analysis and to abandon a broader notion of civil liberties for a more narrow concept of civil rights (Svonkin 1997). The NAACP began to purge socialists and those under suspicion of being communists (including Du Bois, the organization's founder, in 1948). The three large Jewish civil rights organizations—the American Jewish Congress, the Anti-Defamation League, and the American Jewish Committee—declared communism now an anathema to Jewish interests and cut ties to a number of other Jewish organizations blacklisted for being communist fronts. The American Civil Liberties Union conducted an internal purge, ousting leaders such as Elizabeth Gurley Flynn and refusing to support those under attack for being communist such as Du Bois. Even labor unions purged their socialist and communist members (see Horne 1986, Svonkin 1997).

The U.S. government also needed to sever the ties between the United States and international peace movements that socialists and civil rights activists had developed. Using anticommunist legislation, the government curtailed the flow of travel, literature, mail, and other forms of exchange in order to isolate U.S. activities from allies and support abroad. While in the 1940s the old left worked to internationalize the U.S. struggles for racial equality and social justice, the anticommunist climate worked from within and without to change this situation.

For example, the National Negro Congress sent a petition to the United Nations titled "An Appeal to the World: A Statement on the Denial of Human Rights to Minorities in the Case of Citizens of Negro descent in the United States of America and an Appeal to the United Nations for Redress." This petition created a tremendous stir domestically, as U.S. racism was embarrassing the U.S. in its foreign policies. U.S. leaders feared that those making racism in the United States an international issue were contributing to the fact that the U.S. was losing the third world to the Soviet Union (see Horne 1986, Svonkin 1997). Part of the public relations problem for the United States on these issues was that in the 1940s the USSR was doing more publicly on the international front to stand by minorities. It was the Soviet Union that actually brought the Negro Congress petition before the United Nations; the Soviet Union was also a stronger supporter of independence for the emerging state of Israel than was the United States. By the Korean War, integration of African Americans into the U.S. army was the subject of much self-serving media attention; within Black communities, however, many wondered why they did not enjoy basic civil rights at home, but were sent abroad to kill other people in the name of democracy.

But policies in the Soviet Union and the United States would change this orientation. Over time, news of racism within the Soviet Union was publicized, and the American Jewish community also responded to reports of the repression of Soviet Jews and the USSR's turning against the new state of Israel. In the eyes of many (particularly younger) U.S. citizens, the USSR's Berlin blockade set up the Soviet Union as the unjust, and the young John F. Kennedy as the symbol of international democracy. If U.S. progressives and radicals still saw the need for change domestically, they no longer viewed the Soviet experiment as utopian. By 1968, as U.S. police were beating up demonstrators in Chicago, Soviet soldiers were beating up Czechoslovakian citizens in Prague.[13] Further, one could argue that the new left's emphasis on decentralization was as much a reaction to notions of Soviet and old left bureaucracy as it was against postwar U.S. bureaucratization and alienation.[14]

Despite its many contributions as a theory seeking to overcome oppression, class-based theory was being broken down by influences from within and without as a paradigmatic analysis of oppression and power. Domestic anticommunist pressure was extreme. Looking to the breakdown of the U.S. left, leading French intellectual Jean-Paul Sartre exclaimed, "Watch out, America has the rabies" (cited in Anderson 1995, 14). Although France still had an active communist party, the spirit of student revolts was as much alive in Paris as in New York. Millions of French students and workers staged sit-down strikes across the country.[15] In Paris, poststructuralism/postmodernism became the major response to this breakdown in the international communist old left. Michel Foucault, Jean-François Lyotard, and others called all grand narratives oppressive, and named identity and truth as social constructions. A new generation of radicals diligently deconstructed social institutions and ideas (for the most part) without trying to reconstruct them, claiming such building would end in new discourses of power.

Later, when these works were translated into English, postmodernism helped move progressive praxis in the United States. In later chapters we will also, therefore, look to the ways in which postmodernism and multiculturalism both cross and diverge. For now, however, let me merely suggest that the new generation in the United States, traditionally less philosophically inclined than their continental peers, took to the streets first, stimulated by broad ideas about freedom and the inadequacy of Marx's faith in the revolutionary potential of the working class. But the question we must now turn to is: how can we understand this change within the historical context of the development of democratic ideas within the United States?

DIVERSITY IN THE (U.S.) AMERICAN DEMOCRATIC IMAGINATION

With such a heterogeneous population, one of the distinguishing factors of (U.S.) American political history has been the constant grappling with the challenges of difference to a well-constructed union. In the founding period, the signers of the Declaration of Independence and the framers of the Constitution were engaged in debates about representation and issues of race, class, religion, gender, and ethnicity.[16] In the first century of its existence, the republic continued to battle over these concerns, at times literally. The nineteenth century was the century of the Civil War and the demise of Reconstruction, of westward and southward expansionism, of more genocidal policies toward Native Americans, of the suffrage movement and debates over poll taxes and literacy tests at voting sites. These struggles raged on through the twentieth century, generating new responses to the challenge of diversity in the United States and bringing us to the specific, domestic ideological conditions from which a multicultural engagement with diversity and democracy grows.

This is not the place to offer a long historical account of racist and sexist practices and responses in the U.S. tradition. The injustices of the slave trade, genocidal policies toward the native populations, indentured servitude, and the lack of basic civil rights also for women, Jews, Japanese, and others who did not fit the Anglo-Christian norm stand alongside the revolutionary fight against the injustices the colonial elite suffered under British rule. Basically, our grand national and state-level documents stand as evidence that U.S. democracy is founded in exclusion and prejudice as much as it is founded in an elite aspiration for rights and freedoms. The following discussion traces the historical context for three basic responses to difference in (U.S.) American democratic thinking central to developments in the twentieth century that most directly influence contemporary diversity politics. The three responses are: the *melting pot* version of assimilation, *pluralism*'s break that allowed for more cultural diversity, and *multiculturalism*'s embrace of diversity and critique of assimilationism in both the melting pot and pluralist forms.

Factions, Melting Pots, and U.S. Diversity into the Twentieth Century

It is common for critical historians to argue about which set of tensions more deeply characterizes the (U.S.) American national foundation, north-south or east-west. Grounded in the catastrophic U.S. Civil War, the north-south divide casts race, on the scale of black and white, as the main prism through which to see (U.S.) America's heart. The east-west line, which is based in Frontier mythology, presents culture and colonialist expansionism as the defining feature of (U.S.) America's political imagination. If our founding documents such as the Declaration of Independence and the Constitution most clearly represent north-south debates about slavery, then the notion of Manifest Destiny and the Monroe Doctrine (by the 1840s extended also to Hawaii) form the foundation of the policy of westward expansion. Frederick Jackson Turner's nineteenth-century thesis, "The Significance of the Frontier in American History" (Turner 1893), serves as a major written representation of the ideology involved in westward expansionism. As numerous cultural practices, laws, and even the census are often cited as defining the racial norm as white against Black, Turner's work is often acknowledged for its discussion of the creation of the new "American" man on the frontier through his encounter with and difference from the "savagery" of the natives.

Trying to make sense of the relationship between these two grids, some would say that insofar as difference in the United States can be left on an ethnic, cultural plane, we will be capable of meeting democratic aspirations of an inclusive polity.[17] None of these approaches alone, however, can help us grasp the broad-based nature of exclusionary thinking and practices. Further, aside from positing a vague extension of Manifest Destiny, neither the north-south nor the east-west theories can adequately explain how U.S. imperialism with respect to "nearby" island cultures (such as Puerto Rico, Cuba, Hawaii, Guam, Samoa, the Philippines, etc.) has been inherently related to the creation of an "American" identity. Numerous historical experiences crossed with antisemitism, sexism, and homophobia as the United States, being a modern nation-state, has attempted to invent and reinvent itself over time: the conquest of indigenous peoples, how this conquest is complicated in the twentieth century with U.S. expansionism to the south and into various island peoples, the forced influx of slaves from Africa, the servitude of Chinese immigrants, as well as the indignities and exploitation faced by immigrants who were not Anglo or Protestant, and more recent anti-Arabism.

Although originating from what was in fact a blend of Northern European Christian cultures,[18] U.S. policies and norms from the founding period to the early twentieth century set strict limits on what additional differences would be allowed to meld into the grand narrative that was the developing national image and way of life. Assimilation was in practice the only mode to incorporate difference. If you were deemed "too different" to assimilate, your lot was to remain officially at the margins. Thomas Hobbes, the seventeenth-century Liberal British political philosopher, best characterizes this approach when he writes about compleasance, what he terms a fifth law of nature.[19] Hobbes notes that there is a natural diversity among men, but that individuals must accommodate themselves to what is necessary for society. (As will be critically addressed in later chapters, questions regarding the politics of *who* deems *what* is necessary and according to *which* standards—as well as how, where, and why—would have appeared self evident to Hobbes as disinterested, rational considerations by men capable of discerning them.)

Hobbes calls those who observe the fundamental law of compleasance, of accommodation to the rest, sociable. Those who do not are called stubborn, insociable, and intractable. Those who cannot be corrected to fit into a certain mold are to be cast out of society as too cumbersome; they themselves are "guilty of the warre that thereupon is to follow."

U.S. founding father James Madison placed Hobbes's approach to diversity into a U.S. context, inscribing it constitutionally as well as intellectually. In his famous defense of the proposed Constitution, Madison wrote in *Federalist Paper* 10: "Among the numerous advantages promised by a well-constructed Union, none deserves to be more accurately developed than its tendency to break and control the violence of faction. The friend of popular governments never finds himself so much alarmed for their character and fate as when he contemplates their propensity to this dangerous vice." Like Hobbes, Madison also finds difference natural, as he writes, "the latent causes of faction are thus sown in the nature of man." Madison then explicitly grounds "the most common and durable source of factions [in the] verious [sic] and unequal distribution of property," between "those who hold and those who are without property." Thus, since this country's conception, diversity and group interests have been cast as that which introduces "instability, injustice, and confusion" into our "public councils." Differences among the people have been marked as a "mortal disease under which popular governments have everywhere perished," and "the favorite and fruitful topics" of "the adversaries of liberty." Group difference and the expression thereof was meant to be broken at all costs, and those who favor diversity were labeled the enemy. Thus, wiping out difference, slavery, segregation policies, and legalized discrimination were the primary responses to the majority of people inhabiting U.S. territories.

At the turn of the twentieth century, when the United States was faced with yet another large-scale diversity challenge, a name was given to this version of Liberalism's response to difference. It was a Jewish playwright from England who introduced the term *melting pot* into the (U.S.) American vocabulary. Zangwill's 1908 play by that name was set in the then current conditions in the United States. Although a pivotal time for U.S. colonialism in Hawaii and Puerto Rico, the relatively brief period from the 1880s to 1920 saw the country absorb millions of new (predominantly European) immigrants on the mainland.[20] As the Anglo-Christian tradition in the United States had within it a framework of struggling to include ethnic diversity among Northern European Christians, the most promising avenue for including the new arrivals was within the ethnic/immigrant mode. The melting pot concept focuses on that which will be included. The method of inclusion in this mode is wholesale assimilation. In keeping with the basic Madisonian response to difference that "faction," or a natural group-based diversity, is the greatest threat to a well-constructed union, the first twentieth-century response, known by the metaphor of the melting pot, reflected a perceived need to melt away all differences in order to "naturalize" the new immigrants. The melting pot concept demanded sameness across the board, encompassing both personal-cultural and public-civic characteristics.[21]

Within this rubric, certain groups had more possibilities than others to become enfranchised. The closer one was to the cultures of white, Northern European, Christian peoples, the more likely one (as an individual and as a member of a group) was to be pressured to, and to ultimately, give up other remaining ethnic and cultural distinctions as the price of entry into the recognized (U.S.) American public.[22] Attitudes about which differences were too different to be allowed assimilation were encoded legally from the earliest days of the republic. As Rogin points out, marriage across ethnic and religious lines has symbolized the making of "Americans" (1996, 8). But even this method of assimilation has actually been distinctly bounded. Twenty-four states forbade white-Black intermarriage until the 1967 Supreme Court decision in *Loving v. Virginia*.[23] As another example, within the first years of the country's existence, the new government passed the Naturalization Law of 1790, which denied citizenship to foreign-born people of color. One example of gender crossing with such racism was that if a woman with U.S. citizenship married a foreigner, she forfeited her citizenship.

A brief comparison of Irish and other European immigrants to the East Coast and Asian immigrants to the West Coast in the nineteenth century may be seen to represent the capacity of what will be celebrated as "America the melting pot" in the early twentieth century. By 1850, the working class in the United States was mostly foreign born. A wave of immigration of Chinese men in the early 1850s served the demand for underpaid labor that the gold-rush and industrial booms created in the new West. The influx of Chinese workers also set off a series of anti-Chinese legislation, including the Foreign Miners' Tax. The newly invested state of California's constitution included numerous discriminatory policies against the Chinese. Further, the federal Chinese Exclusion Act of 1882 made Chinese immigrants ineligible for citizenship, slowed down Chinese immigration, and barred the reunification of Chinese families by denying Chinese men in the United States the right to bring over their wives.[24] The racial, cultural, and religious differences between Chinese immigrants and the U.S. European Christian norm proved too great for this group to be added to the melting pot. The Chinese immigrants were cast as too different for an assimilationist approach. As will be discussed in greater length in Chapter Five, they remained outside the bounds of even the supposedly universal concept of citizenship.[25]

The majority of the foreign-born working class of this period, however, was clustered in the East and came from Ireland. Due to the position of the Irish working classes in the British empire, what might be seen today as the classic white-skinned Irish person was cast in U.S. politics as colored. The immigrants were called sometimes the Black Irish, or white Negroes. For the vast majority of Irish immigrants, life was harsh and discrimination and violence the norm. If, however, Protestant (U.S.) America was going to expand its conception of "acceptable difference," then Catholics would eventually be recognized as, at least, Christians. And the Irish are, after all, Northern Europeans.[26] By the end of the nineteenth century, when more "olive-skinned" Europeans came from southern and eastern Europe, the Irish slowly began to be considered *comparatively* white. As time passed into the twentieth century, southern Italian immigrants, largely Catholic and therefore capable of falling under a Christian U.S. self-image, for example, gained access to white privilege more smoothly than Jewish immigrants from Europe who arrived around the same time.[27]

But the immigrant story (especially its more often discussed European version on the U.S. East Coast) runs parallel to, only at times intersecting with, the incorporation of peoples of Spanish and native descent from territories the United States acquired in its colonial conquest in the Americas. Most often noted as victims of the European conquest are Native Americans (at times self-identified as American Indians, Indigenous Peoples, or First Peoples). Although Natives had been subject to a multisided genocidal policy (killing by outright massacre and disease, and forced assimilation) since the first Europeans came to the Western Hemisphere, the assimilationist mode did not become distinctly dominant until the 1870s. At this time Natives *as* natives were cast by white

Christians as beneath contempt, but if removed from native culture and brought up as Christian "Americans," these people could be brought into "society."[28]

Native American tribes, however, are not the only indigenous peoples upon whom the United States descended. Native peoples in Hawaii and Alaska fell victim to U.S. expansionism as well. Further, despite late-twentieth-century racialized news stories of an endless stream of illegal immigrants arriving from Mexico, much of Chicano/a (Mexican American) culture has not been an immigrant culture, but emerges from communities long living in areas that the United States has come to claim as its own through war. As U.S. expansionism moves into the Pacific and Caribbean, the United States takes over additional territories, making places such as American Samoa and Guam U.S. protectorates, and Puerto Rico a commonwealth.

Kymlicka's work explicitly challenges the work of Glazer and others who rely on the myth of the United States as the land of immigrants. He points out that even within the formal legal arena, the official response of the U.S. government to these new and diverse peoples incorporated into its jurisdiction was to aim at diluting the power of these minority populations as distinct collectivities. Kymlicka writes that many other countries use a federalist system to "accommodate national diversity" through which the distinctive collective rights and powers of national minorities are respected:

> In the United States, however, a deliberate decision was made not to use federalism to accommodate the self-government rights of national minorities. It would have been quite possible in the nineteenth century to create states dominated by the Navaho, for example, or by Chicanos, Puerto Ricans, and native Hawaiians. At the time these groups were incorporated into the United States, they formed majorities in their homelands. However, a deliberate decision was made not to accept any territory as a state unless these national groups were outnumbered. (1995, 28–29)

Related to issues we will discuss later in this book, Kymlicka offers examples of how this was accomplished. He continues, "In some cases, this was achieved by drawing boundaries so that Indian tribes or Hispanic groups were outnumbered (Florida). In other cases, it was achieved by delaying statehood until anglophone settlers swamped the older inhabitants (e.g. Hawaii and the south-west). In cases where the national minority was not likely to be outnumbered, a new type of non-federal political unit was created, such as the 'commonwealth' of Puerto Rico, or the 'Protectorate' of Guam" (1995, 29).[29]

Pluralism and U.S. Diversity at Midcentury

Scholars and the defenders of democracy might have difficulty grasping a framework which would apply to the histories of both the East and West coasts, the Midwest and Southwest, African slaves, natives and European and Asian immigrants. But, interestingly enough, those against democracy seem to have had little trouble understanding the connections. For example, in the twentieth century, Adolf Hitler himself praised the American form of Lebensraum, whereby we expanded over the native lands and peoples as he intended to do over Eastern Europe. Hitler studied the racially based nature of U.S. citizenship and the race-based 1924 U.S. Immigration Act. In *Mein Kampf,* Hitler singled out the United States and its racial policies as *the* model after which Nazi Germany should construct itself.[30] Hitler's interest in U.S. policies was reinforced immediately upon our entry in to World War II. The United States entered the war on December 8, 1941, the day after the Japanese launched a surprise attack and bombed the U.S. naval base in Pearl Harbor. Within hours the FBI had arrested nearly 1,300 Japanese community leaders. The numbers arrested kept growing, and within two months' time President F. D. Roosevelt signed Executive Order 9066, the first in a series of policies put into effect to round up and intern Japanese residents and U.S. citizens of Japanese descent. Through these policies, nearly 120,000 people (more than half of whom were U.S. citizens) were forcibly removed from their homes and were concentrated in policed camps. Those individuals obtaining leaves through the programs initiated in 1942 remained as registered persons. The last camps were not officially closed until March 1946, immediately prior to the escalation of U.S. anticommunist sentiment and legislation.[31] Friends of democracy must take notice: if fascists and dictators are studying and praising U.S. policies, then we have both a lot to be held accountable for and much further to go in our quest for democracy.

The economic boom for certain segments of the U.S. population following the war, however, contributed to the postwar self-images of (U.S.) America as both distributor of largesse and as "leader of the free world." By this time, theories based on the inadequacies of the assimilationist melting pot response to difference gained currency. Even as the cold war was born and domestic anticommunism revived (as will be discussed in the next chapter), pluralism emerged out of the mainstream critique that an emphasis on (at least cultural) sameness was unnecessary for "American democracy." Trying to distinguish itself from totalitarian regimes then known to have murdered millions of people for their difference, the U.S. promoted a vision of itself as the colorful land of many peoples, living together harmoniously under Liberal democracy.

By distinguishing between what it called private and (*politically* relevant) public aspects of diverse group life, the pluralist idea marked a move toward the incorporation of difference. Pluralism did not demand a complete homogenization, only assimilation in public. It called cultural characteristics "private" matters and celebrated the varieties of (U.S.) American subcommunities. In what it considered the public realms of politics, law, and economics, pluralism demanded an "American" citizenry unified in its commitment to Liberalism, the rule of law, and the basic principles of free-market capitalism.[32] As much of this book will be concerned with the specific response of multiculturalism to the perspective of pluralism, I will not engage a deep analysis of pluralism at this time. I will, however, offer what I find to be a most poignant illustration of pluralism as a midcentury development and its contradictions.

Although Horace Kallen is credited with introducing the term "cultural pluralism," its academic roots extend back to a little-known social scientist named A. F. Bentley, and it was truly put on the map as an ideology by democratic theorist Robert Dahl.[33] In 1908 Bentley published a book called *The Process of Government*. It marked a shift in political analysis from traditional studies of the three formal branches of government and the grand documents. Bentley said we must study groups and their dynamics if we want to understand the process of government. Beginning around the same time, and increasingly into the pre–cold war era, mainstream minority and civil rights groups emerged, forming what those involved later during the 1940s and 1950s would refer to as the "intergroup relations movement."

The broad range of organizations involved developed an ideology that posed "membership in a group—conceived in terms of race, religion, or ethnicity—[as] . . . a meaningful (or even the best) way to understand individuals' relation to one another and to their society" (Svonkin, 1997, 5). As discussed above, with increasing pressure to disassociate from "communism" and therefore from class analysis, the mainstream groups focused less and less on the economic causes of racial discrimination, and worked less on labor-related and systemwide civil rights issues. More mainstream communal organizations began to define "groupness" according to cultural identity rather than to "class" and class conflict.[34]

It was during the height of the intergroup relations movement that political scientist David Truman revived Bentley's analysis in his similarly titled book, *The Governmental Process*, published in 1951. At the time of Truman's publication, the intergroup relations movement had been through a number of strategies aimed at reducing prejudice and enhancing civil rights. In these early days of the midcentury Red scare, most of these groups had begun to be targeted, but were still able to publicly resist anticommunist pressures. Thus, the ideas for a group-based interpretation of U.S. American politics had begun to circulate widely when a young Robert Dahl embarked on his important and ultimately influential study of city politics in New Haven published as a book called *Who Governs?* By the 1960s, however, when Dahl's work was published, what remained of mainstream minority and civil rights groups were advancing a campaign for civil rights practically devoid of analyses of fundamental power structures and economic exploitation.

As his title makes plain, Dahl had a primary thesis question: Who governs? By using the small city of New Haven as a case study, Dahl hoped to examine the intricate workings of the political process. The larger import of his study would be that if he could answer the question "Who governs New Haven," he would, by implication, be able to tell us who governs the nation as a whole.[35] This interest in figuring out who governs is significant in light of the discussion above on the pivotal decade of the 1950s in terms of the demise of the old left in the United States. For although Dahl was a critical thinker and was obviously concerned with injustice, he writes at a time when the left is in disarray. Without participating in simplistic anti-Red mania, Dahl, as demonstrated in his later works as well, does not find the answers to the questions of democracy in European-style socialism. Further, as an offshoot of socialist analysis, elite theories were also popular at the time, arguing that U.S. politics is run by a wealthy elite. Both socialist and elitist critiques called into question the U.S. claim to be a democracy and thus threatened our (particularly) postwar self-image. However, Dahl's study of groups in New Haven (along with the companion volumes from the same data set) arrived at conclusions different from those of elite theorists. It will be these conclusions that capture the heart of mainstream "America" at midcentury, providing a new conception of this as a democratic nation enhanced by its cultural—if not political—diversity.

From a detailed analysis of Yankees, Italians, Jews, Blacks, and various ethnic and other groups (and despite the fact that Dahl is clear that Blacks, for example, are disadvantaged and that the wealthier the group the more influence it has), Dahl concluded that no one group governs New Haven. Instead he offers a portrait of complex intergroup struggles: sometimes certain groups or clusters of interests come out on top, other times different interests win. This is the key to the pluralist self-image: we are a nation of myriad groups, each struggling to advance its interests. As will be discussed again in Chapter Seven on majoritarianism, the nature of (U.S.) American pluralism, however, ensures that no one group will always win or lose in these struggles. This is why we can call ourselves democratic, rather than oligarchic.

There was, however, a significant deficiency with this wonderful self-image. By 1960 the organized old left might have been decimated, and radical critiques of inequality may have been temporarily absent from wide-ranging media, but people continued to live the realities of oppressive social, economic, and political structures. Few minorities actually experienced the even-handed "pluralism" implied by Dahl's analysis. At the very time that Dahl's book was gaining popularity in the early 1960s, our cities were again erupting. Dahl wrote that "violence is not and seems never to have been a weapon of importance to New Haven's rulers" (1961, 311). Minorities—and later distinct groups of diverse women and students—however, had long been experiencing the violence of injustice, and they began to respond en mass. In the period immediately following the publication of *Who Governs?* these groups rioted and staged demonstrations, taking to the streets to protest what has been in fact a deeply and inexcusably inegalitarian reality. In the very town of New Haven, which gave us the materials for Dahl's and others' nice pluralist vision, African Americans and Puerto Ricans explode. The city is set ablaze.

(U.S.) American politics cannot be said to be a pluralist democracy, if by this one means that numerous groups interact in the political process and each is sufficiently enfranchised to have its vital interests met over time. Dahl and other early pluralists saw this clearly and quickly refor-mulated their perspectives.[36] But the question arises: is the problem with pluralism merely a practical problem, or is it a deeper philosophical problem? Is the mid-twentieth-century pluralist version of Liberalism basically a good idea? If not a current reality, is pluralism at least a pos-itive vision we seek to strive for? Or is the framework of pluralism itself part of the problem? Must we hold Liberalism itself responsible for the incredible lack of freedom and equality that hinders our democratic strivings? Since there have been numerous articulations of this ideology, how could we hold Liberalism accountable in this case? In response, many answer that Liberalism as a general ideological orientation is still the best shot we have at becoming a functioning democracy, and that the litany of abuses performed in its name are incidental to its essential promise. They may very well be correct, and there are certainly many strands of Liberals. But we have also seen the rise of an alternative set of ideas about how best to engage in the challenges of difference.

Out of the movements arising in the 1960s, activists themselves have been putting to use an array of ideas that challenge the adequacy of prior (U.S.) American responses to diversity. Some of these ideas developed in critical exchange with Liberalism and old left ideologies; some have come from different practices and traditions of minority cultures. From these various sources, a new cluster of ideas emerges in the vacuum cre-ated by the destruction of the old left and as explicit alternatives to the earlier (U.S.) American melting pot and pluralist responses to diversity.

Diversity-Based Politics and Multiculturalism

What I refer to here as diversity politics, as a newer form of democratic theory and action grounded in cultural diversity, took Marx's group-based vision and expanded it to include class as one form of identity-based oppression, along with race, ethnicity, religion, sex/gender, sexual orientation, ability, size, and age. The form of politics I am concerned with that is emerging out of, and drawing lessons from, the histories of many cultural groups long marginalized in society maintains a radical critique of power when discussing group-based identity issues. It responds directly to pluralists by: (1) clarifying that culture is, in fact, political: many experience some of the most profound aspects of politics (i.e., discrimina-tion, marginalization, oppression) due to cultural differences; and (2) challenging the demands for a politically unified public as if the norms of Liberalism and capitalism are acultural. Thus, filling a void remaining from the post-Stalin/post-McCarthy disintegration of the old left, diversity-based politics emerged as the third major twentieth-century democratic response to the challenges of difference in the United States.

In the remainder of this chapter I want to provide some highlights of the concrete developments of this period. The ideas that we will struggle with in the following chapters grow out of these concrete movements and legislative battles. Therefore, I offer a brief survey of the new social movements and legislation of the 1960s and early 1970s that are born in the intersection of the shifts in leftist modernism and (U.S.) American democratic traditions and that provide the material grounding for the newer form of diversity-based democratic theory this book articulates.

It is important at this point also to reground a discussion of identity politics emerging in the 1960s (which challenges the U.S. American democratic theory of pluralism) in its roots in old left activism. Large organizations that helped found and give support to new movements of the 1960s include CORE (Congress of Racial Equality), the NAACP, the Urban League, the American Jewish Congress, and various religious groups. These are pre–cold war institutions that survived the McCarthy period's attacks on even mainstream civil rights groups. The Red scare is self-destructing as the 1960s unfold. As a survival tactic, however, these groups have become more "professionalized" and have toned down their analysis and critique in order to distance themselves from "radicals and subversives." The limitations on economic analysis imposed during the Red scare diminish cultural critiques of the period, but ironically they also allow for a broadening of democratic analysis in other ways. Many problems faced by the marginalized cannot be reduced to economic exploitation only. In the post-McCarthy period the intellectual and activist climate will be more tolerant of analyses that include additional facets of oppression.

The relationship between cultural critiques and economic critiques, political analysis and social analysis, was to be a challenge to many groups emerging in the 1960s. As we will discuss in later chapters, these tensions and the tensions between what some call universal concepts and particular concepts have contoured much of progressive and radical democratic debate to the current day. As the political climate opened up in the early 1960s, many of the mainstream groups that survived the Red scare turned inward to their own communities, and intergroup work became more fraught. These will be legacies that theorists and activists continue to struggle with for many years to come. Though it struggled to rebuild itself, the labor movement remained an important venue for democratic activism. After the fall of Senator McCarthy, however, there was also increasing political freedom and room for cultural diversity. It is in this climate that young people came of consciousness in the 1960s.

Union organizing continued to be a primary outlet through which workers challenged exploitation. Looking beyond unions, however, reveals that actions taken particularly by African American young people and students (and later non–African American young people and students) in the early 1960s revitalized the civil rights movement and the public sphere in the United States as a whole. It was four Black college students who claimed victory the day they demanded service at a Woolworth's lunch counter on February 1, 1960, in Greensboro, North Carolina. Within a week or two hundreds of Black, and later other, college students began protests demanding desegregation in the South. From there, at the prompting of the great civil rights leader Ella Baker, local Black student groups across the South came together to form the Student Nonviolent Coordinating Committee (SNCC; Carson 1981, Morgan 1991). National victories, simply not possible in the 1950s, now bolstered the grassroots movement. The combination of Republicans, a preponderance of conservative southern Democrats, and anticommunist pressures on others (targeting civil rights as procommunist) created a Congressional climate largely antithetical to civil rights lobbying in the 1950s. By the mid-1960s, however, anti-Red fever had (relatively) died down, making some inroads possible. The work of coalitions of older adults in more established organizations began to pay off in the passage of the Civil Rights Act of 1964 and the Voting Rights Act of 1965. The growth of civil rights as a mass movement in a post-McCarthy atmosphere opened up space for more radical groups such as the Black Panthers, the Nation of Islam, and the Black Power movement more broadly. A politics of those Americans of African descent expanded to include Afro-Caribbean activists and more recent immigrants from various African countries.

Jewish activism also significantly changed shape in the post-McCarthy period. Ongoing domestic difficulties of anti-Semitism and its intersection with sexism, homophobia, and economic exploitation of Jews in the United States were also mixed with international Jewish issues. The 1961 trial of Adolph Eichmann, a notorious perpetrator of war crimes during World War II and head of the Gestapo's Jewish section, and resurgences of neo-Nazi activity generated attention to the Holocaust (a term that does not come into use until the 1960s). The war in Israel in 1967 also served as a catalyst for a renewed Jewish-identified Jewish progressive movement (including an increase in progressive, labor, and socialist Zionist youth movements). The recent removal of anti-Jewish quotas at many U.S. universities meant a rise in the Jewish student population. That these specific factors occurred in the slowly opening climate after the Red scare—and in conjunction with a renewed African American civil rights movement—meant that Jews once again rekindled their tradition of activism on a mass scale across the community. This time, however, more explicitly Jewish progressive and radical groups emerged as avenues for Jewish participation in leftist politics in addition to intersecting with civil rights and later renewed women's and gay liberation, multicultural coalitions, environmentalism, and economic justice.[37]

At this juncture, it must be made clear that the new left that emerges in the 1960s builds on the nascent civil rights movement within the African American community and is made possible, at least in part, by the sudden rise in the student population. By the 1960s, more students were able to go on to college than at any other time in U.S. history. One factor key to this rise in college enrollment was the GI Bill, which stipulated that the government would pay a veteran's college tuition. In 1965 Lyndon Johnson enlarged the student loan program, and the state university system began a period of massive expansion in order to make college more accessible to those beyond a minority wealthy, white and male Protestant elite. The baby boomers were now of college age and a third of high school students were going to college—three times the percentage of the previous generation (Anderson 1995, 93). In the early 1960s many Jewish and Christian white students from the North joined the civil rights movement. Activism on college campuses increased and branched out to other issues. After four students were killed by police during an anti–Vietnam War rally at Kent State University in 1970, students at 350 universities went on strike, and protests resulted in closing about five hundred campuses (fifty for the remainder of the semester). Anderson also notes that "protests were so common that wire services began reporting campuses that did not have demonstrations" (1995, 350; see also Morgan 1991, 125). We will look again in Chapter Six at some interesting effects of generational politics, including the effect on diversity-based democratic movements.

The student vein of the antiwar movement joined a larger movement across the country at this time. In 1961, Women Strike for Peace held local peace strikes in sixty cities across the country in response to concerns about radioactivity from above-ground weapons testing. Eventually JFK passed the Test Ban Treaty and formed a Women's Commission. The ranks of the peace movement—backed by such groups as Mobilization for Survival, the War Resisters League, the Women's International League for Peace and Freedom, the Jewish Peace Fellowship, and the Fellowship of Reconciliation—swelled during the antiwar phase of the Vietnam era. It is true that most (U.S.) Americans went on to conduct their daily business as usual, but most younger activists today probably cannot visualize the scope of a movement in which over 170,000 men were conscientious objectors, over half a million committed draft violations, over 3,000 went to prison, nearly 100,000 were military deserters, and over 60,000 U.S. citizens emigrated to Canada and other places in order to avoid the draft (Morgan 1991, 128).

In this period women beyond the college campus and the peace movement began to organize explicitly for women's liberation. Activities of the 1960s came to be referred to as the second wave of women's movement (after the first wave of suffragist activity). In 1963 JFK signed the 1963 Equal Pay Act, which prohibited "discrimination on account of sex in the payment of wages by employers" and labor unions from causing/attempting to cause an employer to discriminate on the basis of sex. In 1964 women in SNCC raised their own issues. By 1965 predominantly white women began to raise feminist issues in SDS. In 1966, when the EEOC was found to not be enforcing the sex discrimination provisions of the 1964 Civil Rights Act, female delegates demanded enforcement. Officials blocked the vote and two dozen women walked out. It is from this act that NOW—the National Organization of Women—was formed. Although still working on issues of reproductive rights, including an end to forced sterilization of many minority women, an early significant victory of the movement came when a young lawyer named Sarah Weddington argued in the Supreme Court, legalizing a woman's right to choose to have an abortion. Increasingly in the context of antiracist, counter-anti-Semitic, antihomophobic, antiableist, and antiageist politics, feminist groups worked on empowerment for women, antiviolence projects, alternatives to and within mainstream religious movements, labor and economic issues, peace and antinuclear issues, and environmental and animal rights concerns.

The rise of women's liberation provided an important base for a newer activist gay and lesbian liberation movement. Despite the midcentury emergence of a national self-image of the United States as pluralist, where group difference and activity is seen as the hallmark of democracy, anyone deemed too far out of the mainstream suffered greatly. In the period of the Red scare, homosexuals were also targeted as "un-American," disloyal, and a security threat. This was a time when homosexuality was considered a disease, same-sex dancing was illegal, it was illegal to refer to homosexuals in the movies, and those thought to be homosexual frequently faced severe discrimination, violence, raiding, and entrapment. Three important organizations emerged under these conditions of repression: the Mattachine Society in 1951, the Daughters of Bilitis in 1955 (by lesbians who found the Mattachine Society unwelcoming to women), and a magazine called *One, Inc.* But the nature of gay and lesbian activism changed in the 1960s. The emphasis changed from an assimilationist mode to one of pride in difference, becoming more similar to the new women's, student, Black Power, Jewish, Chicana/o, and antiwar movements.[38] The riot in response to a raid at Greenwich Village's Stonewall Inn at the end of June 1969 marked a fundamental shift to a mass, diverse, organized movement.[39] Over time the movement grew and changed to include bisexuals, transsexual and transgendered people, queers, two-spirited, and same-sex loving people, and other sexual outlaws.[40]

It is also at this time that we see the growth of a new Latina/o empowerment movement. As a major part in this process, in 1965 the Filipino/a farm workers joined by Caesar Chavez declared a strike and within a month the national grape boycott began. The power of this action is most often credited with galvanizing a new Mexican American civil rights movement, drawing on support from CORE, SNCC, student activists, clergy, and labor people (Del Castillo 1980, Gutiérrez 1993). Between 1965 and 1968 Mexican Americans were organizing in cities and states throughout primarily the mid-southwest such as Texas, New Mexico, Denver, and Los Angeles. In the 1970s Chicana/os and Puerto Ricans joined together in Crystal City, Texas, staging a mass walkout to protest discrimination in education. La Raza Unita Party won control of the school board and eventually of the city government (Anderson 1995, 333; Anzaldua 1987, 63).

In Texas and in cities across the country Puerto Rican activism reemerged, aiming both at problems for the community living within the United States and at independence for Puerto Rico itself. In the aftermath of the Red scare, new anti-imperialist organizations were forming in Puerto Rico (with supporters in the United States) and domestically (such as the Young Lords Party in New York City in 1969). Many Puerto Ricans refused to serve in the Vietnam War, and the movement for Puerto Rican independence grew as resistance to the draft strengthened. Many argued that U.S. exploitation was ruining their country. By 1970, a full 70 percent of Puerto Ricans were eligible for food stamps. In the post-McCarthy climate of the 1960s, socialism had become a major influence in the Nationalist Movement, and many radical Puerto Ricans had come to identify with Che Guevara and Fidel Castro.[41] These developments among Chicana/os and Puerto Ricans helped create the broader Latina/o movement with Central and South Americans living in the United States.

In 1970 Native Americans occupied Alcatraz Island. Activist organizations such as United Native Americans and the American Indian Movement were formed to reestablish native control over Native American policy, and take their issues out of the U.S. Bureau of Indian Affairs. In the early 1970s AIM occupied the Bureau of Indian Affairs office in Washington, D.C., and in 1973 three hundred AIM members occupied the town of Wounded Knee, South Dakota (where the U.S. cavalry had massacred hundreds of Sioux in 1890).[42] A collective Native American political movement grew and challenged U.S. policies harming Native populations and lands and the devastating force of genocidal programs and assimilationist pressures. For both Latina/os and Native Americans, the 1960s marks the first major period where an historical diversity of ethnic and tribal groups came together to form a new, wide-ranging and overarching form of community politics. For example, members of many different tribes participated in the occupation of Alcatraz Island. Such a joint effort might have formerly been thought of in these communities as a coalition. In the 1960s, the popularity of a more "panethnic" version of minority group politics served as a catalyst to a new "pan-Asian" identity and activist base.

Pan-Asian activism began in the 1960s, largely on college campuses. The community consisted of an expanding immigrant population from Asia and the Pacific Islands. The nations of this panethnic identity grouping forged in the United States since the 1960s include: China, Japan, Korea, Vietnam, Laos, Cambodia, the Philippines, India, Thailand, Pakistan, Samoa, Guam, Hawaii, and numerous smaller Asian groups. As a politically active ethnic grouping in the United States, Asians and Pacific Islanders may include those from families that have been in the United States for many generations, or those from among the millions who have come to these shores since the 1960s. These groups target anti-Asian and other racist views, have been active in the campaign against discrimination in college admissions, in labor disputes for restaurant workers in New York City's Chinatown and other cities, in the struggle to end sweatshop labor and the exploitative situations for women brought from Asian lands to work in the United States as domestics, and in raising awareness about and stopping international environmental abuses, child labor, and sex trafficking.[43]

Although civil rights advocacy on behalf of workers and consumers, for health insurance, other health-related issues, and housing had been targeted as too "procommunist" during the McCarthy period, in the 1960s more of this work became possible again.[44] A consumers' rights movement reemerged that targeted big businesses in major industries. In response to activism against the German tranquilizer thalidomide, linked to birth defects in the infants of women who used the drug while pregnant, the 1962 Kefauver amendment to the Federal Food, Drug, and Cosmetic Act was passed, setting testing procedures for drugs before marketing. Ralph Nader entered the consumer advocacy scene in the early 1960s on the issue of motor vehicle safety and then meat inspections. The early efforts by Nader and his teams met with legislative success and encouraged increasing numbers of ordinary people to stand up to corporations. Among other organizations, Nader helped to create the Public Interest Research Group, which would later attract many young activists into local campaigns. Consumer rights groups have also been particularly important for women, given the large role of, for example, U.S. pharmaceutical companies in women's health and reproductive care. Minorities have also made significant use of these groups to confront companies that market harmful products to their specific communities.

Civil rights and other activism dedicated to "the poor" as a group had come under virulent attack during the Red scare as being too close to communist ideology. In the post-McCarthy climate, however, there was a resurgence of grassroots workers organizing in low-income neighborhoods. Many worked explicitly to fight for and protect tenants and their rights. Their cause was somewhat aided by legislative success at the federal level with the Fair Housing Act of 1968. The 1968 FHA was the first such legislation on housing since an 1866 Civil Rights Act that did not prove effective to combat the issues minorities actually faced. Significantly, the 1968 FHA also provided both loans and mortgage programs for minorities, opening up the possibility of future legal protections against discrimination in lending and housing in later decades.[45]

A host of additional and related activist movements also emerged at this time. For example, in 1970 twenty-million people in the United States participated in a week's worth of events for the first Earth Day (Anderson 1995, 349). By 1972 Congress had passed some of the first legislation arising out of demands of the new ecology movement: the Federal Environmental Pesticide Control Act, banning DDT, and proposing the Endangered Species Act. Movements emerged to deal with the different ways that age can play a factor in keeping certain individuals without equal rights. We saw the beginning of a political movement by and on behalf of children.[46] Also, in 1970, the Grey Panthers came onto the political scene and succeeded in getting passed some of the first significant legislation responding to the needs of senior citizens. The 1973 passage of the Rehabilitation Act marked the first major Congressional response to a new movement by and for those with disabilities, beginning the process of mandating free appropriate public education for all children in the least restrictive environment. In each of these movements, women of various communities and racial/ethnic, gender, sexual, and religious minorities have been able to address specific challenges that disability, age, and ecological devastation pose to them.

As with the emergence of pan-American and pan-Asian identities over these years, we also see a newer development of self-conscious Arab-American identity communities. Domestic religious demographics continue to shift, and Islam becomes the fastest-growing religious minority in the United States. Many mosques for Muslims of all ethnic and national groups are being built. Numerous cultural and political organizations for and on behalf of Arab-Americans from all religious affiliations and of Muslims in their diversity are being formed. Members of these communities and their allies are creating self-help and anti-defamation associations in response to anti-Arab and anti-Muslim prejudice. These networks are essential as too many people in the United

States stereotype and demonize Arabs, Muslims, and others from the Middle and Near East—particularly during periods of U.S. crisis (such as the Gulf War, the Oklahoma City bombing, and events resulting from the September 11, 2001, hijackings and attacks.)

CONCLUSION

Undoubtedly numerous individuals, incidents, movements, and communities that one could well argue are central to the development of post-1960s politics from the margins have not been addressed. The above discussion does not seek to be exhaustive, but instead suggestive. Furthermore, the point of this brief recounting is not to cast the 1960s and 1970s as some simply revolutionary time, where all citizens were moved to act against injustice. In fact, in the next chapter we will address some of the limitations of the new diversity politics of the 1960s, given its roots in both pluralism and the old left. Throughout this book we will continue to challenge diversity politics in order to help us develop a radical democratic theory. The 1960s was, however, the beginning of a new form of activist democratic participation in the United States. Emerging as it did in the aftermath of the Red scare, this newer form of politics was both constrained and made possible by the historical circumstances within the United States and internationally.

Class and economic analyses were no longer privileged, but became factors among many that stimulated activism and theoretical investigation. The new form of 1960s activist politics was largely spurred by drawing on and responding to additional aspects of individuals' group identifications. A politics of communal identities exploded at this time, becoming a prism through which to view politics and issues of oppression and liberation, and directly informing other, not explicitly identity-based, movements in such areas as health, ecology, work, housing, and ethics. With identity having become central to the newer form of activist politics emerging from the 1960s social movements, we now turn to an explicit and critical analysis of this particular phenomenon of identity in politics.

3   Who: Identity

BACKGROUND

IN OCTOBER 1997 the *San Francisco Chronicle*'s business section reported that for every dollar that white male managers in the United States earned, the average amount earned by others was significantly lower. The *Chronicle* article tells us that in comparison to this one dollar, on average Asian men earned ninety-one cents and Asian women earned sixty-seven cents. Other groups fared even worse: African American and Hispanic men earned sixty-five cents, white women earned fifty-nine cents, African American women earned fifty-eight cents, and Hispanic women earned forty-eight cents.[1]

Why did someone research this information? Why did the newspaper see fit to print it? Why do we as readers find this list significant? Increasingly such information *is* deemed important. We recognize the injustice the comparison suggests. We should know that this situation composes an aspect of our current reality in the United States. With this knowledge perhaps we can more coherently work to challenge and change such an injustice. But that statistics such as these are available, that someone saw fit to research and write about them, that the *Chronicle* saw fit to print the piece, and that we eagerly read suggests a convergence of interests and, for this example, a convergence of values that deem the information such a list conveys as worthy information.

This is a relatively new phenomenon, for only recently would a listing of wage comparisons, suggesting economic inequality, be understood according to gender, race, and ethnicity. We are living in a time when these factors of identity are consciously shaping our understanding of our

Some materials in this chapter are reprinted from "Jewish/Feminist/Queer: Identity Challenges for Moderns and Post Moderns," *SHOFAR* 17, 2 (Winter 1999): 8–15, by permission of the University of Nebraska Press. © 1999 by the University of Nebraska Press. Also reprinted with changes from "Theorizing Diversity from a Jewish Perspective," *Race, Gender, Class: American Jewish Perspectives* 6, 4 (1999): 13–23; reprinted by permission.

lives and what we will deem politically relevant material. We are also living in a time when a critical view of such factors of identity is contributing to how we understand the capacities and limitations of political agency. Race/ethnicity, gender, and class from the above example—and I will also add at least sex and sexual orientation, ability, and size—are not merely a random grouping of identity signifiers. They are important in current political and sociological terms due to the way that we are coming to see that they fundamentally constitute power dynamics and thus affect human relations and agency.[2]

I understand this increased attention to identity seen on the streets, in the academy, through the halls of government, and in philosophical thought since the 1960s as an expression of a new mode of democratic politics. As activists and scholars question "democratic" principles that seem less than democratic, the issue of identity restimulates the specific question, with whom is democratic theory concerned? Although the answer historically has been "the populace," the reality has never been that simple. Democracy is supposed to be a system of sociopolitical organization by, for, and of the people, and yet we know that who counts as "the people" has long been the subject of controversy.

At pivotal periods, activists and thinkers have revisited this *who* question of democratic theory, expanding and/or revising older conceptions. With the rise of diversity-based politics we find ourselves again at such an historical moment. For example, we can see that the mode of governance in ancient Athens was participatory and has become a model for more modern notions of democratic organization. This form of political system that we call democracy was, however, an extremely elitist regime. Only a certain group of Athenian men were counted as citizens and were therefore enabled to participate in the benefits and responsibilities of what we in the United States would refer to as democracy.[3] We have, perhaps, learned the important notion of democracy from ancient Athens, but we certainly would not want to accept the quite limited and elitist definition of who are democratic participants as was understood in that historical context.

In premodern Europe, a version of the aristocratic model extolled by the Greek philosophers was employed by the nobility and their supporters. Students interested in this period might find the work of Edmund Burke a particularly illustrative example of thinking from this era. Burke is interesting because it was in his time that this model came

to be seen as inherently antidemocratic in that the franchise was so limited. This direct challenge to the feudal norm crystallized these long-held
ideas, enabling Burke to defend them with clarity. The new radicals of
the modern period sought explicitly to shift the notion of who counts
politically as members of the populace. The Liberals of the French Revolution for democracy sought to extend the notion of "the people" from
the aristocracy to include middle-class male heads of household.

In another revolutionary turn, in the nineteenth century Karl Marx
took issue with the Liberal understanding of the democratic populace. An
extreme representation of this can be seen in Marx's pre-twentieth-
century vision of the dictatorship of the proletariat. We should be careful
not to use our twentieth-century experiences of devastating dictatorships
in understanding this conception. Marxists argue that this vision was
even more democratic than those previously put forward, actually, as
dictatorship means "full rule" and the majority belonged to the working
class. Throughout history, however, most people have never been fully
included in "democratic" notions of the people.

For the most part, women and most minority groups have historically been left out of the category of people included as legitimate actors
in a democratic polity. This has been the case even when some in these
populations might also have been considered members of included
groups such as "the working class" or "male heads of household" and
the rare occasions when select individuals achieved a measure of "elite"
status. If we want to consider ourselves democratic, we must look again
at the definition of who counts in a democracy and rethink our understanding of an enfranchised populace.

What we see emerging as a new form of democratic theory in the
post-1960s era continues the extension of the ancient Greek notion of
participation and qualitative enfranchisement further. In contrast to
Liberalism's tendency historically to focus on the individual, however,
this more multicultural vision of democracy seeks to explore the nature
of, need for, and barriers to enfranchisement based not only on our
rights as autonomous human beings, but also as members of identity
groups. Thus, since the 1960s, identity groups have become a base from
which to engage in politics at an unprecedented level, forcing democrats to ask critical questions about *who* gets to speak, *who* is it important that is listening, *who* sets the terms of debate and the parameters of
the public agenda, *who* decides on behalf of *whom*?[4]

The development of such a focus stems from the awareness that many of us belong to groups that have been marginalized *as* groups. It could be said that we are learning from the difficulties and failures of, for example, the Emancipation of the Jews in France following the 1789 Revolution.[5] In this paradigmatic case, Jewish men were extended many of the new rights of citizenship if they would enter the new political arena as individual men, not as members of the Jewish community. In this way, Jews, for the most part, remained marginalized, although select persons who assimilated to the Christian/civic culture were enfranchised. Contemporary diversity politics demonstrates that women, different peoples of color, those who are disabled, bisexuals, gays, lesbians, transsexuals and transgendered people, as well as other groups, continue to face this very challenge. For example, these still marginalized groups can now vote and are theoretically entitled to equal protection under the law. These groups increasingly have been clarifying the limitations of democratic participation defined in such terms, however, in a society still so dominated by identity-based standards relating to race, ethnicity, religion, sex/gender, sexual orientation, ability, size, and age.[6]

In this chapter I will develop one sort of grounding to the discussion of the identity politics of race/ethnicity, sex/gender, religion, ability, size, class, and sexual orientation in philosophical terms. This chapter examines a perspective on contemporary identity politics in relation first to Marxism and then to postmodernism in the context of a post-Marxist debate between modernists and postmodernists. Here I take identity politics seriously as I also approach it critically. New conceptions of identity have grown out of the politics engaged in by those on the margins of society. Below I will discuss the visions of identity that have been emerging as *multiplicitous* and as *mutually constitutive*. I will argue that appeals to subjectivity on the part of minorities are not necessarily modernist appeals. Without essentializing the array of views known as postmodernist, I explore why minority groups have had trouble with some of the, even important, contributions postmodernism has made in the critique of oppression. Identity politics has helped clarify how a politics must take into account oppression and privilege based in identity. Similarly, it has helped us to understand that a democratic theory attending to identities must be grounded in the historical, changing, and adapting processes of politics, power, and social relations. Understanding identity politics in this way enables us to see that it is not exclusively the domain of the marginalized or minorities. Democratic theory must attend to the *who* question in order to critically assess and articulate aspects of justice, policy, ethics, and social dynamics for everyone. Building on the analysis of Chapter Two, let us now turn to a discussion of the philosophical debates out of which identity became foregrounded in a radical activist politics in the United States during the second half of the twentieth century.

MARXISM AND THE DEVELOPMENT OF
CONTEMPORARY MULTICULTURAL THINKING

To begin, we must clarify that contemporary diversity-based democratic thinkers seek to extend the Greek notion of participatory enfranchisement, but not on Liberalism's individualistic terms. One of the significant contributions of the new form of democratic thought is that it incorporates an understanding of individuals as also members of groups in need of enfranchisement. Marx is a complex thinker and probably would not have thought of himself as a group theorist. Still, Marx gave modern Western political thought (particularly in the United States) the first full-scale group-based vision of an emancipatory politics. In contrast to Liberalism, which not only focuses on the individual but claims neutrality with respect to the various life plans and claims of groups, Marxism is a class-based philosophy and practice that makes explicit its bias toward ending the oppression of the exploited class.

As one of the precursors to multiculturalism, pluralism is a more recent form of Liberal thinking prominent in the United States with significant links to the developments here attributed to Marx. Until the twentieth century, political science in this country tended to focus its inquiry into the formal institutions of government and central documents such as the Constitution. Early pluralists realized that there was a lot more happening that scholars ought to look at in order to understand politics. They needed to look beyond the Congress, the presidency, the courts, and the Declaration of Independence. Aware of Marx's approach to politics, political scientists began to look toward extragovernmental forces. They found the group notion of political activity helpful, but Marx's group category of class too broad to apply in order to understand the workings of U.S. politics. Pluralists began to look at a host of smaller groups, including those organized around specific economic interests such as farmers or oil manufacturers, as well as those connected to specific communities such as ethnic and racial groups.[7]

In this new use of group studies in politics, pluralists broadened traditional Liberalism's exclusive focus on individuals in the political arena, but they did not adopt Marx's expressly radical political imperative to understand and overthrow oppressive classes and social structures. More recent diversity-based thinking uses the United States form of pluralism's view of politics as composed of myriad groups but retains Marx's political imperative. Another way to see this, given the historical picture painted in the previous chapter, is to take philosophical note of the roots of identity politics in Marx's radical and class-based understanding of groups in politics. To the extent that the contemporary identity politics also has roots in Marxist philosophy, the development of identity politics has had to overcome some of the limitations of Marx's vision, as well as those of its ties to Liberal pluralism.

If the origins of contemporary identity politics are found in both U.S. pluralism and international Marxism, then both of these democratic theories enabled multiculturalism's capacity to critically attend to groups and communities in politics. But identity politics also inherited certain problematic assumptions found in both pluralism and Marxism. For example, there is a tendency toward essentialism in pluralism that must be addressed. What I mean by this is that there is a tendency in pluralist thinking to see the groups fighting it out in politics as having "essential," or given and fixed, interests. One finds in pluralism a tendency to refer to "women's interests" or "Asian interests" as if these are known and static, rather than constructed in the course of politics over time. Additionally, there has historically been a related problem in Marxism. Marxists tend to base a liberatory politics explicitly on class grounds, often prioritizing class as *the* universal group experience. It is no wonder, perhaps, that early efforts at diversity politics lie in identifying individual characteristics—such as race/ethnicity, ability, or sexual orientation—that are singled out for analysis. This one identity aspect was often universalized and set at the center of visions of ending oppression. Pluralists tend to view each group as distinct with essential interests. Marxists tended to argue that we must focus exclusively on a class-based revolution after which other oppressions will end. Similarly, we often found feminists countering that the primary root of oppression is gender, gay activists assuming that heterosexuality is the crucial oppression. Such prioritizing emerges from the Marxist paradigm, and relies on the pluralist tendency to see these groups and their interests as separate to begin with.

Even with these problematic origins, however, on this point of identity in politics what multicultural work has done specifically to Marx's group-based view of enfranchisement is to complicate it. In the view of a politics of diversity, class becomes one of many axes of oppression. Class-based exploitation must be challenged, but it must be challenged along with other forms of exploitation and injustice. Let us see how this works in comparison to some choices that Marx made in his life and work.

As is well known, Karl Marx was descended from a long line of rabbis. During a period of liberalization in the constant turnover of regimes, Marx's father had taken advantage of a new opportunity for Jews to attend university and enter into the professions, eventually becoming a lawyer. When the tide swung back to conservatism, given the shifting of state administrations over the region in which he lived, and Jews in such circumstances were told that they must convert to Christianity or lose their positions, Marx's father chose conversion. We know only a little of the Jewish customs Marx's mother continued to keep alive privately, and we know that Marx was involved with many of the Jewish radicals of his day, including of course Moses Hess (one of the founders of radical Zionist theory). But the group-based vision Marx developed, breaking out of the individualist paradigm of Liberalism, was not based on the self-understanding of the Jewish community. Marx would not have seen his version of group-based politics as an identity politics. Of course, in "On the Jewish Question," Marx disturbingly utilizes Jews as the paradigmatic case of the inherent failure that an historically marginalized group seeking Liberal rights will encounter. This was the problem Jews faced during the period of Emancipation after the French Revolution as mentioned above. Instead, the group vision in which Marx invests himself is an economic one based on class. Despite his significant contribution to a potentially radical democratic praxis, Marx understood class to be the universal group, fairly blinding him to the *multiplicity, intersectionality, and mutually constitutive tendency* of group-based oppressions.

During the early explosion of what is often called identity politics in the United States in the 1960s, many new groups intent on liberation followed a similar path to the more orthodox Marxist vision. In the excitement of new calls for liberation, much of the rhetoric and analysis offered claimed new axes of group-based identity as the universal basis of oppression. Black Power set race as the most important factor in politics, for example. *Identity,* for Liberals and all moderns, historically meant, from the Latin, *the same.* Identity in this case refers to *identical* or *shared* essential characteristics, as the term is still used in mathematics. By understanding this new group politics based on race, sex/gender, sexual orientation, religion, class, and ethnicity as "identity" politics, many assumed an "identity" as sameness within the groups now active in politics, or essentialized characteristics of the communities rising up as activists. With reference again to Black Power, such an essentialized notion of race originally made it very difficult to argue that Black women, for example, might have something specific to contribute to revolutionary politics and so activists ought to take women's concerns seriously as well. Women as a group were often portrayed as sharing the same oppressive experiences, much as people of color were often presumed to share the same racist predicament.

This new diversity-based form of democracy was also referred to as multiculturalism, suggesting the importance of attending to culture in politics as well as a multiplicity of cultures in politics. However, although this politics aimed at shattering the myth of sameness on the national scale, many involved appropriated modernist notions of sameness when applied to the specific subnational communities. What we see from a twenty-first-century perspective is that we have needed to be wary of essentialism at many levels and to learn the lesson of the cross-construction of identity and power many times over in recent history.[8] For example, the women of SNCC (the Student Nonviolent Coordinating Committee at the forefront of early race-critical politics) found themselves developing new feminist critiques as part of their participation in the Black struggle in the face of the form of patriarchy refashioned by their brothers. A new form of lesbian-feminism emerged that became known as the lavender menace at NOW (the National Organization of Women), as heterosexual feminists had defined the "women's movement" in a way that excluded lesbians and bisexuals. Many Chicana lesbians and other feminists embraced the *malinchista* since the term was thrown at them as a label for being traitors to La Raza when the new radical Chicanos demanded they be Chicana Primero (i.e., and women "only" second).[9] Critique and action emerged from Jewish and working class segments of feminist and minority communities challenging their invisibility. Through these examples and so many more, radical democrats have come to see that the narrow modes of nationalist/identity politics generated at the onset of this sort of movement must be examined in larger, more integrated contexts.

Historically, in the development of diversity politics over time, those who explicitly face multiple oppressions have introduced significant new ways of viewing identities in politics. A central contribution of people who are oppressed based on more than one aspect of their identity (given numerous axes of racism, sexism, homophobia, anti-Semitism, ageism, and ableism) was to show that we can not single out one aspect of identity as the universal category. To privilege one dimension over others did not make sense to Jewish or African American women, for example, or gay Pacific Islanders. Although separatism has been an important answer for many in identity politics, it has not been the primary response. To join a separatist movement of women, for example, often did not make sense in the context of the lives of women who had other communal bases of existence and in which they also made meaning. Chicanas as a group may have significant affinities with other women, particularly other Third World women, as they might with Chicanos. Similarly, the demand that Black women work against racism or to build up the race in a way that ignored their situations as women was not very appealing either. Caribbean and African American feminists insist on an emancipatory politics that takes into account gender as it does race and ethnicity. We came to learn that oppression works through multiple mechanisms, and that identities cannot be seen in isolation from one another. This level of analysis brought about new ways to conceive identity as politically relevant.

One of the earliest discussions of multiple identity oppressions and their interlocking nature came from the Combahee River Collective. The collective was a Black feminist group that began meeting in Boston, Massachusetts, in 1974. After a few years of engaging in activism and study together they wrote the Combahee River Collective Statement, which offered a brief analysis of the history and theory of their activism as Black feminists and Black feminist issues and practice. The political work and coalition participation of the group, the process of the group's development and direction, and the wisdom gleaned in its studies made the collective important. At a certain stage the group also committed itself to writing "as a means of organizing Black feminists as we continue to do political work in coalition with other groups" (281). In

1977 the group wrote the brief statement, which had a tremendous effect on Black women. It also helped to transform the entire feminist movement, offering the women's movement a clearly articulated statement of the "synthesis" of racial, sexual, heterosexual, and class oppression that "create[s] the conditions of our lives" (272).

From the Combahee River Collective Statement on, discourse about multiple identities gave way to self-criticism, including the recognition that identities were not simply many, but interconnected in an indefinite variety of ways. We could not just add critical race theory to feminist analysis, for example, because the way that one's life is gendered does not stand on its own as clearly distinguishable and then get added to the way that one's life is raced. A person is not a woman first, and then Puerto Rican, and then middle class. One does not have a single essential "identity" such as race and then add other identity characteristics as secondary or tertiary. As Elizabeth Spelman (1988) suggests, all women might be women, but no woman is only a woman. With these insights, many from an array of communities began to talk about the connection between identities or even the ways that oppressions intersect.[10]

Talking about the connection between identities or even their intersection might still suggest, however, that each identity stands on its own. With this way of seeing multiple identities, one may still presume that each distinct identity gets created through a discrete set of social dynamics that form a bounded and separative identity such as race or sexual orientation. Thus, some thinkers even went further than this in their work on identity. Intersectionality was not enough, and they began to theorize the ways in which identity signifiers were actually mutually constitutive. What they meant is that gender itself, for example, is a raced category, as race is a gendered category. Gender, in another example, came to be seen as mutually constitutive of the construction of sexual orientation so that being male or female only made sense in the context of compulsory heterosexuality.[11] As Sojourner Truth's famous speech makes clear, for many, the category *woman* has been historically constructed as a category of and for elite white women. Let us look at this a little more closely.

Sojourner Truth was born in New York State with the name Isabella. Being born into slavery, she was sold numerous times before she was twelve years old, was raped by one of her masters and escaped to freedom in 1827. After some years of working as a domestic in then "free"

New York, she took the name Sojourner Truth and began traveling, preaching, and singing in an effort to end slavery and later for women's suffrage. At a religious meeting in 1851 some of her words were recorded and later came into the public domain under the title "Ain't I a Woman?" Among other things, in this speech she said, "That man over there says that women need to be helped into carriages, and lifted over ditches, and to have the best place everywhere. Nobody ever helps me into carriages, or over mud-puddles, or gives me any best place! And ain't I a woman? Look at me! Look at my arm! I have ploughed and planted, and gathered into barns, and no man could head me! And ain't I a woman? I could work as much and eat as much as a man—when I could get it—and bear the lash as well! And ain't I a woman? I have borne thirteen children, and seen them most all sold off to slavery, and when I cried out with my mother's grief, none but Jesus heard me! And ain't I a woman?"

One of the things that this speech helps us to see is that the category of gender is simultaneously a raced and classed category. In elite discourse, the category of *woman* is a category that is raced white and classed as rich enough to be riding around in carriages. We do not need to accept the elite categorizations that would not include Sojourner in the category *women*. We do, however, need to understand and analyze the ways that our multiple identities are mutually constituted. Sojourner Truth stood up at that meeting and asked, "And ain't I a woman?" I respond to her: "Yes, Sojourner, you are a woman." If you answer thus as well, then you must realize that the way some females become gendered as women differs from the way others do. In this example, race and class makes some women *women* in certain ways and others in other ways. Sojourner Truth is a formerslaveBlackwoman. Her gendering as a woman is incredibly different from the class-based gendering of some white women who, by being helped into carriages and carried over mud-puddles, become elitewhitewomen. One might say that both are women. One would also have to say that they are women in significantly different ways and recognized as such through a system of different signs, histories, and characteristics. This is an example of how we may understand the discourse concerning the mutually constitutive character of multiple identity signifiers.

Activists and thinkers have suggested numerous metaphors for this conception of identity as they have worked to articulate the experiences of our multiple and mutually constitutive identities and theorize from that basis. Some speak in terms of hybridity or hyphenated identity.[12] Anzaldua (1987) writes beautifully of the "mestiza," one whose identity signifier is inherently and historically multiply situated. The mestiza is a mixed breed, a cross-cultural being traversing boundaries. Anzaldua offers us this concept of identity out of her historical experience as a Chicana. Chicana/os are a community created in the mixture of Spanish conquest and indigenous people of Mexico now facing their fates on the borderlands created in the U.S. conquest of (what are now) the U.S. southwest territories. Others have used the concepts of the synchronism of jazz and chemical formulas to help us think about identity in a way that is complex rather than "identitarian." In these examples, in jazz and chemical formulas, when two or more elements or rhythms are combined, each discrete element is not only transformed but can no longer be separated to its original.[13] Phelan talks about a coyote politics, and a number of writers utilize food-based references to name their mixed, multiple, and process understandings of identity in politics. We have heard of borscht, curries, and masalas, and also of curdling in the literature.[14]

Many have also drawn on these metaphors not only to claim the multiplicity of identity as an empirical description, but also to suggest a normative dimension to the discussion. Identities are interesting in politics not just as descriptions of an individual's personal statistics, but in terms of how identities are part of our engagement in life practices and enable viewpoints and different strategies for such engagement. Although in dominant theories identities are singular, static, and essentialized, in much of multiculturalism we can see an alternative conceptualization of the multiple, constructed, and changing nature of these identifiers. From the static conception, to theorize from a place of identity in the traditional mode would be to theorize monologically. If one *is* Chinese American, then one thinks or has a particular set of interests that are Chinese American. But when Cherrie Moraga, a Chicana feminist, writes "My brother's sex was white. Mine, brown" (1983, 94), she uses a multiple and mutually constitutive view of identity to help guide her way in political struggles. Her complex understanding of her identity enables her to understand and to navigate in politics. In this mode, identity does not equate with a viewpoint or ideology simply. Instead, the point is to make clear our subjective aspirations in a liberatory politics that might suggest new forms of thinking and practice. *Being* Chinese American, as in being a member of a particular identity community, does not mean one *thinks, acts, is* Chinese American in any a priori, given, or fixed way. *Being* Chinese American does not necessarily mean that one has a simple Chinese American perspective on things, as if there could be one Chinese American perspective on anything. But diversity politics has looked to people from a variety of identity communities to see what they might have to offer as perspectives that have been made possible in the complex of their lives as members of different communities.

In this newer form of politics, identities, identity communities and experiences are taken seriously as part of what enables us to develop alternative visions, conceptualizations, and engagements toward more radical democracy. For Anzaldua, the mestiza is not only the term applied to a woman from the Chicana community, but names a new form of consciousness that operates in multiple worlds at once, historically, seeing on numerous levels simultaneously. Some have looked to concrete circumstances of other minority communities to suggest similar notions of dialectical thinking from this multiply situated understanding of identity. For example, some have suggested a dialectical component to the strategies and analyses of some Jewish activists and thinkers related to the hybrid structures of various Jewish languages.[15] The idea of the double consciousness of African Americans given segregated life worlds between the races points in this direction as well.[16] James Baldwin writes: "The American Negro has the great advantage of having never believed that collection of myths to which white Americans cling: that their ancestors were all freedom-loving heroes, that they were born in the greatest country the world has ever seen, or that Americans are invincible in battle and wise in peace, that Americans have always dealt honorably with Mexicans and Indians and all other neighbors or inferiors, that American men are the world's most direct and virile, that American women are pure" (1963, 136).

As many activists and scholars involved in diversity work are coming to understand, no longer can all oppression be crystallized into one single aspect of our group identity. Certainly, we often must abstract out, or focus on, some particular component of our group selves for focused deconstruction, analysis, reinterpretation, reconstruction. There are also times when practical politics demands prioritizing certain identity-based oppressions in the course of social struggle. However, given that we all have multiple identities and that power dynamics exist on multiple grids simultaneously, the new mode of democratic thought emerging from many marginalized groups more broadly analyzes and challenges power in its multiplicity. In contrast to the traditional Marxist paradigm of privileging one category, in Marx's case class, we have the vision of—Black, socialist, lesbian, feminist, partnered to a Jew, and ultimately victim to cancer—Audre Lorde: "There is no such thing as a single-issue struggle because we do not lead single-issue lives." [17]

MULTICULTURALISM AND THE POST-MARXIST MODERNIST/POSTMODERNIST DEBATE

What differentiates this critical diversity-based understanding of identity from a postmodern view? There are many points of convergence between the two perspectives. As they have played out in public discussions in the U.S. context, in many ways each has enhanced the other, offering modes of critique and extended analyses. I do not find the view that casts multiculturalism and postmodernism as wholly at odds helpful. To argue that they are at odds, one must first posit that they are also separate. To do so, scholars of one perspective must often essentialize the other, paint it in stark terms that would rarely be recognized by those ascribing to the demonized perspective. Having said this, thinkers often do portray postmodernism and multiculturalism as opposing philosophies. Thus, in order to understand such portrayals and how they may be used in political discourse, we will have to explore some of the differences between the two. For example, although both perspectives rely on the assumption that identity is constructed historically through the workings of power in society, one might sum up the divergences in the following manner: work that falls into a more multicultural paradigm seeks to liberate our identities from their oppressive social ascriptions, rather than to liberate us from our identities. What may be characterized as a more postmodern view uses various methods to demonstrate the oppressive nature of our identities historically, surmising that we must shake off these oppressive binds. As an alternative, the first notion (as an example of multiculturalism) suggests utilizing critical deconstruction, multiplicity, and change to work *with* identity in politics, in order to create conscious politics from our identities, and seeks to transform our political arenas so that they may better address issues generated in identity explorations.[18] But this is a complicated comparison needing further explication.

Staking out this new, multicultural approach to identity politics has been difficult due to the way that the post-Marxist debate has been corralled between modernists more generally and postmodernists. Although in the United States we are all actually living through the tensions between moderns and postmoderns, unless we are philosophers or literary critics we may not be familiar with the terms of the discussion. Therefore, at the risk of simplification for brevity, in this section I will lay out certain features of the basic parameters of the modernist/postmodernist discussion on identity, clarifying the central ideas at stake in this current debate. I will then challenge the parameters of this narrow space with perspectives from a more multiculturalist attempt at theorizing.

Identity: Modernism and Postmodernism

By way of introduction to this section, we should note that questions concerning identity have been a focal point in the debate between modernist and postmodernist theorists. Previously in Western historical discussions, political, theological, and cultural disagreements about identity tended to focus on the nature of "the subject" or who would be considered such. (As explained further below, a subject is one who "counts" politically and philosophically, as opposed to an "object" or one who is "objectified.") The postmodern contribution to this discussion has been to challenge the biases and exclusions of historical constructions of subjectivity. In the course of analysis, such a challenge has usually brought these thinkers to the point of negating the very existence of the subject itself. If the subject has been a category constructed through exclusion, a postmodernist might argue that she therefore has no use for the notion. The postmodern project has certainly been informed by an awareness of both micro and macro systems of domination and has relentlessly challenged the oppressive nature of modernity. In this, postmodernism has often been an ally and of service to marginalized groups. But some have also found its specific means of negating modern subjectivity unhelpful, if not explicitly threatening.[19] This issue has pitted many in marginalized groups against postmodernists. However, those of us in marginalized groups can take little solace from an alliance with the modern vision that, despite its motto of "Liberté, égalité, fraternité," has long been antithetical to our liberation. In this section I seek to explore these ideas. Let us begin with the problem of subjectivity in Liberalism.

The Liberalism of the modern period introduces the "subject" as a

particular understanding of human being. To some, this new understanding was liberatory, part of the move to broaden those included as
participants in the public sphere beyond a tiny elite of lords and nobles
as found previously under feudalism. The modern subject is an atomistically (as in a separate, thickly bounded atom) autonomous and rational actor, to be distinguished from the vast majority who had been
without a voice in the highly stratified social structure of the feudal system. In modernity, those recognized as subjects are accorded person-
hood: it is respected that they have interests to protect and promote, and
that they are the bearers of rights. These particular characteristics are
presented as universals and are thus seen as the basis for full citizenship.

Although the new subject did open up European society to some
degree, it was based on numerous exclusions of its own. Many have criticized the unified, autonomous subject as actually radically particular,
rather than universal. Such a view of subjectivity is generated from the
specific experiences of a small group living in the West (i.e., white, elite,
Christian men). Relying on such particulars (these men's whiteness, their
elite class status, etc.) as if they were universal, or applying to all people,
has also been used as one of the main mechanisms to justify and perpetuate the disenfranchisement of many whose lives have not appeared to
fit the universalist paradigm. Thus, the modern "I" has been critiqued, for
example, as problematically Christian, masculinist, racist, ethnocentric,
heterosexist, ageist, ableist, and culturally imperialist.

Based on this critique, postmodern thinkers, for example, seek to
write without an assumption of a coherent and rational subject. The
main idea here is that we cannot separate modern notions of subjectivity (even as they have been historically important to the enfranchisement of some) from the oppression necessitated by and as an effect of
such a subject (a condition historically affecting many). In this view, the
notion of subjectivity is inherently oppressive, not just incidentally
problematic historically. This means that attempts to reform the politics
of who might count as a subject are misguided. If the concept is inherently oppressive, then we must do away with it if we are concerned with
disrupting that oppression. Postmodern thinkers thus focus their energies on challenging the modern notion of identity as essentialist, as ahistorical, and as narrowly unified in the service of dominating power
relationships.[20] This mode of thinking unmasks identities as, instead,
social constructions, fractured, and fluid.

As I have been arguing, postmodernism has not, however, been the only critical response to Liberalism and modernism. In the United States, for example, activists and thinkers were busy developing their own critiques and were also confronting the inequities of power. In the 1960s, as intellectuals and other radicals in France were developing what we often refer to as postmodernism, U.S. Americans were taking to the streets to name and overcome racism, sexism, homophobia, anti-Semitism, and other identity-based oppressions both domestically and globally. Most thinkers and activists in the United States did not read French. They did, however, know some Marx. The 1960s version of U.S. American radicalism discussed in Chapter Two emerged out of the ashes of the old left, contextualized in the rather multicultural basis of politics in the United States. In contrast to Marx, however, these thinkers and activists began calling race, gender, and sexual orientation, as examples, identities constructed in the interests of the privileged in the political, economic, and cultural power hierarchies operating in the United States.

This period of movement placed marginalized groups in a difficult position. Within the framework of modernity, enfranchisement has been marked by the move to see previously objectified individuals and groups as subjects. One needed to be seen as inherently independent and rational in order to be taken as a self-representing agent in political society. Hobbes (1968, 217) wrote that "a person, is he whose words or actions are considered, either as his own, or as representing the words or actions of an other man." The represented and the representing then get incorporated into one being, that of the person doing the representing. Hobbes explains this by likening the situation to actors in the theater "[s]o that a *Person*, is the same that an *Actor* is, both on the Stage and in common Conversation." In that erasure of one's very being, the represented loses all agency. Waves of emancipatory movements in the United States have sought to remove whole groups of people from those cast as among the "represented" and instead included as agents of their own representation.

This classic formula for liberation was successfully utilized time and again by marginalized groups in the United States. Take for example the interrelated histories of struggle by women and by slaves as a group. Manumission of the slaves and the women's suffrage movement were central aspects of the work to overcome the oppression of women and all Americans of African descent. The model relied upon for these two monumental steps toward ending racist and sexist discrimination was to broaden the notion of who gets to be counted as a subject and as a self-representing agent. Abolitionists and suffragists argued for the person-hood of both women and Blacks (and eventually those who were both women and Black) so that they could be counted in at least the broadest and most basic terms of modern citizenship: to be free people who can vote. In these examples, significant steps toward ending oppression were made by extending the definition of subjecthood to include former slaves and both Black and white women. And yet, also in the name of ending oppression, postmoderns are challenging the very premise of subjectivity. It was through discussions about the concept of subjectivity that philosophers imagined people as agents: as capable of acting, ratio-nal, and able to speak for themselves. As Disch (personal communica-tion) asks, then, what kinds of agency are possible in the wake of the critique of the autonomous subject? We must push this inquiry further and ask, is postmodernism even best situated to answer this question? Although certainly informed by the often excellent work done under the banner of postmodernism, there are some voices from minority com-munities which would suggest that it might not necessarily be the best grounding for a liberatory multicultural politics.

Although similar to postmodernists in their critique of the biases of the modern formulation, many marginalized groups assert that in prac-tical politics they cannot necessarily afford to abandon their struggle for subjectivity. Now, in the late modern period when more and more groups are finally beginning to be recognized as subjects, leaving behind their status as objects, it is too dangerous to challenge the very notion of the subject as we find happening in postmodern circles.[21] Some feel, as Moraga puts it, that "the fact that some aspects of that cul-ture are indeed oppressive does not imply, as a solution, throwing out the entire business of racial/ethnic culture" (1983, 127).[22] It is important to stress at this point, however, that this does not mean that members of these marginalized groups accept the modern view of subjectivity either. What is at stake here, and what other options are there? A help-ful critique might not enable a politics that can actually take subjectiv-ity to task. Deconstructing problematic notions of separative autonomy does not necessarily provide modes of disrupting problematic practices. If we agree that the postmodernist critique of subjectivity is generally philosophically persuasive, we might still want to ask: are there models of agency other than the modernist subject available to democratic thinkers from historically marginalized communities and previously unrecognized modes of politics?

Some activists in the Third World and others in marginalized groups in the West have found themselves in an interesting dilemma. It seems that when the parameters of debate are set by the discussion between modernists and postmodernists, the possibilities for such marginalized groups are hopelessly bound. Identity in the modernist frame has been oppressive, and postmodernists want to jettison such oppressiveness from our politics. But what do you do if you want to end oppression and do it still within the context of identity? What do you do if you want to end sexism, homophobia, ableism, racism, and anti-Semitism, for example, but want to continue living in and re-creating Jewish-Latina/o-African-Asian-Queer-Deaf culture? Given the terrain of the contemporary philosophical debate, how are we to place the self-understandings of nondominant communities that, although affected by dominant currents of modern/postmodern thought, have their own particular cultural frameworks of meaning and which have long histories prior to mainstreams of Western culture informing their identities? Further, how are those in such communities to pursue an end to their marginalization when, regardless of their "difference" from dominant paradigms, it is the power structures and paradigms of meaning of the mainstream that they must confront? What do we do when neither the dominant paradigm, modernism, nor the major opposition at present, postmodernism, seems to address our understandings, needs, orientations and liberatory struggles with identity?

One way to begin to look at this dilemma is to ground oneself in some specific identity discussions and struggles waged by marginalized groups. I will ask, in light of the above discussion, how am I to make sense of these communities, their engagement in identity politics, and their struggles for agency in the United States?[23] Historically marginalized groups are important to explore at this point in a discussion of identity because they are among those seen as outside the modern definition of proper subjects. On the one hand, however, many claim to have good reason to be wary of the postmodern pronouncement of the death of subjectivity. On the other hand, they also have little need for a modern notion of the isolated subject.

A Multiculturalist Response to the Modernist/Postmodernist Debate

As affected by modernity/postmodernity as many marginalized groups are in their current incarnations, many are certainly not-modern communities. As different as they are, many communities with hyphenated "American" identities, such as African-Asian-Jewish-Latina/o-Native Americans, have as central components of their identities premodern cultural traditions. Although significantly reshaped in the modern West, many of these communities still rely on various languages, calendars, rituals, histories and other cultural markers that distinguish them from modern Christian, European-American norms in the United States.[24]

In other ways, other aspects of our identities with political relevance in our time are clearly creations of the modern period, and to some degree of postmodernity. Strong women, gender challenges, and same-sex loving through the ages notwithstanding, contemporary feminists and queers, as examples, significantly forge their senses of identity and political programs out of the circumstances of identity in modernity.[25] Though skin pigmentation has long differed around the globe, racial classifications are modern creations.[26] The transformation of the poor into a political class as we know it is a nineteenth-century development.[27] Thus, although feminist, queer, race-based, and class-based communities and actions long existed, the creation of "feminist," "queer," "class," and "race" identities are historically and culturally specific to either modernity, or to a transition out from modernity. Politics based on the multiplicity of such identities has become a significant force only primarily since the 1960s.

This is all to say that, as diverse as we are, the life experiences and visions of many marginalized communities in the contemporary period have been forged in an incredible intersection of historical—and often ancient and relatively contiguous—communities, modernity, and postmodernity/post-1960s multiculturalism.[28] These mammoths of communal identity are thus neither neatly modern nor postmodern. It is no wonder that neither liberatory option—the modern one of the universal and naturalized subject, nor the fractured and fragmented, purely deconstructed and never reconstructed model of postmoderns—seems to fit for many in these groups.

To push this point further in the context of contemporary multicultural politics, we find nonnormative members of various marginalized communities now speaking up as well. For example, we not only have a politics based on race and a related critical race theory; we are increasingly hearing from the marginalized populations among racial minorities such as women, the poor and working class, queers, and non-Christians as well as those of biracial backgrounds. The very existence of these multiply situated voices has been predicated on the deconstruction of certain categories of identity. Latina feminist and queer identities, as examples, or the development of working class ideas and the actions of economic justice taken as their result in feminist movements, in whatever particular forms, have become possible only with the fracturing of the idea of unitary authoritative identity categories. These identity constellations have been given life in identity communities bursting into multiplicity. But such vitalization is not happening in a postmodernist mode of fracture and deconstruction simply. There is often an aspect of the feminist, queer, class-based, and racial/ethnic and religious movements that has kept such developments in a more multicultural mode. What I mean by this is that such discussions still tend to operate within contexts, accepting frameworks, remaining situated in identity, reaffirming community, and honoring membership. Many engage in deconstruction, but also significantly in reconstruction. Does this mean that we are, therefore, stuck in a modernist discourse? Not at all.

At this point we must address the limitation of the postmodern argument highlighted by this focus on the multiplicity identity constellation discussed above. Although deeply affected by modernity, the very condition of marginalization for many minority groups rests on their difference from the modern Western paradigms. It is therefore confusing to many members of marginalized groups when their discussions of community are critiqued according to the same rules as modern Western theories. There is no doubt that community-talk might be, and often is, universalist in its own way (as discussed above). However, the tendency in postmodernism which assumes that any talk of identity, community, vision, or creation is necessarily totalistic and disciplinary on the model of modernity is itself a colonialist reduction. It presumes categories or concepts that may be used in subaltern communities are used in the same way, or mean the same things, that they do in the dominant paradigm. To be not postmodern does not mean that one is simply modern. The postmodern critique of identity politics usually misses this fundamental point. How can we understand this idea?

The affirmation of numerous identity groupings within community has a life beyond itself as a re-creation in modernity. As examples noted previously, Asian-Latino/a-Jewish-Native-African-American communities cannot be reduced to a modern Western specimen simply. These identities consist of components that antedate modernity historically and cannot be subsumed under Western culture philosophically. Thus, these particulars of identity and community are probably not best understood as simply modern Western categories. For example, factors central to modern notions of the self (such as atomistic autonomy, disembodied and rational preconditions for agency, and separated individual selfhood) are not categories found salient among many marginalized minority groups, nor do they exactly resonate in the philosophies of these communities.[29] We can see this example manifest on two levels of these communities' struggles to overcome oppression.

We must first look at the philosophical premises of the developments within these various communities. The logic of liberation for those who experience marginalization within their particular community (such as women and queers in the various Jewish, Asian, and Pacific Islander communities, or working class African and Caribbean American communities) has generally not been one of a modernist, individualistic subjectivity, as one now with selfish interests to promote and protect. Those concerned with ending marginalization in their communities have not made their plea on the basis of their status simply as rational speakers or actors. Instead, much of the call coming from African, Asian, Latina/o, Jewish, and even women's, queer's, poor and working class communities more recently, for example, has usually relied on the conceptions of honoring membership in the community. The legitimacy of their self-representing agency, then, depends on acknowledging that membership. They have argued on the basis that such marginalization has deprived them of making their full contribution to the whole, and that the whole has thus also been deprived. As will be discussed further in the next chapter, these diverse subgroups have marked their marginalization as a failure of their communities to recognize and appreciate them. Their call for inclusion has come not simply in the form of demanding their rights of free speech as autonomous agents, but as a call to listen to their voices and welcome their participation.[30]

In her highly critical and very cautious discussion of identity in politics, Phelan (1989, 170) writes, "If we are to be free, we must learn to embrace paradox and confusion; in short, we must embrace politics. Identity politics must be based, not only on identity, but on an appreciation for politics as the art of living together." She will, however, hold politics equally responsible to identities: "Politics that ignores our identities, that makes them 'private,' is useless; but nonnegotiable identities will enslave us whether they are imposed from within or without." Phelan is not simply accusing any identity-talk of being "fixed." Instead, she appreciates identities and their potential role in a radical democratic politics. But if identities are to fill such a democratic role, then those of us who rely on them, and those of us who are sympathetic to them, ought to be careful about how we understand and how we use them in our discourse and practice. I wonder what we can learn for this radical democratic praxis from those for whom identity figures largely in their political self-consciousness *and* whose notion of identity is fluid and contextual.

When we get beyond the academic discussion and look to actual groups and communities engaged in concrete power struggles, we can find, in fact, many involved in identity politics who understand identity not as a nonnegotiable possession, a static and historically given reality, but as a social relation. As a relation, identity is always ever reconstructing itself because relations are dynamic processes. In this light, many discuss identities not only in terms of "being," but also of "becoming." In this view, identities are seen as creations of communities in specific historical contexts. To say this does not mean that the varieties of identity that we see currently are not inherently related to the histories of the particular community. It suggests, however, that the historical understanding of a particular community's identifications are not inherent within them, as unchanging essences, but are developed over time in relation to other communities, events, and to the shifting relations among the community's members themselves. Thus, we find other voices in identity politics which clearly indicate that by identity they do not mean only a turn to the past, but a deliberate move into the future.[31]

For example, the category of Asian ethnicity is decidedly a creation of modern U.S. politics and power dynamics. Myriad and quite different Asian communities were cast together in their transplanted lives in the United States in ways likely unimaginable in their former homelands. In their encounters with the United States, and in the permutations made possible through their encounters with one another in the U.S. context, a form of "panethnicity" developed for certain cultural and political purposes. On college campuses with small Asian communities, students from Cambodia and students from China might engage with the "Asian Students United" group as they each seek community, means of minority survival, cultural expression, and political leverage. When they were in Asia, or for their parents whose identity might be more rooted in the context of Asian politics, such a joint project might seem absurd. But it will likely be easier to raise funds for cultural and intellectual programming of interest to these students, or to put forth an appeal for a well-equipped writing center available for students for whom English is their second language, together as the A.S.U. with thirty student-members than as separate communities with a few students each. For the few Asian students, although they might long for other Laotians or Japanese, their minority status on a particular campus might make finding *any* other Asians a priority. The relational dynamics of identity politics for such students involves at least (an understatement to be sure!) negotiations with the complexity of Filipina/o communities and concerns historically and today, for example, as well as with "pan-Asian" communities and concerns historically and today.

Further, if identity is seen as a relation, then it is fundamentally political and ought to be approached in the context of politics.[32] The "creation" of pan-Asian groups, in the above example, is itself not a given. There are any number of possibilities to enable various Asian communities to face their situations as minorities in the United States. The pan-Asian notion comes about through politics: through historical developments, yearnings, aspirations, repression, discrimination. Pan-Asian identity is not always the best strategy for specific individuals or for particular communities. It will rarely be forged without costs of its own. A pan-Asian movement risks the loss of specificity of the many subgroups. Movement dynamics may replay dominant hierarchies based on class, immigrant status, sex/gender, sexuality, age, ability, religion, ethnicity, ideological orientation. To insist on the political nature of such relations is to insist that, even when helpful, the very creation of a panethnic identity be critically interrogated and practiced. To call relations between these individuals and groups political is to say that those involved in identities as "becomings" are attendant to the vicissitudes of their formations even as they are ever in the process of transposing. Keeping transmutation as an aspect of identity itself enables its own possibilities for resistance and construction. As part of the process of politics in this way, working with identity can point us also to deliberation on ethical relations.

For example, on criticizing claims sometimes made to authenticity, West (1993b, 25–26) writes in *Race Matters* how this relational aspect of identity leads to ethics and politics. West writes, "First, blackness has no meaning outside of a system of race-conscious people and practices. After centuries of racist degradations, exploitation, and oppression in America, being black means being minimally subject to white supremacist abuse and being part of a rich culture and community that has struggled against such abuse." West states clearly that "any claim to black authenticity beyond being a potential object of racist abuse and an heir to a grand tradition of black struggle is contingent on ones political definition of black interest and ones ethical understanding of how this interest relates to individuals and communities in and outside of Black America. In short, blackness is a political and ethical construct." Thus, a significant contribution that those involved in identity politics are making is clarification of how categories of identity once thought to be simply given, are actually social constructions that shift over time. Prior to the contemporary mode of diversity politics, "the change in the meaning of the term 'race' from nobility, blood, family, household, to arab, Asiatic, Jew, Israelite, Negro, Black is one which passed almost unnoticed" (Guillaumin, 1995, 44). It is, however, central to the current project of diversity politics to make such changes explicit so that we can problematize them and submit them to ethical deliberations.[33]

So how does this affect the level of oppression and liberation for these community groups vis-à-vis national politics? The above discussion helps explain why many minorities and marginalized peoples seem to be in a dilemma. The means to end oppression in the dominant paradigm of modernity is to become a self. This is not, however, what the marginalized tend to be asking for. True, when the options within the current hegemony are subject or object, the oppressed want to reject their placement as object. The nature of the more multiculturalist call for subjectivity, however, proscribed by the duality of the modernist paradigm, is of a different sort than the modernist notion itself. Oppressed groups are asking to end explicit injustice and to be allowed to participate as particulars, as members of identity communities, and not as the culturally stripped universal individual agents demanded at least since the Enlightenment. There is absolutely a call for selfhood, because that is the vocabulary that will be understood in the prevailing power structure. The individualist and selfish criteria for the modern self are, however, often absent in this instance. The call for selfhood we are more likely to find emerging from the interactions of those historically disenfranchised in a hegemonic modern Western world tend to be in the group-defined form of being self-determining of diverse cultural practices, art, relations, self-esteem, and ideologies.[34]

The wonderfully critical alternative of postmodernism, however, is not always particularly applicable to the predicaments of many minority groups either. The option for an alternative basis for agency of endlessly multiplying, opening, and fracturing everything is not necessarily a viable option for all peoples with a communal sense of self and a continued commitment to history. The postmodern liberatory motive for fracturing in the face of solid signifiers that exclude is understandable, but does not necessarily relate to the specificity of needs named by many minority communities. When the specifics of one's community's oppression have been marked, at least in part, by the fracturing of bonds, relations, connection to history and group knowledge, then further fracturing actually represents further oppression. It is no wonder that the frameworks of liberatory feminist and minority praxis come often in the form of reclaiming, recovering, rebuilding, repairing, reconstruction.[35] As Shokeid writes, for example, in his work on Congregation Bet Simhat Torah, the Gay and Lesbian synagogue in New York City, the combined processes of anti-Semitism and homophobia create a "broken image of one's identity," and for many congregants, joining the synagogue was an act of "restoring their cracked self-image and identity" (1995, 239). As another example, Dyson's work draws on Malcolm X to address directly "a daily political ethic of care for fractured black bodies and spirits" as part of his larger radical democratic social activity and structural analysis (1995, 181). In the emphasis on the potentially emancipatory move of fracturing and deconstructing everything, some postmodern critics seem unself-conscious of the tendency to further alienate and repulse minorities for whose liberation they claim to be working. In this, these postmodernists have fallen into the all-too-typical mode of oppressors as actors in dominant traditions, using abstractions that are out of touch with and actually detrimental to many.[36]

With this critique of a postmodern tendency to invest in fracturing and unending variation as a liberatory model, I am not arguing for a simplistic politics of "wholeness," "oneness," or "oneworld-ism." Often, communities must face the devastation and unusual possibilities that fracturing has occasioned for them historically. Postmodern theories and methods of deconstruction can be of service in this difficult work.[37] But a simple celebration of identity as fractured and displaced, in either/or opposition to the subjugation entailed in Western notions of subjects as seamless selves on firm foundations, may be more oppressive than liberatory for certain groups. As a more general caution, philosophers ought to be wary of overarching notions and theorizing in such a polarized fashion. What multiculturalism has to offer to this discussion is also, therefore, the idea that theories and pronouncements about identity and subjectivity need to be accountable to specific identities and subjectivities. In the process of holding philosophy accountable in this way, we tend to find that identity struggles, and struggles with subjectivity, are often different for different groups and in different eras. If we are concerned with interrupting oppressive practices, then we are best off remembering that there are myriad such practices, and therefore myriad community-specific interruptions are called for.

CONCLUSION

In my view, a new perspective on the identity politics of race and ethnicity, class, religion, ability, size, sex/gender, and sexual orientation helps us to locate certain important components of a new democratic theory. There have been many philosophies that have been called democratic, though none has taken the *who* question seriously enough. The political vision emerging from many feminists, minorities, and those with whom they stand in solidarity challenges democrats to ask: who is it that our theory and practice are serving? As Audre Lorde suggests, "by seeing who the *we* is we learn to use our energies with greater precision" (1984, 137). New understandings are developing from those engaged in certain aspects of identity politics, understandings that offer a critique of other philosophies and seek to reintegrate their contributions according to a contemporary politics in which those from minority communities and previously marginalized groups will be included both as individuals and as groups.

New diversity-based politics works with a conception of identity that differs significantly from the dominant Liberal notion. With respect to the two more recent critical theories on identity, Marxism and postmodernism, this newly emergent democratic theory helps us to understand some of their limitations, as well as draw on their strengths. Although borrowing heavily from Marx in its critical historical grounding, the contemporary and more multicultural way of thinking is not properly modernist. Despite its shattering of unitary and ahistorical constructions, the emphasis on reconstruction significantly distinguishes it from postmodernism. As I have discussed in this chapter, this newer democratic theory remains committed to the critique of oppression, but also retains a constructive notion of justice. As another example, this form of critical diversity politics is working within the framework of multiplicity and change, but within a more Marxist dialectical scheme rather than one of unrepaired fragmentation. Finally, the democratic vision currently emerging from marginalized identity groups is self-conscious of re-creating oppression, but will not sacrifice its activism.

Nor does a diversity politics that utilizes identities mean that it can therefore respond only to identity questions or rely solely on those with marginalized identities. To separate out identity issues from other issues is to miss the point of a diversity-based democratic notion that we must increasingly utilize identity views and critique in all aspects of politics, as these cannot be separated. Further, as Michael Eric Dyson puts forward in response to the notion that, for example, only African Americans can know and make use of African American experience: "Unquestionably, African-American history produces cultural and personal experiences that are distinct, even singular. But the *historical* character of such experiences makes them theoretically accessible to any interpreter who has a broad knowledge of African-American intellectual traditions, a balanced and sensible approach to black culture, and the same skills of rational argumentation and scholarly inquiry required in other fields of study" (1995, 61–62). Affirming multiculturalism's focus on identity politics does not necessitate a reduction of all politics to identity relations. Similarly, addressing identity politics well does not necessitate proof of any particular identities.

Such a view supports Narayan's response to Linda Alcoff's "Problem of Speaking for Others." Narayan demonstrates the cultural essentialism constituting the cultural relativism that results in a diversity politics where only an "X" can speak about "Xs," make sense of "Xs' " historical experiences, and make use of any lessons gleaned from them. Narayan explains that such a quandary happens when we rely on a Package Picture of Cultures that sees different cultures as "neatly wrapped packages, sealed off from one another, possessing sharply defined edges or contours, and with each package having a distinct content inside" (1998, 10). Every culture is composed of heterogeneity and contestation that might very well make the views of certain segments of a community more than able to understand, relate to, and critically judge segments of other communities. From an informed position, and in the service of exchange, everyone can speak for themselves.

Finally, we see that multiculturalism points to identities as political constructs. This does not mean that only the marginalized have a place; it means that everyone must take identities and their relations to power seriously. In addition, multiculturalism as referred to as identity politics is a *politics, particularly a democratic politics.* Doing this kind of politics thus also points to—as does any democratic politics—ethics, theory, insights, justice, social construction, and change in addition to experiences and histories.

Having explored some of the contributions that marginalized groups are making to discussions about *who* counts, and ought to count, in politics, we can now turn to yet another fundamental question for democratic thinkers and actors. In the next chapter I will examine the *what* question. Building on the perspectives on identity politics developed in this chapter, I will specifically ask: *what* is it that these groups are demanding and in what ways does this shift political discourse and our visions of democratic goals?

4   What: Recognition

> I am an invisible man. . . . I am invisible, understand, simply because people refuse to see me. . . . it is as though I have been surrounded by mirrors of hard distorting glass. When they approach me they see only my surroundings, themselves, or figments of their imagination—indeed, everything and anything except me. It is sometimes advantageous to be unseen, although it is most often rather wearing on the nerves. . . . you're constantly being bumped against . . . you often doubt if you really exist. . . . out of resentment you begin to bump people back. . . . You ache with the need to convince yourself that you do exist in the real world, that you're a part of all the sound and anguish, and you strike out with your fists, you curse and you swear to make them recognize you. And, alas, it's seldom successful.   —Ellison 1947, 3

THUS RALPH ELLISON opens his first novel and now legendary tale of the *Invisible Man*. Published in 1947, Ellison's work seemed to express something central to the experiences of many African American men due to the historical development of racism in the United States. Men and women from various communities of color responded to the chilling rendition of their peculiar form of invisibility: to be somehow invisible at the same time one and one's people are so explicitly and violently *seen* in order to both mock and mark one as abject.[1] Ellison's invisible man was taken also by European-Americans as metaphor for a broader alienation increasingly endemic to late capitalist forms of society.[2] Inherently related to vast economic inequality, "[t]he deeply ideological nature of imagery determines not only how other people think about us but how we think about ourselves."[3] Cultural forms of oppression

Earlier versions of the arguments in sections of this chapter were presented as papers at: The American Political Science Meeting, Atlanta, Georgia, September 1999; The Annual Foundations of Political Theory Workshop on Political Myth, Rhetoric, and Symbolism, Atlanta, Georgia, September 1, 1999; the Conferences of North American and Cuban Philosophers and Social Scientists, Havana, Cuba and Guantanamo, Cuba, June 1998; The Pennsylvania Political Science Association Meeting, Pittsburgh, Pennsylvania, April 1994; and the Western Political Science Association Meeting, Albuquerque, New Mexico, March 1994.

and the ways one and one's communities are reflected in a culture, then, are deeply political.[4]

I begin here because the central question of this chapter is: how are we to understand *what* new democratic actors and thinkers demand at the heart of their political vision? In the 1950s in particular the state mobilized its vast network of coercive resources in order to squelch political activity and cultural production that it deemed threatening to the hegemonic power structure. This phase of state-sponsored repression, commonly referred to as the McCarthy period, had devastating effects on radical organization and thought in the United States. In response, the left was forced to recouch its demands. In the process, those involved also came to reconceptualize the terrain of radical democratic praxis and redefine core concepts of Western political philosophy.

As this book argues, the forced disintegration of Marxist, mass-based leftist organization in the aftermath of the Red scare gave way to new levels of political action that would also center on the oppression of peoples of color, women, Jews, homosexuals, those with disabilities, and other groups in addition to economic agitation by the working class. Thus, rather than stopping progressive activity in the United States, the McCarthy period ended up extending the group-based politics of class, drawn from Marx's work, outward to additional fronts of the political battles being waged. Here in the United States, even Marxist understandings of economic oppression must be translated into multilayered, peculiarly identity-based, manifestations of coercive power that include racism, sexism, ableism, anti-Semitism, and homophobia.

One of the key elements of the new thought generated in the transformation of radical politics in the United States is the place of the demand for recognition coming from the oppressed.[5] What we get from this politics of recognition are new understandings of a number of important philosophical and political concepts. It is also through the process of redefining these other concepts themselves that recognition comes to take on its various meanings in contemporary diversity politics. One must have a clear understanding of a politics fueled by demands for recognition if one is to comprehend the development of post-1960s community-based activism and new ways that core concepts of Western political thought are currently being redeployed.

For example, Ramón Gutiérrez characterizes the development of self-conscious Chicano/a politics as follows: "The Chicanos, largely a contingent of educated students, in a revolution sparked by rising expectations, demanded equality with white America; demanded an end to racism, and asserted their right to cultural autonomy and national self-determination" (1993, 45). In order to enable activists and thinkers to have a clearer sense of such historical accounts, as well as understand and engage more effectively in activist politics today, in Part I this chapter will explicate the significance of answering the "what" question of democratic theory with the notion of recognition. In Part II we will sketch how this has led to a reconfiguring of certain key concepts in Western democratic thought and how such reconfiguring can clarify debates about identity-politics and which lessons might best serve a new democratic theory. Part I explains a critical politics of recognition in historical context as related to performativity. Here we will also address issues of obligation and social equity to make sense of the peculiar not seen/seen as abject (or contemptible) dynamic that a politics of recognition seeks to challenge. Although numerous core concepts of Western political thought are being redefined in this emergent alternative democratic praxis, in Part II I will sketch some newer ways of understanding three of the more commonly relied upon concepts: equality, freedom, and justice.[6]

PART I: RECOGNITION

In the public sphere where individuals and differing groups come together, we find that in answering the "what" question, diversity-based activists begin with a political demand for recognition. Previously, more common initial answers to the question "what are we after in a democracy?" might have been freedom, equality, or justice. In the United States today the meanings of these terms appear self-evident: in democracy we want to be free from oppression/outside imposition, to be treated equally/or the same as others, and to aim for a fair distribution of goods and services among the populace (justice). To many students of, and participants in, democratic practices in the United States, these ideas seem right, good, purposeful, and even energizingly lofty. Unfortunately, such definitions are not *the* definitions of freedom, equality, and justice. Instead, they are a specific, ideologically based set of definitions most commonly articulated in the context of Liberalism. Although a label claimed by an array of different political philosophers,

Liberalism as the dominant political philosophy and operating ideology in the United States is also therefore inherently implicated in the forms of discrimination and oppression existing here. Those marginalized within the supposedly free, equal, and just democracy that "is" the United States are exposing certain problems with defining the "what" of democratic praxis in that way. Marginalized groups may seek freedom, equality, and justice, but what they tend to mean by these terms differs significantly from mainstream Liberal meanings. Moreover, it is the very ideas and practices related to these Liberal definitions that are themselves part of the problem for marginalized groups. If we are to understand new calls for freedom, equality, and justice emerging from diversity-based politics in the United States and find ways to respond to them appropriately, we must pay attention to another concept that has become central to radical democratic politics in recent years.

New democratic thinkers and activists are more likely to begin their response to the question "what are you after in democratic politics?" with the notion of recognition: of our individual and group selves, as we engage in the processes of naming ourselves over time. Because traditional democratic answers (freedom, equality, justice) to this question are important, but themselves major facets of what is up for contestation in diversity politics, new democratic actors begin the answer to the "what" question by naming recognition.[7] Once we have explicated what this new politics of recognition is, we can address the ways in which the more traditional answers—freedom, justice, and equality—are themselves being redefined.

A politics of recognition as it is emerging from the margins concerns 1) shifting internal and external perceptions of differing communities' origins and 2) an ongoing struggle to develop equality in society, as well as 3) the very character of social structures and their potential for justice. First, in a combination of contemporary Liberal and communitarian perspectives, diversity politics brings our attention to the importance of our identity-communities-of-origin and those that have been chosen, and their effect on agency, on our sense of self, and on our resultant multiple relations to power in society. Second, in society we are steered away from our course in the pursuit of central democratic aspirations such as freedom and equality because we are stuck inside definitions that have grown out of the experiences of a relatively homogeneous segment of the population. Third, narrowly envisioned cultural standards have shaped our social institutions, thereby limiting our opportunities for equal freedom to live, love, work, and struggle.

Bell hooks (1984) and other members of marginalized groups have clarified the concept that as we are positioned differently in society and the labor market due to various aspects of our identities, we also have different ideas about and perspectives on society. Gilligan (1982) has shown that we often speak in different voices and those at the center tend to ignore or misunderstand the life language of those who are more peripheral conceptually. Fraser's (1989) analysis demonstrates that these differing cultural means of interpretation and communication are at the heart of political movement to overcome oppression. The idea of recognition here suggests that there are new democratic lessons to be learned from the experiences of groups that have historically been marginalized. Whether contributions from previously ignored communities' rich cultural legacies or from their specific coping and resistance strategies, we all potentially can benefit from new insights and understandings and find alternative methods for overcoming oppression in democratic politics more generally.

Seen/Not Seen: Politics of Recognition, Misrecognition, and Nonrecognition

The form of identity politics emerging out of diversity-based activism is exposing a peculiar dynamic in the politics of who is oppressed and how, and who becomes dominant and why. This newer form of democratic praxis is concerned with achieving new dynamics of recognition, given the present problematic nature of positive modes of recognition for the privileged and methods of misrecognition and nonrecognition for those marginalized in the current system. But how is it that those on the margins are seen through as if they do not exist, and at the same time seen so debasingly in order to fuel stereotypes and the institutions that both add to and respond to the stereotypes?

Let us examine some examples. In Malcolm X's speeches we find one suggestion of how creating destructive images of minorities causes them to be seen and to then see themselves negatively. He shows us that this occurs in such a way that it is inherently implicated in the exploitation of Black labor in public institutions such as slavery for the benefit of whites and the simultaneous segregation of Blacks into separate spaces to keep them out of sight in white culture. In one of Malcolm X's last speeches he stated:

> When you teach a man to hate his lips, the lips that God gave him, the shape of his nose that God gave him, the texture of the hair that God gave him, the color of the skin that God gave him, you've committed the worst crime that a race of people can commit. . . . This is how you imprisoned us. Not just bringing us over here and making us slaves. But the image that you created of our motherland and the image that you created of our people on that continent was a trap, was a prison, was a chain, was the worst form of slavery that has ever been invented by the so-called civilized race and a civilized nation since the beginning of the world. (1989,166–67)

As a result, Cornel West writes, "Malcolm X also realized, as do too few black leaders today, that the black encounter with the absurd in racist American society yields a profound spiritual need for human affirmation and recognition" (1993b, 143).

A look at the role of holidays in a national calendar can illuminate other examples of the dynamic of not seen/seen as abject at work in the current mode of politics that a demand for recognition is designed to disrupt and overcome. In the United States national holidays are often scheduled around Christian holy days and commemorations of the European conquest of these territories (and the subsequent protection of that conquest). "Independence Day" and all the annual hoopla create pride and a sense of autonomy and strength only if one identifies with the cultural nation that performs the celebration of independence. Native Americans have long protested the militaristic and other reenactments of their condition as objects of conquest and cultural destruction performed yearly at Independence Day and Columbus Day and therefore residually at Memorial Day, Veterans Day, and even to some degree Thanksgiving.

In the peculiar dynamic of not seen/seen as abject, Native Americans are unrecognized, nonexistent, to the degree that as the major mode of celebration for Columbus Day is a sale at The Gap, non–Native Americans do not even consciously engage with what the holiday commemorates. They are unrecognizable to the extent that one does acknowledge what the holiday stands for. Since Columbus, Native Americans have in part been seen by European Americans as naturally simple and their culture, therefore, essentially necessitating conquest by the more advanced and civilized Europeans. Columbus found the native peoples he met on his journey simple because they were friendly and willing to trade whatever they had with these newcomers. Further, Columbus wrote in his log of the Arawaks whom he encountered when first landing in "the new world" at the Bahama Islands: "They were well built, with good bodies and handsome features. . . . They do not bear arms, and do not know them, for I showed them a sword, they took it by the edge and cut themselves out of ignorance. They have no iron. Their spears are made of cane. They would make fine servants. . . . With fifty men we could subjugate them all and make them do whatever we want."[8] These representations are unrecognizable in relation to Native American images of themselves.

Jews, Muslims, and other non-Christians are told from every official outlet that public and most private institutions do not discriminate on the basis of religion in the United States. They are also usually told that they must take "personal" or "sick" days off from work or school on their religious holy days when the public school, university, government, and most businesses organize their calendars around days free for Christian holidays such as a Sunday Sabbath, Christmas, New Year of the Christian calendar, Thanksgiving (remember, this is actually a Puritan holiday), and often Easter. Citizens are told that these are now national holidays sometimes referred to as the weekend, winter break, spring break, and so on.

In more recent years, in response to charges of discrimination and cultural insensitivity, many have begun to call Christmas, for example, a secular, national holiday. Many schools have been careful to rename as "winter break" the time off they schedule for the Christmas holiday and the Christian New Year. This skirts the problem: calling Christmas and the Christian New Year winter break does not change the fact that the calendrical norm is Christian and alternatives are privatized and/or seen as diseased (thus the need for "others," meaning non-Christians, to take "personal" or "sick" days for their own holy days). In fact, it only pushes the problem underground. The nationalistic reappropriation of Christian holy days makes it more difficult to see the insight of the criticism of cultural erasure. It also therefore makes those who still do not participate further removed from membership in the nation (or on the micro level as uncooperative, troublemakers, stingy, or unfun for not participating in the requisite Christmas season joy of parties and gift giving).[9]

By the repeated reenactments of these observances and celebrations, as well as their commercialization, certain groups are clearly recognized as belonging to the nation. These constant reenactments designate these groups as worthy: independent, autonomous, powerful, sacred, and hard working/deserving of time off. Others are unrecognized, as their existence and cultures are erased from public commemoration posing as inclusively national. As some are designated to the void, they are at the same time seen but unrecognizable, at least according to their own systems of self-imagination. A politics of recognition is intended to confront these negative images and the practices that both set them in motion and result from them on the level of their play in the dominant culture as well as on the level of their internalization within the marginalized communities themselves.

Recognition And/As Performance

The demand for recognition in politics is, however, particular to and made possible by the nature of state and civil structures of modernity. For example, Taylor's (1994) historical and philosophical discussion of the developments leading to the current demand for a politics of recognition demonstrates that in feudalism, under the ancien régime (the "old order") where there were stable social hierarchies, recognition was as impossible for the masses as it was useless for the elite few. In the change to Liberalism with its pretense toward equality and social mobility, a demand for recognition on the part of the masses, long necessary, became possible.

In the current period, since the 1960s, groups marginalized under Liberalism itself came to bring this conception of recognition to the fore in new ways. We can see why this is necessary by looking at Rawls's Liberal articulation of a theory of justice. An eminent contemporary Liberal theorist, John Rawls writes: "the basis for self esteem in a just society is not one's income share but the publicly affirmed distribution of fundamental rights and liberties. And this distribution being equal, everyone has a similar and secure status when they meet to conduct common affairs of the wider society. No one is inclined to look beyond the constitutional affirmations of equality for further political ways to securing his status" (1971, 544–45). But what if the "distribution of fundamental rights and liberties" is not now, and never has been, equal? In contrast to Rawls, note Phelan's explanation of the rise of gay and lesbian politics: "beginning with the realization that self-respect, an essential ingredient of happiness, has been denied them by virtue of definitions and perceptions of lesbianism and homosexuality, lesbians began the fight for an identity that would foster self-respect and pride" (1989, 4). For lesbians, the "publicly affirmed distribution of fundamental rights and liberties" has not been equal and the status of lesbians has not been secure. Lesbians have thus not merely been *inclined* to look beyond formal affirmations of equality, but have been *compelled* to develop alternative political methods for securing status.

In the modern period certain groups have been marked in various ways as less than fully human. Social structures and relations that were developed to enact and reflect back on differing human endeavors and relationships constitute the kind of politics as recognition that was made possible in the turn to Liberalism. This early Liberal form of a politics of recognition was also related, then, to the social position of the primary class responsible for the Liberal turn. The rise of the middle class, a merchant class, and its demand to have its interests recognized and responded to in the old order run by and for the aristocracy was the main catalyst for the French and American revolutions of 1789 and 1776 respectively. In successfully overthrowing the ancien régime, the newly dominant bourgeoisie set up institutions that responded to their needs for social order and recognition broadly as a class.

In the changing shape of intersecting power dynamics, acts of recognition are performed repeatedly that bolster the sense of worthiness and actual superiority of this dominant class. Those enfranchised tend to have also a sense of themselves as enfranchised and as entitled because the repetition of these acts of recognition over time forms our capacity to conceive of what is our "real" situation and ultimately the development of our identities.[10]

In a society, for example, where a certain class of white men not only have been leaders of government and bosses in the workplace, but have been constantly represented as those fit for leadership, those of this class (or those hoping to become so) are recognized in cultural production as having the desired qualities for such roles. In popular arts, advertisements, decrees, and actions this group is seen performing the acts of leadership and responsibility repeatedly over time. This group also lives in a context where characteristics associated with success and mastery are portrayed by players who are and/or look and appear to be like them. Those who make such performances possible are most often either darkly figured in the background, presented as smaller in physical stature, or not there at all. In response, made possible by the transformed social order in which the bourgeoisie rose to power, the contemporary incarnation of a politics of recognition targets this very social order, Liberalism and capitalism, itself.

Recognition and Obligation

The recent incarnation of a politics of recognition will best be understood as a kind of politics in which those differing from Liberalism's elite—expressed in group terms as those enjoying the privileges associated with membership in collectivities of people who are white, straight, Christian, able, middle-to-upper class, and male—can and will be recognized according to their own changing assessments of what such recognition entails politically. This diversity-based view has become increasingly necessary for democratic praxis because acts of recognition politics performed more traditionally under Liberalism have produced a "privileged irresponsibility." Attending to and recognizing others' needs is relegated to the background; it is the negative, what the performances of the elite or leaders, known as the responsible, stand in relief from.[11] In a postcolonial context, colonizers construct the fiction of their own superiority and mask it with civility. This mode of enacting the civility of the colonizers "precludes the recognition of the colonized's humanity."[12]

The notion of privileged responsibility is a newer version of a long-disputed conception of the problem of political obligation under Liberalism. It is not those involved in contemporary diversity politics and postcolonial studies who first challenge Liberalism's capacity to honor a set of relationships in which one has responsibilities. Liberalism was explicitly breaking away from a conception of rule related to the aristocracy's idea of noblesse oblige (the responsibilities and obligations of the nobility). The ancien régime held duty and obligation as core facets of social relation. This form of political obligation was, however, necessary to uphold the social stratification of societies ruled by the aristocracy. The masses had a duty to know their place and obey the nobility, those naturally fit for governance. The nobility had a paternalist duty to protect the masses and the obligation to make sound decisions on their behalf. Whether it was early Conservatives writing at the time of the French and American revolutions or more recent neoconservatives,[13] defenders of the old order against Liberalism criticize this new form of social organization as lacking the grounds necessary for a well-ordered society due to Liberalism's quite bold rejection of earlier forms of political obligation.

Since the development of Liberalism, other critics have examined the same question and provided a rather different analysis of its problem of political obligation. Like Conservatives, radical democrats of various kinds have found a distinct callousness operating within Liberalism. In contrast to Conservatives, however, radical democrats point to the *class*- and *group*-based biases in Liberalism's celebration of supposedly egalitarian individual *self*-interest. The problem of political obligation for radical democrats has been related to various manifestations of alienation, ruthless corporate management, and lack of responsibility for the community, other humans, and the environment. Rather than lamenting the decay of aristocratic forms of social hierarchy because people forget their duties, radical democrats find the problem of obligation in Liberalism to be that it makes possible new forms of vast inequality. It then also makes it nearly impossible to hold people and institutions accountable for attending to the devastation left in its wake.[14]

The more recent incarnation of this discussion growing out of diversity-based politics refers to the privileged irresponsibility of elites in modernity and includes the variety of cultural forms of oppression that such irresponsibility both relies on and causes. Issues of recognition are fundamental to the operations of this dynamic. In understanding this dynamic of recognition and irresponsibility, the mythic character of recognition for dominant groups fabricated and repeated in popular culture and social-structural relations becomes important. What we find is that the system of repeated performances of acts that serve to recognize the dominant class rely on a fallacy in what is being recognized. The dominant myth recognizes the apparent humanity of elites as "civilized," and through reflecting their "civilizing" mission. Those in the cluster of dominant groupings are represented through repeated acts as being quintessentially freedom lovers, equality protectors, democracy defenders, and justice pursuers.

Under critical scrutiny, however, we can see that certain types of performance expose a problem of political obligation of concern in contemporary diversity-based democratic politics. It is not only that the lack of responsibility is exposed—as a form of benign neglect or a gloss on Liberal democracy's self-image as actively just—contemporary critics further argue that the problem more seriously lies in a kind of irresponsibility that is actively unjust. The nonrecognition of the current pain and historical horror of the European genocide of Native Americans involved in the national holiday Columbus Day is one example of the irresponsibility of the privileged. European Americans not only commemorate Columbus's conquest, but then celebrate it by forgetting it, through commercialization and the rush to get a bargain on a pair of blue jeans. Not only is this deeply irresponsible on the part of the privileged; this irresponsibility is possible only under the conditions of such privilege. Members of Native American communities do not have the "privilege" of forgetting about the European conquest.

In the theater of privileged irresponsibility, some performances show the "reality" of the elite as extending freedom and breaking down racial inequality as an imaginary appearance. Instead, those performances that can expose the dominant self-view as imaginary, and not "true," can also at times show us that dominant practices of democracy are at times ineffectually political and culturally colonizing practices. As an example, in his work on the politics of blackface in the history of popular culture in the United States, Rogin argues that "democratized from court and plantation, minstrelsy enacted the urban white desire to acquire African American expressive power and supposed emotional freedom without actually freeing the slaves" (1996, 22). Although appearing to be democratizing acts that promote racial freedom by breaking oppressive social boundaries, performances of minstrelsy and blackface in effect mask the lack of action; they cover up white passivity in the face of injustice.

Ironic imagery in film, advertisements, and television that "switch" roles in a playful manner also expose a quite serious oppressive use of representation in the dominant performances of the politics of recognition. What is the potential of intentionally inverted performances of whites awkwardly trying to look like hip hop–styled Blacks, men placed in the sexualized contortions of female models, gay scriptwriters having fun with queer icons and jokes in straight sitcoms, the raced and gendered classic 9 to 5/The Associate corporate role reversal between lone irresponsible white male bosses and colluding smart white or Black women? Each instance of this sort is intended to disrupt current inegalitarian performances of recognition as part of the demand for opening up acts of recognition by and for marginalized groups in ways they themselves will name empowering, rather than oppressive, over time.

Recognition and Social Equality

Nancy Fraser places this newer demand for recognition as part of the "postsocialist" condition. This assessment is correct, but it is not postsocialist in terms of the breakup of the Soviet Union in the late 1980s. The turn to a politics of recognition as central to social justice activism is rooted earlier in the shift in political possibilities for those on the margins in light of the Red scare. The civil rights movement, which emerged as a mass force beginning in the 1950s and grew during the disintegration of the old left, actually relied on a politics of recognition for its first major victory.

Many would argue that the Supreme Court decision of *Brown v. Board of Education of Topeka, Kansas* (1954) marked the start of new mass movement politics related to identity and diversity. Many today think of the civil rights movement as the icon of the 1960s, and the 1950s as simply repressive given the cultural chill from the cold war and Senator McCarthy's anti-Red crusade. This is not an entirely accurate portrait of the era. It was actually in the 1950s that the civil rights movement new in strength began to emerge, and the activity related to *Brown v. Board* was central to that work.

In *Brown v. Board* the Supreme Court decided that the separate educational facilities for white and Black students created an inequality in the schools that is constitutionally unjustifiable. This case specifically overturned the earlier explicitly racist decision in *Plessy v. Ferguson*, which argued that equality could be found in racially separate facilities. (Minority views on integration as the best solution to end inequality have changed over the years and will be addressed below.) What is less often remembered is that the organizations sponsoring the case relied heavily on new ideas becoming popular in intellectual currents of academia. Professionals such as Kenneth Clark played significant roles in the *Brown* decision and the strategy used to succeed in the case.

Kenneth Clark was a civil rights activist and psychologist by professional training. Clark served as coordinator of the social science testimony for the NAACP (National Association for the Advancement of Colored People) Legal Defense and Education Fund. He was the main author of the social science statement signed by one hundred psychologists that was submitted to the court as an appendix of the NAACP brief. Clark relied on work that he and his wife, Mamie Phipps Clark, had done on racism and self-esteem among Blacks. The social science statement discussed the notion of an "inferiority complex" in order to ground the court decision, arguing that responding to a sociological interpretation of such a psychological state is part of the mission of our public schools (Keppel 1995). What we see from this is that a politics targeting issues of cultural recognition was central to a newly racialized form of radical social politics aimed foremost at ending exploitation.

Thus, although in many ways helpful, we must be careful about Fraser's characterization of the diversity politics version of a politics of recognition. She writes that "Many actors appear to be moving away from a socialist political imaginary, in which the central problem of justice is redistribution, to a 'postsocialist' political imaginary, in which the central problem of justice is recognition" (1997, 2). She perceives that "the result is a decoupling of cultural politics from social politics, and the relative eclipse of the latter by the former" (1997, 2). It is probably more helpful, however, to understand this decoupling as an historical legacy that effects the possibilities of recognition politics today. Thus the decoupling of which Fraser warns us may be better understood as a possible result (and not *the* result) in a shifting social justice politics in the United States.[15]

In any mass and diversely grounded form of activist politics, there will be those who comprehend social problems from their roots and demand radical changes, as there will be those whose vista remains more on the surface and/or demand reforms. It is true that not every individual, organization, or representation of recognition in contemporary diversity-politics is inherently related to radical critiques of exploitation and engaged in radical strategies of social transformation. Mass movements have historically relied on this diversity for attending to different levels of problems in their complexity. Diversity-based democratic theory must also be "large" enough to critically encompass and strategically interface with these many dimensions of movement and vision.[16] However, as Chapter Two discusses, Fraser's awareness of "decoupling" cultural issues from economic ones is a direct result of the struggles progressive groups faced during the McCarthy period. The mainstream civil rights organizations that survived the Red scare did so in part by distinguishing civil liberties and structural analysis from civil rights so as to avoid being the target of even harsher racism, anti-Semitism, and anticommunist hysteria. This move enabled some progressive organizations to come through the storm and be there to help pick up the pieces of political action when the craze died down. This legacy helped pave the way for current deep examinations of the issues at stake in a politics of recognition, even as it suffered from the lack of economic analysis. But once beyond the form of repression experienced by radicals and progressives in the 1950s, much activism and thinking in the nearly forty years since has again tied cultural to economic issues. For politics today, however, we must also note critically that in the ways hegemonic powers continue work to co-opt new challenges to the status quo by softening their radical edges so as to fit them into existing social structures, the commercialization of diversity has attempted explicitly to sever recent recognition politics from a more radical democratic notion of power and equity. This is a path many democratic activists and thinkers are, and must be, wary of.

Fraser is correct that recognition and economic redistribution, when presented as antitheses, are actually "false antithesis."[17] It is not, however, most helpful to understand the target of socialist agitation as distribution simply. A reading of Marx and much old left activism places distribution in the deeper context of the unequal power dynamics of exploitation that seek and result in unfair distribution. Although critical of Liberalism, however, much of socialist politics also avoided addressing head-on forms of oppression connected to but not exclusively economic.[18] For now we must distinguish that which has followed the path of decoupling from those working on a politics of recognition who are actualizing a different potential in this form of politics. In this chapter I am drawing on a host of democratic writers and activists who consider the cultural politics of recognition to be inherently bound to the social politics of economic class, "interests," "exploitation," and "redistribution." What I refer to here as a diversity-based politics of recognition involves the explicit attempts of what Fraser calls postsocialists to bring facets of cultural recognition into democratic politics aimed at ending economic exploitation.[19] In this view of the role of recognition in diversity-based democratic politics, recognition responds to injustices in Liberalism as well as unacceptable lapses in the old left imaginary and its resultant form of mass politics.

In *Race Rebels*, Kelly discusses how in his time working for McDonalds he saw many on the margins of society engaged in acute political struggles. Traditional socialist definitions of counterstruggles that are political, and the parameters of their political movements, however, would need to be redefined in order to see, incorporate, support, and build on the acts of rebellion in which he and the other workers were engaged. Kelly writes: "that we were part of the 'working class' engaged in workplace struggles never crossed our minds in part because the battles that were dear to most of us and the strategies we adopted fell outside the parameters of what most people think of as traditional 'labor' disputes." In responding to their exploitation as workers, Kelly explains that a different kind of politics was occurring: "the employees at the central Pasadena McDonalds were constantly inventing new ways to rebel, ways rooted in our own peculiar circumstance. And we never knew where the struggle would end. . . . But *what* we fought for *is* a crucial part of the overall story; the terrain was often cultural, centering in identity, dignity, and fun" (1994, 2–3).

That Fraser might characterize an example such as Kelly's as post-socialist seems fitting. She is also correct to warn us of the dangers of splitting a politics of recognition from a politics of social and economic equality. Many engaged in diversity politics have already been enacting Fraser's theoretical proposition that "the cultural politics of recognition ought not simply supplant the social politics of redistribution. Rather, the two need to be integrated with one another."[20] According to many involved at the time, the movements of the 1960s offered both a distributive and what they would call a qualitative critique of the United States (Morgan 1991). It is this form of a politics of recognition that I suggest we understand as answering the question "what are we after in democracy?" for newer diversity-based democratic activists and thinkers.

Diversity-Based Democratic Theory and a Critical Deployment of a Politics of Recognition

This does bring us, however, to other critical considerations in the new form of demands for recognition in democratic politics. A skepticism regarding recognition is understandable and healthy. Do we simply want to revalue any undervalued community and its ideas, including white-Christian supremacists? Does the call for recognition presuppose some essentially "good" characteristics of minority communities to replace "bad" stereotypes? Must we accept Berlin's (1969) fatalistic characterization that sometimes we may want recognition for our group so intensely that we may accept bullying from members of our own race or social class?[21] These questions are important ones to ask for democratic actors and thinkers. They do, however, miss certain crucial aspects that a new politics of recognition can contribute (and is often already contributing) to democratic theory and practices.

The call for recognition emerging out of diversity politics can help democratic theory stay grounded in and respond to the visions and needs of a variety of groups, particularly those historically marginalized that are making demands within a democratic framework. It places the cultural facets of politics on the agenda, demanding that democracy be attentive to the cultural dimensions of oppression and interrupting disrespectful and prejudiced performances that make possible and are made possible by exploitative practices. This does not mean, therefore, that what ought to be recognized instead of problematic images, or the alternative processes of diversity-stimulated recognition politics, are straightforward or simply known by segments of the population waiting to be put into place.

Democratic practitioners and theorists must remember that when referring to a politics of recognition it is *politics* that is being dealt with. To assume that there are stable identifiable identities out there waiting to be represented more truthfully is not a *politics* of recognition, but merely the implementation of a prior knowledge of real or essentialized identity. As discussed in the previous chapter, on the question "with whom ought democratic theory be concerned?" what we may best take from identity politics for a new democratic theory concerns a group-related notion of agency that involves a complex and multilayered political process of group and individual self-identification and the intentional inclusion of the lessons learned and the demands derived along the way from such a process in the public sphere. When we move to the question, "what are we after in democracy?" and answer by naming recognition, this means that we must make issues of recognition part of the conscious agendas in politics. There are usually multiple and competing negative images and methods of underrepresentation of women and minority groups in the history of Western democracies. Part of what the newer form of a politics of recognition is about is the explorations, dialogues, and disagreements within and among communities as they try to gain understandings, analyze, and transform these images and methods. Let us look at some examples.

African American women are simultaneously portrayed in mainstream U.S. culture as strong, hardworking single mothers in the face of the supposed breakdown of their community's traditional family structure, and as lazy and spoiled "queens" in collusion with their men and extended families to milk the welfare system. Jewish women are portrayed as simultaneously rudely direct, strong-willed over-achievers, and as manipulative—somehow both—promiscuous and frigid "princesses." Latinas are portrayed as wildly oversexualized roaming whores, and simultaneously repressed strict Catholics mothering large families. If Native American women are portrayed as "happy and simple" but "passive," it does not mean that happy and simple are better external stereotypes for them than passive. A politics of recognition is bound with a complicated historical process of communities themselves, in their own spheres and in relation to many other spheres, figuring out who they are, were, and aspire to be, what they do, did, and will need from themselves and intersecting larger society. Sorting through multiple and often contradictory bases of differing acts of recognition/nonrecognition/misrecognition in a system plagued with inequality, and designing alternatives, is a complicated political process occurring over time.

Thus, when democratic thinkers such as Michael Eric Dyson (1995) write of African American cultural styles, and ask if it is possible that this community can be let into the democratic process on its own terms, we must interrogate such a question. Is there one African American cultural style, is there one uncontested set of African American terms? Obviously not, and Dyson would not suggest that there is. When Mullings (1997) writes *On Our Own Terms*, her vision makes explicit racial, classed, and gendered differences in "the lives of African American women." The call to be let in on one's community's own terms is a popular way to demand that the internal and external processes of valuation and the ongoing, changing social-structural implementation of the fruits of such processes be more inclusive of the dynamics within the communities themselves.

Gutiérrez writes: "Reciting the psychic violence that racism and discrimination had wrecked on African Americans, Malcom X noted that the most profound had been the emasculation of black men. In the eyes of white America blacks were not deemed men. Thus whatever else the Black Power movement was, it was also about the cultural assertion of masculinity by young radical men. Chicanos faced what was undoubtedly a rather similar experience—social emasculation and cultural negation—by seeking strength and inspiration in a heroic Aztec past" (1993, 45). Does this mean that justice will be done simply by recognizing Black Power and an Aztec myth? We must be careful and subject this to critical

inquiry. That many Caribbean and African American men came to identify with Black Power, and Chicanos with an Aztec myth was a deeply
complex and political process not without contestation and alternatives
even among fellow radical Blacks and Mexican Americans. The processes
of emasculation from a white, Anglo, middle-class, Christian, able, heterosexual performance of masculinity involves modes of denigration
(disrespect, casting aspersion on the reputation of by blackening or dark-
ening) that have been clearly oppressive. Does this mean that for a politics of recognition to counter such oppression, Black men and Chicanos
should be revalorized as members of the dominant gender in its classed,
sexed, cultured, able, and raced form? Certainly not, and there are many
other possible responses to this question from the history of Caribbean/
African American and Chicano identity politics.

In the conclusion to Chapter Three I introduced Narayan's (1998)
notion of the Package Picture of Cultures. Critics of new demands for
recognition (as if these demands represent some fixed and obvious portrait of the historically despised) are relying on a concept, whether their
own or as an interpretation of identity politics, of communities as neatly
wrapped packages. When responding to simplistic demands for the correct representation of the distinct content of these sharply defined packages of cultures, critics may themselves accept such notions as the truth in
order to criticize the whole of the politics of recognition. The version of a
politics of recognition that I am suggesting can keep political theorizing
grounded in radical democratic visions, because it includes a broader
view of the more intricate dynamic between (using the above example)
vast segments of African/Caribbean American and Chicana/o communities. If some in Black Power named part of the oppression of Black men as
emasculating and sought to counteract it, other Black men and women—
including feminists, queers, and socialists—critically engaged with their
brothers in an intra- and intercommunal process of self-identification and
analysis and social transformation. Current performances that represent
Chicanos and Black men as less worthy than white men must be inter-
rupted. The methods of doing so, however, and the alternative more
empowering representations to be performed are still being figured out in
the processes of intra- and intercommunal politics. It is the conscious
attention to this multilayered dynamic within, among, and along with historically marginalized communities that makes the current incarnation of

a politics of recognition a potentially significant contribution to a more radical democratic praxis.[22]

Part II: Recognition Politics: Redefining Core Concepts

With some of the major ideas of a critical politics of recognition emerging from the margins and their potential contributions to new democratic theory, it is now time to assess how such a basis in recognition leads those involved to redefine certain core concepts of Western political thought. Although many on the margins would also claim they are after freedom, justice, and equality, what they mean when using these terms is often significantly different from mainstream, meaning default Liberal, definitions. The very ideas and practices of freedom, equality, and justice as employed under Liberalism are themselves involved in the modes of oppression experienced by those on the margins. Using notions of recognition put forward in contemporary diversity-based politics, we can now examine these three crucial concepts directly.

Justice

From a base in this politics of recognition we find that activists and new democratic thinkers offer a vision of justice that attunes us to a democratic politics fundamentally aimed at, in the words of Iris Marion Young (1990), overcoming oppression. Significantly, Young will characterize this notion of justice in relation to oppression as having numerous faces, rather than a single one: exploitation, marginalization, powerlessness, cultural imperialism, and violence. West (1993b) delineates lines of critical inquiry that aim also at examining subjugation, domination, and repression in order to keep notions of justice more responsive to the call of nondominant groups in a democracy than will starting with the more common distributive notion.[23] Laswell's (1936) idea of who gets what, when, and how is an important democratic concern even for radicals, but in a capitalist system it has tended to degenerate into a merely possessive vision of justice focused on regulating competing interests. Vision, dignity, voice, and fulfillment are reduced to static things rather than seen as functions of social relations, creating and created by social structures in institutional contexts. Nondialectical

Marxist approaches have similarly tended to remain on a macrostruc-
tural level of class, labor, and economics in a way that has blinded them
historically to many of the cultural aspects of oppression central to the
situations of various minority groups and more recently to the pre-
spectival difference of the working class.

Young reconceptualizes justice as "calls, pleas, claims *upon* some
people by others" (1990, 5). We might see this in contrast to a Kantian
or, in more contemporary terms, even a Rawlsian conceptualization of
justice as the quest for first principles. Phelan (1989) understands
oppression in terms not only of actions, but also the "psychic condition
of the individual." This occurs not just from discrete actions by the state,
or we could add in the labor market, but "from the entire social matrix
of which politics is a part." She writes, "in this broad sense, oppression
involves the denial of one's voice through the imposition of an external,
alien standard for the interpretation and judgement of one's thoughts,
actions and being" (16). This notion of oppression is a more helpful
grounding for justice work due precisely to the reason Liberalism has
avoided it: its ambiguity.

The tendency among Liberals to rely on positivism, which requires
objective proofs of certifiable and repeatable data, would thus catego-
rize this notion of oppression as too subjective. This is specifically the
situation a diversity-based politics of recognition seeks to address. As
Phelan points out, "the other side of the positivist's concern for facts is
a remarkable obtuseness and inability to deal critically with questions
that suggest the world of 'fact' is socially constructed and interpreted"
(20)—which we must acknowledge occurs within a highly charged field
of power relationships. It is by attending to issues of recognition as discussed above that justice work might be able to, as Phelan suggests,
"reconcile subjective perception and objective structure and meaning in
order to provide a fulcrum for social criticism" (17), and I would add,
concrete social transformation.

The foundationalist desire for first principles, for the "truthfulness" of
facts, is important to Liberalism's notion of justice as distributive. The
move to ground justice in (what appear to be) quantifiable things that we
have and can therefore split up and distribute in various ways relies on
a capacity to first limit matters of justice to things one is able to posses.
The possessive notion, as C. B. Macpherson (1962) has characterized it,
is not one built on core justice issues (as named by the oppressed in the

contemporary period) of recognition, dignity, human rights, the division of labor, self-respect, marginalization, and cultural imperialism. These are not all things, quantifiable, that can be distributed. Certain good-faith capitalists have tried, however, to heed the call of these new social justice movements and thus have attempted to at least extend this possessive notion of justice as distributive to these nonmaterial aspects. This is a misguided move both philosophically and politically.

The problem with merely extending the distributive paradigm to nondistributive aspects of justice, rather than rethinking justice as a whole, is that a variety of claims made by the oppressed are reduced to static things rather than understood as functions of dialectical social relations, creating and created by social structures in institutional contexts driven by power. As Young points out, it also "conceptualizes justice primarily in terms of end-state patterns, rather than focusing on social processes" (1990, 25). Political theorists are honing these ideas about justice being developed in activism—as a way of thinking about justice in terms of social relations and processes—combining some of these newer philosophical insights of postmodernism with Marxist dialectical notions of power.

Marx saw that as important as the redistribution of goods is, it is not necessarily in his view the core of the problem in society. We could say that for Marx, exploitation is the core of the problem and the foundational relationship in exploitation is one of power. Viewed in this way, the current form of diversity-based politics of recognition is potentially very much related to a socialist vision and need not be understood in contrast to justice demands for redistribution.

In some ways, however, even much of Marxist-based agitation has missed the crucial point, about justice being a relation and not only a problem of distribution, by largely focusing on the redistribution of wealth. This has happened particularly in reformist versions of trade unionism that look either at specific workplaces, rather than the class system, or seek to alter discrete allowances rather than involving a deeper conception of the relationship of exploitation. We cannot excuse the narrower version of trade unionism as simply a piecemeal or reformist strategy, as fighting for pay or benefit increases in an individual factory or even industry, or working to eliminate biohazards for a select group of workers might be in a nonrevolutionary era. There are even now alternatives to the distributive model in labor disputes.

Corporations that set limits on the ratio differentials between everyone in a company get closer to implementing shifts in the power relations over time.[24] Usually, a union must fight for a specific raise for workers in each contract. This most often requires a battle, whether ultimately successful or not, that is not only costly, but time consuming and time bound. It also sets workers off from owners and casts the problem as a problem for labor. When ratio differentials are the corporate structure, although employees might fight for altered ratios, the salaries and benefits of all those in the company are bound together. If those at the upper end of the pay/benefit scale use their power to increase their standing, they can only do so to the degree that the company can afford to increase the standing of every employee. Including workers effectively in decision-making processes is an example of a change that also gets beyond immediate distribution issues and enters more deeply into ongoing power imbalances that are structurally secured. In the current labor-management structure, workers usually have different perspectives from management on how to assess and address the needs of a company and its employees. Including workers in decision making involves including the politics of recognition of workers' views in traditional politics of redistribution.[25]

An important vision of justice emerging out of diversity politics places an emphasis on oppression. Discussions of recognition are aimed at addressing the variety of modes of inequity in our system. In this the argument is also the notion that discussions of distribution must take place in the context of a politics of recognition. This does not mean that one must see recognition as in some way lexically prior to distribution,[26] or vice versa. We do not need to argue whether recognition ought to come first and then distribution issues, or the other way around. This would involve a severing of recognition from redistribution. Because issues of recognition are imbricated with issues of equity, exploitation, and distribution, such a severing does not make sense. I place recognition first in this chapter for explanation simply due to the tendency of many people, whether Liberals or socialists, to jump to a discussion of distribution when exploring justice. Moving immediately to a discussion of distribution in the possessive context of capitalism begs the significant political questions of how a polity decides what goods could be up for distribution publicly, how to distribute goods according to what principles and assessments of whose needs, and how to reevaluate any particular set of decisions regarding the above. But this is not all. Such questions still assume that the only issue for justice is distribution, as if all matters of justice involved quantifiable things.

Inequality in concrete material goods is certainly an issue for democratic politics. Without an awareness of the need for recognition, however, it will be difficult to assess who needs what. A central lesson of postcolonial thought is that fair distribution is meaningless if people and groups themselves cannot determine and discuss with others what they need distributed to them and what might be the best means to do so. But there are two additional points to keep in mind. First, a politics that acknowledges the importance of recognition will also be able to examine fair methods of determining what various individuals and groups might have to offer in the social, political, and cultural process, rather than focusing only on what is to be received. Second, without including an end to multilayered modes of oppression involving exploitation, violence, marginalization, cultural imperialism, and powerlessness—much of which does not occur only in problems of goods or things—justice will not relate to the actual problems faced by the oppressed.

Equality

It is not clear what a conception of justice is that demands equity in terms of distribution, an equal respect for the dignity and moral worth of people, equal human rights and so forth if we do not clarify what understandings of equality are currently being employed in diversity-based politics. Additionally, we will not understand this idea of equality if we do not place it in the context of recognition. To return to a Liberal characterization of the relationship between recognition issues and equality, note Rawls's view: "in a well-ordered society, then, self respect is secured by the public affirmation of the status of equal citizenship for all" (1971, 545). But Liberalism has a tendency to presume that being a democracy means that members of the polity enjoy "the status of equal citizenship for all." One might want to call the United States a democracy, but one could hardly argue that all citizens enjoy equal status in terms of our concrete social conditions. Jefferson wrote in the Declaration of Independence that it was "self-evident that all men are created equal." There is not much for democratic thinkers and actors to problematize politically if equality is presumed a settled matter philosophically. Hawkesworth presents a differing view, that equality is "the consequence of participatory citizenship and a goal of democratic politics" rather than the presumption in Liberalism that equality is a pre-political given (1997, 13).[27]

How are diversity-based democratic thinkers and actors conceiving of this goal of participatory citizenship called equality in the context of recognition? The most helpful way to engage with the theories and activism emerging since the 1960s on this point is to think in terms of difference and sameness. When some characterize early identity politics as caught in a dilemma between equality and difference, they express debates central to new social movements since the 1960s even as they misrepresent them.[28] It is probably more helpful to clarify that the debates were about equality, and the differing perspectives on how best to conceive and strategize this equality relied on notions that drew on the concepts of sameness and difference. As Minow reminds us, "the problems of inequality can be exacerbated both by treating members of minority groups the same as members of the majority and by treating the two groups differently" (1990, 20). It depends on the context, its capacity for complex (or not strictly Liberal) political workings, and who gets to set the terms of the debate. By the 1980s those involved in radical democratic politics were increasingly presenting a more nuanced form of this discussion, so that "equality" and "difference" were not pitted against each other as opposites, but seen in a more dialectical relationship of sameness and difference in their composition of equality.

In order to set this dialectical reworking of sameness and difference in motion, this form of diversity politics represents a practical reinterpretation of the ancient Greek notion of proportionate equality. Greek philosophers, as well as more modern Conservatives, employed a version of equality that set likes equal to one another. This idea of equality was used to bolster a distinctly inegalitarian social structure. As unlikes were distinguished, as among the different classes, they were to be treated unlike one another. How may we understand this as a notion of equality?

In his *Republic*, Plato delineated three parts of the soul that relate to three classes in society. According to Plato, three parts of the soul—the appetite lodged in the belly and genitals, the spirited element lodged in the chest, and reason lodged in the head—exist in different proportions among people, leading to distinct classes. Some people are like bronze and are ruled more by their appetites, some are like silver and their sense of honor stands out, while others are like gold and are guided by their wisdom. Justice exists in the state when membership in the three classes is clear and each performs its appointed duty: bronze commoners and tradespeople are productive, silver guardians are executive, and gold philosopher kings perform deliberative and governing functions. For Plato, to treat guardians as commoners or common tradespeople as philosopher kings would be the height of injustice.

Burke (1969) as another example of a similar approach, drew clear lines between the aristocracy and the lower classes, each having their distinct characteristics, capacities, and duties. For Burke, a society where the lower classes would engage in governance suited to the elite, or one where the nobility would be treated as mere men and women, is a society gone mad. In this line of thinking, to treat commoners according to a standard designed for them, and not according to a standard designed for nobility, is to treat all equally by treating them differently. In each case, this view of equality as proportional was used in societies as different as Plato's and Burke's to maintain systemic hierarchy.

In response, Liberalism redefined equality in such a way as to avoid the hypocrisy of arguing for an equality that would justify hierarchy. It did so, however, by jettisoning the notion of difference. Liberal equality, since Hobbes defined it as the same ability each of us has to kill another, has relied on sameness as its defining principle. Hobbes's assertion in 1651 in *Leviathan* that "[n]ature hath made men so equall, in the faculties of body, and mind . . . when all is reckoned together . . . the weakest has strength enough to kill the strongest" (1968, 183) is perhaps the first great statement of equality in the modern period. This emphasis on sameness, however, has an effect of a violent exclusion of all who are different from the professed norm. Hobbes wrote "that every man [should] strive to accommodate himselfe to the rest;" that despite "a diversity of nature" if some do not fit—like irregular stones when building an edifice—or "[take] more room from others" and it cannot be "corrected," they are "to be left, or cast out of Society, as cumbersome thereunto" (1968, 209).

As radical as were claims for women's suffrage, manumission of the slaves, early civil rights work against segregation, early second-wave feminism's and gays' and lesbians' calls for equal rights, much in these struggles relied on the dominant Liberal understanding of equality as being treated "the same as." If those with disabilities are discriminated against because of their difference from those with abilities, the first move to end discrimination was to stop their differential, in this case meaning discriminatory, treatment. Inequality also for women, African Americans, Jews, working-class folks, Asians, Latina/os, Native Americans, and queers, as other examples, is seen in that they are treated differently from heterosexual, middle-class, white, Anglo, Christian men. In these cases, "differential treatment" meant power differentials so that some enjoyed privilege and access and some did not. The call for equality meant ending differential treatment for these groups, meaning ending discriminatory treatment. But this is a problem when ending differential treatment that is discriminatory gets confused with the need to be blind to the potential differences between groups, whether due to histories of discrimination, cultural practices, and/or varieties of needs.

As stated, the Liberal notion sees equality as a sameness. To treat x *equally* with y is to treat x *the same as* y. In this case, the historical treatment of y becomes the standard for the "equal" treatment of x. This has created a colonizing practice of coercive assimilation to the dominant paradigm if one is to be treated equally or accorded equal rights. The social movements since the 1960s in the United States have drawn on Liberalism's rejection of hierarchy, but themselves increasingly reject the sameness model. Often enough, ending discrimination does not mean being blind to what is, or has been historically, different among groups.[29] What we now find is a radical reclaiming of a proportionate form of equality that, in contrast to the Platonic and Conservative uses, purposely aims at overthrowing relations of domination and institutionalized hierarchies.

Audre Lorde, an African American lesbian feminist socialist, offers some important insights on this point. She reminds us that "institutional rejection of difference is an absolute necessity in a profit economy which needs outsiders as surplus people" (1984, 115). Consequently, we have all been taught to see differences in simplistic opposition such that one signifier is always dominant and the other subordinate. We must, instead, look across difference in equality. In this light we can see such concepts as affirmative action as attempts to reclaim the Greek, and later Conservative, notion of proportionate equality for contemporary social justice politics.[30] For example, I must treat Sandra, a student in my political theory class with a hearing impairment, differently from hearing-abled students and according to her specific needs in order to actually be treating her equally in the classroom setting: that is, to ensure the quality of her education as I would other students'. I must allow her an assistant to take notes if she requests this, keep a space open in the front row of the class for her to sit in, and attend to my own enunciation so that she may be able to read my lips. I do not necessarily have to care for such things for my hearing-abled students who are the majority, but ensuring an equal education for Sandra requires that I do care for these things for her. Approaching difference in its specificity for the goal of overcoming oppressions in their myriad manifestations means treating individuals and groups equally often enough not by treating them "the same" but by treating them differently.[31]

Freedom

In the United States, perhaps the first answer one would have expected to the question "what are the oppressed after in democratic politics?" would be freedom. Freedom has become so equated with the myth of "America" that its meaning is rarely questioned in mainstream politics and its use is of great service to advertising specialists. "Freedom" is simply a good, so we can name a gas station chain in South Dakota "Freedom," or boost the sales of products on the market if we suggest that somehow buying this foot powder or other product will "set you free!" We will have to look critically at what is usually meant by freedom in these settings in order to understand the rather different meaning of cries for freedom emerging from the oppressed in the current version of diversity-based recognition politics. Before we do so, however, let us address why many might have expected this to be the first section of this chapter, and not the final one.

Freedom and equality are often coupled concepts in politics; together they provide the vocabulary for explorations of justice. I would suggest that the phenomenon in my predominantly white classrooms in U.S. universities where most of my students would first say they want "freedom" is a cultural specificity based on an ideological assumption. Students do not have to have read Thomas Hobbes, John Locke, or Adam Smith to have been schooled in Liberal ideas. Because Liberalism is the dominant ideology in the United States, "commonsense" understandings tend to reflect Liberal conceptions and thus constitute the default position of most of the populace from Arkansas to Pennsylvania to Los Angeles. In Liberalism freedom is the dominant conception in the couplet with equality. Equality in this mode is therefore defined in terms of freedom. A common definition of equality in this version is that in the

United States we are all equally free to pursue our individual life plans, in other words, to do what we want. As Berlin puts it, in this tradition we have an "equality of liberty" (1969, 125). But this is not the only possible relationship between the two terms. Other approaches set equality as the dominant conception and define freedom in its terms.

Compare the Liberal, or common U.S. version, with Marx's coupling of freedom and equality or with that of Theresa Asago'n de Valdez. In the *Communist Manifesto* Marx envisions a society where "[i]n place of the old bourgeois society, with its classes and class antagonisms, we shall have an association, in which the free development of each is the condition for the free development of all."[32] Valdez, a Chicana political activist and writer, says that "true freedom for our people can come about only if prefaced by the equality of individuals within La Raza" (1980, 11). Marx refers to society as a whole and suggests that in order to say that there is freedom, or that one or a group is free, everyone must be free. A perception of individual freedom in a society where others are unfree is a misperception. Valdez refers to this on the level of intra-communal politics so that there must be equality among the members of a community in order for the community as a whole to be considered free. In these two accounts, freedom's constitution through equality relies on a relational model rather than an individualistic one. This is an important distinction if we are to make sense of the ways that calls for freedom from those on the margins of society are made in the context of recognition politics and potential contributions to new concepts in democratic theory.[33]

On the concept of freedom more generally, Liberalism posits a negative form: freedom *from* outside constraints.[34] As Hobbes puts it so succinctly: "By Liberty, is understood, according to the proper signification of the word, the absence of externall impediments" (1968, 189). This idea of freedom as throwing off the yoke of oppression has energized social movements throughout history and significantly informed Marxist organizing. But Marx and the new social movements include additional dimensions of freedom in their political praxis. This is because when taken in isolation, Liberalism's freedom *from* is often irresponsible, resembling a stereotypical Western male adolescent who wants to be free *from* his parents' rule, free *from* all authority, so he can wreak havoc and simply do as he pleases without any attachments. As Nancy Hirschmann describes it, freedom *from* posits a separative subject whose desires come from within, standing opposed to the outer forces that would restrain (1996, 53).[35]

Isaiah Berlin and T. H. Green[36] designate an alternate form of freedom as positive. In this case, freedom is understood as freedom *to* act, to exercise our capacities, to engage, or as Berlin suggests, "to lead one prescribed form of life" (1969, 131). Hirschmann (1996) sees this form of freedom as challenging the duality of the negative form. Currently we find that visions of freedom are not only energizing these movements in their negative form, but also in the positive form of freedom *to*.[37] In the paradigmatic liberation story of the biblical exodus from Egypt, we might focus on the escape from bondage only. This would mirror the notion of freedom *from*. The story is also, however, a story about rising up out of slavery *in order to* be a free people able to make a civilization together. Freedom *from* bondage is a good, but we must also ask, what do we want to be free *for*?

Moreover, I am indebted to Roelofs for help in clarifying these categorizations. H. Mark Roelofs (1992) adds a third dimension to this discussion, that of freedom *with*.[38] Freedom here has a relational quality, rather than being seen as the prerogative of a separative individual for the purposes of selfish interests, or as purely instrumental. This notion of freedom assumes the primacy of intimate and communal attachments. In what we might consider a critique of the Liberal mode of a dimension of freedom discussed above, Bennet looks at freedom as wild and unconstrained and suggests that instead "[m]obility is widest when it's *not* random, erratic, or too fast; space for becoming is greatest when it's *not* an accidental effect; and novelty is most valuable when it's *not* treated as an end-in-itself" (1988, 34). Her alternative view of freedom, rather than individualistic and self-serving, is more relational; she suggests an ensemble of elements—"dynamism-wonder, morphing-reflection, charm-conscience, flexibility-possibility—be mobilized in relation to all the others, for without the ensemble you could end up with a ruthless commitment to your own mobility, or a merely spectatorial caring, or a homesick variant of romanticism" (1988, 35).[39]

In this third conception of freedom *with*, we want freedom to be *with* our loved ones, comrades, fellow community members. This dimension highlights a third perspective on the paradigmatic biblical story as being about not only the imperative to escape oppression, but the freedom *to* become a people, and develop a *joint* communal life. Although the discussion of negative freedom *from* and positing of a positive freedom *to* tied to an alternative freedom *with* have been derived by and often applauded by many on the "left," those in marginalized communities remind us to be cautious of how these characterizations might still favor elite groups, and that we must continue to reshape notions of freedom as new counter and alternative voices are raised. Contemporary movements for social justice in the recognition mode are also often community-based movements demanding an end to unjust treatment, the ability to meet their needs and pursue their dreams and aspirations, together with their communities, loved ones, and comrades in ways they designate for themselves. When consciously connected to the lives of those on the margins, the activism of radical movements in the United States interweaves ethical and communal aspirations of freedom *with* in a dialectic with the powerful freedom *from* and freedom *to* in new ways.

Let us return to Young's alternative conception of justice to offer an example. She argues that we need to shift the paradigm of justice to one that refers "also to the institutional conditions necessary for the development and exercise of individual capacities and collective communication and cooperation" (1990, 39). Here Young merges new notions of freedom *from*, freedom *to*, and freedom *with*. Further, Young writes that "[r]ational reflection on justice begins in a hearing, in heeding a call, rather than in asserting and mastering a state of affairs, however ideal" (1990, 5). This is a nonfoundationalist reworking of justice. It is not based on a need to ground the notion of justice in a universal foundation. It is part of a changing political landscape that comes in the form of a call from the marginalized in society and designates the necessity of the privileged to listen. This makes sense, however, only in the context of freedom redefined and related to equality in a way different from that commonly found in Liberalism.

When asked where our freedoms come from, most students of U.S. democracy will answer that they are granted primarily in the First Amendment to the Constitution, which enumerates freedom of speech, thought, and assembly. In Mill's defense of this view, our freedom consists in the law's capacity to stop others from interfering in our thinking, expressing, and gathering.[40] But "freedom of speech"—as understood commonly in the United States as the freedom *from* external constraints on our expression—is not grounded in the communal presumption of a freedom *with*, nor on the normative good specified in answering freedom *to*'s implicit question: "we want to be free *from* constraints on our speech *in order to* develop what kind of life and practices?"

Often the call from marginalized groups does not focus on this "freedom of speech" alone, but on the larger context in which ideas are produced and the speech is made possible, and on what kind of relationships exist so that there will be folks around who will listen.[41] To describe the politics of recognition in terms of promoting the freedom of means of expression outside culturally dominant norms is to miss the point of the "recognition." It is easy for those already with access to the megaphones to find freedom of expression the quintessential form of freedom. Minorities and those historically on the margins may secure more protection from the external constraints on their various expressions over time, but that does not mean that the majority or those in power will bother to stop and take a look long enough to do more than just market such expressions—such as rap music or hip hop clothing styles—for their personal gain. Promoting freedom of speech does not mean that communities will get the space they need to figure out what their public needs are. It does not mean that the privileged will cross cultural boundaries to understand what I am saying in my language and in my own way. Nor does it mean that even if I learn to speak in the accepted modes of the dominant culture that anyone in that culture will bother to stop and listen to what I am saying, let alone take my voice seriously and possibly respond.

CONCLUSION

A politics of recognition puts issues of communal and individual expression on the table for conscious revaluing as a part of an effort to change the power imbalances of inequality rampant in our current form of "democracy." Justice work involves what it takes to get those with an historically privileged irresponsibility to overcome structural and cultural aloofness. A politics of recognition seeks to create modes of public discourse and processes in which the privileged begin seeing and listening to the complex identities, needs, and visions of those long relegated out of sight. What other kinds of reconceptualizations will this take, and where and how might we be able to put this critical form of a politics of recognition into practice? In the next chapter we will address certain obstacles to recognition in this understanding currently faced by those on the margins. From there we can proceed to the where and the how.

5   Why: Rethinking Universals
and Particulars

INTRODUCTION

AS AN EMERGENT democratic theory attending to oppressed groups and pursuing a politics of recognition, diversity-based politics from the margins has also revived the discussion of *why* we engage in politics, offering new ideas about the empirical and normative grounds that motivate political involvement. Why do people participate in democratic politics, and what grounds ought democratic theory to encourage as the basis of politics? Although apparently contradictory to one another, major democratic theories have posited two main answers to this question. Some thinkers answer the *why* question of politics by pointing to individual self-interest. Others have based their ideas on conceptions of the public good. The prevalence of both these polar opposite answers relies on the tendency in democratic theories to split what is seen as altruistic motivations from selfish ones and to consider them at odds.

We can see at work in much multiculturally oriented activism today, however, an assumption that politics is and ought to be about social relations of dignity and respect. In this view, democratic politics characterizes a process of identifying, interpreting, and developing strategies to meet our ever changing aspirations and needs as individuals and as communities. Such an understanding does not rely on dichotomizing specific and general motivations, striving simply for either self-centered or for

This chapter appeared in an earlier form in "Theorizing Citizenship from the Margins," *The Southeastern Political Review* 26, 3 (1998): 519–544. Reprinted by permission.

For their feedback and the lively discussion, I would like to thank those on the Feminist Theory and Citizenship panel at the 1996 Western Political Science Association Meeting where this was first presented as a paper: Martha Ackelsberg, Patricia Moynagh, Lori Marso, and Shane Phelan. I also owe a debt to Mark Roelofs and Bertell Ollman, whose work has stimulated some of the thinking over the years that has surprisingly found its way into the last sections of this chapter.

collective ends. It is here, then, in looking critically at the relationship between universals and particulars, that we will best be able to understand this newer democratic theory's answer to the *why* question and its significance in terms of the history of democratic thought. Instead of refusing to engage in the theoretical world of universals and particulars, a refusal commonly found in certain postmodern theories, diversity-based democratic theory can continue to make use of these concepts but in new, dialectical ways. In answering the question *why* in politics, much of multiculturalism focuses us again on the historical development of various ideas, offering an important critique of the existing framework of the argument and bringing the debate forward with new contributions.

CITIZENSHIP AND THE WHY QUESTION

In the last chapter I argued that in response to the question "what" are those involved in this new democratic praxis after? we must first attend to discussions concerning recognition, and from there find that those on the margins are redefining core concepts of Western political thought such as justice, freedom, and equality. Utilizing Charles Taylor's essay "Multiculturalism and the Politics of Recognition," I examined the move to incorporate the acknowledgment of cultural differences into democratic praxis and fundamental ideas such as equality. Taylor, however, points out that such acknowledgment generates an apparent contradiction in this new line of thinking. On the one hand, we can see an emphasis on sameness historically in the demand for equality as a universal human right. On the other hand, the politics of recognition seems at first glance to move in the opposite direction—toward the demand for recognition based on all of our differences. In the essay on recognition, Taylor demonstrates that these two demands are not quite as separate as they may seem. He writes that "the politics of difference is full of denunciations of discrimination and refusals of second-class citizenship." Such a statement suggests that the politics of difference rests on a notion of universal equality. This might appear to cause tension, philosophically. What we are more likely to see in this case, however, is an interactive relationship in which particular aspects of difference are not actually standing against universal concepts. Taylor explains this in that "we give due acknowledgment only to what is universally present—everyone has an identity—through recognizing what is peculiar to each. The universal demand powers an acknowledgment of specificity" (1994, 39).

Taylor's perspective is helpful for sorting out the complicated aspects involved in answering the *why* question in political theory. But I would also like to point out an interesting facet of his discussion: Taylor slips immediately into the realm of citizenship to illustrate his point on sameness and difference. This happens easily because when we are recognized in democratic politics, we are usually seen as citizens. In democratic thought, then, theorizing about such issues tends predominantly to occur within the framework of theories on citizenship. Thus, in order to examine new understandings about universals and particulars coming from those on the margins as I attempt to answer the *why* question, I will locate this discussion within the framework of theories on citizenship. What we will find, however, is that we will have to rethink such a framework when trying to bring about a more transformed and inclusive democratic praxis.

One reason we will need to reevaluate the framework of citizenship is that with increasing migration and the tenuous status of refugees geopolitically, we need to attend to those living within any set of juridical borders who are not citizens at all. Uma Narayan, an Indian feminist philosopher currently working in the United States on Third World feminism, explains that demands for justice within the language of citizenship often have a Janus-faced quality. What she means by this is that "on the one hand, the term has had a significant role in struggles to secure greater dignity, rights and participation for members of marginalized groups; on the other hand it has often *simultaneously functioned* to justify the exclusion of other members of the national community" (1997b, 64). Narayan "suggests that concerns articulated in the name of citizenship should often be broadly construed to include all those who are ongoing members of the national community" (49).[1]

We must take into account Narayan's cautions. When we do so, however, we also find that within more traditional democratic theories it is not only noncitizens who experience exclusion. Even most people with formal citizenship status are not included in a politics of dignity, rights, and participation. Utilizing the contributions from those on the margins, how are we to make sense of these limitations for people, citizens or noncitizens, and what does a more diversity-based democratic theory suggest in light of this critical understanding?

In the Western canon there are numerous democratic traditions that utilize the citizenship framework. When we study their underlying democratic theories, we can find numerous significant differences between them. One example of such a difference may be seen between the tradition referred to as civic Republicanism and the Liberal tradition. Republicanism tends to demand that citizens transcend their selfish interests in pursuit of the common good. In contrast, Liberals tend to assume that each member's working to maximize self-interest within the framework of the law will lead society to achieve a state in which individual understandings of the good can be protected in common. Such differences are important to contemporary discussions of diversity politics. However, in order to begin the project of theorizing citizenship from the margins—as we examine the *why* in democratic theory—one must first note the similarities between such divergent democratic visions and be clear about the implications of the convergences. Thus, let us first address certain similarities between these two traditions.

Based on an assumption of an impartial civic public, in both the Liberal and Republican traditions, citizens are expected to be rational actors capable of acting independently and discerning reasoned solutions to social questions. Critical examination of the relationship between identity and power reveals that the philosophical vision of an atomistically autonomous and objective citizen served to justify in practice the exclusion of many who were deemed incapable of assuming the appropriate distance. Such designations tended to be based on economic, cultural (including race/ethnicity and religion) and gender grounds. Feminist and minority scholars have shown how such forms of political philosophizing served to justify and also to reinforce the concrete oppression of these groups.[2] How does this work more specifically?

Rethinking Politics (Public and Private) from the Margins

Through a critical analysis of the *why* question that moves from the margins, one can reexamine the traditional expectations of citizenship. The oppression of women, those with disabilities, people of color, Jews, and sexual minorities relies on multiple and complex mechanisms and philosophical assumptions that often significantly distinguish the oppression of one of these groups from another. There are also times that we might find it productive to focus on similarities among groups' oppressions.

The groups named above have in common the experience of exclusion from public spaces for deliberation and decision making that is a central and operative aspect of each distinct oppression.[3] If these groups have been oppressed in part due to biased presumptions about political motivation, and this has occurred through marginalization in the formal arena of citizenship, a reexamination of the parameters of, and demands one might make on, that sphere is in order. This can be achieved by entering into an analysis of the web of other less formal spheres in which women and marginalized minorities *have* engaged.

However, one encounters a roadblock even before beginning. Of what use is it to look at the informal worlds of "others," interesting as that might be in an anthropological study, if we are trying to rethink the quite formal realm of citizenship for its impact on the polity consisting of both citizens and noncitizens? Such a hesitation is rooted in the hierarchical ordering of the experience of privileged men over that of women and marginalized minorities. What is at work here is what feminists have named the public/private split as a mechanism to legitimize, as well as to give voice to, certain groups . . . and to silence others.

As has been discussed often, a common thread in the versions of the public/private distinction found in much Western canonical thinking is the association of men from dominant identity communities with the public (e.g., Elshtain 1981). Specific characteristics such as rationality and distance marked those capable of autonomous participation in the worlds of formal law, economics, and politics. Conversely, women and members of nondominant groups, with all of the contradictions that the attempt to separate these categories imply, have been associated often with emotion and connection/dependency and therefore deemed fit only for private arenas concerned with the home or with physical caretaking (e.g., Tronto 1993).

Feminist and many minority activists and theorists have reinterpreted these categories. Their work exposes the political nature of the other relationships in which those on the margins have been engaged historically. It is no longer acceptable to relegate all that happens in the home, for example, or in other less formal relationships outside government and the public market, to the private. In doing so we relegate to silence the people and their experiences found within such spheres. Feminists said we must have women's "private" issues (such as housework, sex, rape, and domestic violence) on the public agenda. These are political, by nature public, issues because they concern one of the primary aspects of politics: oppression. This important work brought the negative experiences of the oppressed in the so-called private world out into public view so that they could be acknowledged as social issues, analyzed, and overcome (e.g., Freeman 1975, Rich 1986, Evans 1979).

Scholars can now also look to other aspects of the so-called private spheres in which the marginalized spend their time. One can claim other aspects of our lives as political also because we bring the attention of society to bear on these experiences, subjecting them now to philosophical analysis and critique in the service of the political goals of freedom and equality. Given the importance of citizenship to democratic theory historically, we must engage with the subject of citizenship in our examination of political motivation. To begin, we need to remember that citizenship is a certain kind of relationship. Remembering that citizenship is one kind of relationship calls us also to explore other relationships that might prove interesting for the potentialities of comparative analysis. As citizenship is clearly a political relationship, this chapter explores the politics of, and the political lessons to be gleaned from, some of the experiences marginalized groups have had in other relationships. As feminist theorists have already done much work on the subject of citizenship, I will utilize their insights and often refer explicitly to diverse women's experiences in these other relationships.

ALTERNATIVE SPHERES

Of particular note for the purposes of this chapter are the relationships within families and among friends, neighbors, and comrades. These are areas in which nondominant groups have always been active participants, but they are realms that traditionally have not been deemed political. Looking critically at these other relationships in terms of their political import, we will see that certain problems in democratic theories and practices of citizenship will be set in relief by the marginalized, whether technically citizens or not. In attempting to answer the *why* question, at this point we must ask: what can thinkers learn for a new democratic membership, one that is more inclusive and open to diversity, from the relationships and skills women and oppressed minorities have developed in these spheres? In addition we ask: how do we go about such a project without falling into false essentialisms, reifications of oppressive assignations, and a tendency toward totalizing discourse around extremely diffuse life experiences? In order to proceed any further, one must engage this last question first.

Concerns

How can one claim to look at, for example, "diverse women's experiences in families and friendships, as neighbors and comrades" as I propose to do in this chapter? There is no single way one could even attempt to summarize the characteristics of these relationships from the myriad perspectives of all the individuals involved. The fears expressed by many antiessentialist theorists are certainly legitimate. Antiessentialists might suggest that attempts to discuss these relationships as a whole will necessitate facile and oversimplified generalizations, representations that are monolithic and themselves unproblematized.[4] Yet what follows is precisely such a discussion. Why is it still appropriate, and how can it be done without essentializing?[5]

First, I make no claim to present a new or exhaustive study of people's experiences in these spheres. The purposes that compel theorists to look to these relationships do not necessitate exhaustive accounts or even "new empirical" research (see also Spelman 1988, 140). There is no such thing as an exhaustive account of people's lives. Scholarly expectations of a total rendering tend to rest on the suggestion that there can be a single truth to our lives that could be uncovered and articulated. Looking at why people get involved in politics and linking this to a concern for more inclusive democratic forms of membership and citizenship does not need to rely on empirical truth claims from people's experiences. The aim is, instead, to learn *some* lessons from different people's experiences to see how we may understand political motivation and thus suggest a view of democratic membership that is more inclusive in both form and content. With that normative, philosophical goal, theorists can look for lessons in *some* of the representations and interpretations of these experiences.

Also, as I look in this chapter to a diverse set of women's experiences, this search is consciously limited to representations and interpretations that claim to be explicitly feminist, as it will be feminist lessons that are being sought. Here, I make no claim to objectivity. Therefore it is quite obvious—without necessarily being debilitating—that others may learn different lessons from these same experiential spheres, and then they can write a different sort of theory. If I choose certain characteristics—that at least many recognize as characteristics of certain of these relationships—that is all I am doing. I am not claiming them to be wholly representative of the relationship or to be expressing some essential characteristic thereof. Even if we are looking primarily at one group in this case, women, the chief goal is to let as many different communities of women speak to the issue at hand. If readers are interested in pursuing inquiries further within the specific, diverse communities that I draw on in the following analysis, the notes should provide a helpful outline of the literature. This section thus continues with a brief review of some of the relevant feminist literature concerning women's experiences in families and friendships, as neighbors and comrades from a diverse and interweaving cluster of communities.

Experiences

Families

Most feminist literature on women's relationships in families across diverse communities tends to focus on motherhood. Some feminist scholars remind us that, even with significant transcultural and transhistorical differences, a common characteristic can be found in that there is a division of labor in families and that females primarily mother.[6] The multicultural feminist literature on motherhood[7] suggests a significant aspect of many women's experiences in families is that of relation, and in particular relations wherein *one's* self/role is understood in that one helps, loves, protects, nurtures, provides, cares for, and prepares *others* into their own selfhood in the world.[8]

   In contrast to rather essentialized representations of white, middle-class, Christian women, these texts provide a complicated picture of motherhood that is at the center of so many women's experience in families. Much of the multicultural feminist literature portrays neither simply an idyllic and selfless madonna, nor an hysterical and parochial protector. Instead we tend to find a complex being of love and rage, struggling to survive herself as well as to care for and prepare others for survival and celebration in an often hostile world. That the work of mothering is done primarily by females does not, however, necessarily mean it is performed exclusively by mothers (biological or adoptive). In fact, usually mothering responsibilities extend to females in general in relation to younger females and to males of any age (daughters and sisters/cousins are still usually

expected to mother—that is, to be good listeners, provide emotional support, undertake food preparation, and do housework for—their fathers
and brothers/male cousins). Moreover, in many nondominant communities such expectations extend not only to biological relations, but to
women as neighbors as well.

Neighbors

Therefore, one of the main reasons it is difficult to distinguish declaratively between women's experiences in families and as neighbors is
that, for many women, familial-style relations extend beyond nuclear
configurations to kinship networks throughout their neighborhoods.
Literature particularly on many minority ethnic and racial groups
demonstrates that households in these communities are not isolated
units but stretch out beyond these separate boundaries. Many women's
lives in the context of their neighborhoods are constructed, and play
out, in connection to others through links to formal structures such as
parent-teacher associations and civic organizations, religious centers,
and work in local shops and factories. The web is woven also through
less formal spheres women specifically help to initiate, such as arrangements for health care and services, care for the communities' children
and elders, as well as extended kinship and cultural ties that women
create and maintain.[9] Although there are significant specificities across
many communities, such a characterization of relatedness in bonds of
mutual support seems appropriate for many women as "neighbors."
This understanding is developed from an examination of life not only
in many country towns, but also in the presumably more alienating
neighborhoods found in suburbs and urban environments. We can also
find numerous incidences of this dynamic among neighbors who do not
live in "neighborhoods," such as rural, college, and "homeless" women
(see Ackelsberg 1984, Gould 1995, Roesenthal 1993).

Friendships

It may not be surprising, then, that I will have trouble separating out
women's experiences in the sphere of friendship from their experiences
in the spheres of families and neighborhoods. Zavella (1987), for example, discusses the work and family/kin/neighbor-related friendship
networks among Chicana cannery workers in the Santa Clara Valley
that were central to the women's lives. As another example from a dif-

ferent ethnic minority, Hareven (1982, 85) stresses the importance of friendships that emerged among women as workers and through their joint experiences in factories and mills in a New England industrial community. Due to the homophobia in their towns and families of birth, many lesbians often migrate to new locations explicitly for their queer populations and form new, nonbiological families and kin structures among the friends they make in their new neighborhoods. For many women their sisters, cousins, mothers, or other female family members are their closest friends, and lesbians often discuss the difficulties of distinguishing between friends and lovers. Many lesbians also experience their relationships with other women not necessarily as being split definitively between the categories friends and lovers/families, but more on a continuum between such relationships.[10]

The more well-known philosophical writings on friendship have been done by elite men. A central feature that stands out in these writings is that friendship transcends the dichotomous split philosophers often impose between egoism (self-directed activity) and altruism (other-directed activity). Moreover, friendship is often understood as interwoven with human relationships in other spheres of life, such as religion, family, and politics. It has been suggested that friendship is so little discussed among male theorists precisely because it seems to merge these categories otherwise assumed distinct in much of canonical literature (see Pakaluk 1991). Although the male literature mostly does not reflect on men's friendships with women and does not conceive of friendships between women, there are a growing number of feminist philosophers who do address women's experiences.[11] Different women's concrete experiences as offered above indicate that friendship among women seems to be an extremely important, life-sustaining component of many women's lives and leads feminist philosophers to cross the same kinds of boundaries earlier male philosophers had to.

Comrades

Finally, into what specific relational category are we to place the experiences of young women such as Minnie Fisher? She worked as a hat maker in a millinery shop and lived in a "commune" with others of her cultural peer group. These comrades studied together at a university of their own making that they called the Yiddishe Arbeiten Universitet (Jewish Workers' University). The group worked, played, studied, celebrated, lived, and were activists together.[12] Actually, it does not seem at all uncommon for women to make politics in the places they live, grounded directly in their relations, and based on their concerns, as relatives, neighbors and friends.[13] Concomitantly, it is also not uncommon for women to create specifically political spaces that are also places to live, love, socialize with friends, and create culture.[14]

The reader may wonder why a discussion of women as comrades is included here among spheres presented as alternatives to the traditionally elite male-valued sphere of politics. Aren't comrades inherently political sorts of folks? It is interesting that what might otherwise be understood as women's "political" consciousness and activities are often devalued by elite men as not "real" politics. It has been one project for feminists to articulate the political nature of women's actions and relationships that elite theorists traditionally deemed outside the political realm. It is another project to have the activities of marginalized groups that elite theorists would otherwise name "political" actually valued as such. Students and marginalized minorities have faced the same reaction on this point as have women as a group. When these marginalized groups "have acted outside their homes, their activities have often been ignored or ridiculed, defined as lying outside the domain of politics properly construed."[15] Thus, as we will discuss again in Chapter Six, although elite theorists have excluded the political activities of the marginalized from formal definitions of politics, people from diverse marginalized communities have long been engaged as participants in activism, based also in their other relationships and drawing both strength and direction from these relationships (Weisen Cook 1977).

Implications for Citizenship

Much in the Western canon has relied on dualistic pairs of concepts: public/private, self/other, rational/irrational, emotion/intellect, body/mind, interest/altruism, passion/reason. These realms are mutually exclusive: aspects on one side cannot include the other, and they are always at odds. It seems, however, that this scheme thus far does not describe much of women's experiences from a diverse selection of communities. By looking at women's active experiences in some less formal spaces that they have carved for themselves out of the collective life, we are presented with an alternative possibility for their lives as citizens in the more formal arena of politics.

What is most significant about this in theorizing the *why* question, is that for many women, the alternative realms discussed above are often characterized by relationships, many specifically designated as relationships of care. What is also worth noting is that not only does a combination of concern, care, and interest exist, but these characteristics are directed both inward and outward. Women's often fierce feelings and actions tend to extend not merely to the limits of their atomistically defined selves, but out to others in their lives, be they children and relatives, friends, neighbors, or comrades. Further, not only do care and interest cross between self and other, but the different realms in which women are active participants and which texture their lives cross between the worlds of family, friends, neighbors, and comrades.

Some feminist scholars have explored the political consequences of many of these social relationships. Relating to a notion of political motivation quite different from that espoused in traditional theories, they have offered visions of a politics that takes into account both specific and general characteristics of individuals, appears more attentive to concrete needs and feelings, and assumes responsibility as a relational norm.[16] Thus, emerging from the notion that women seem often to live in both the worlds delineated and then separated in Western patriarchal philosophies, we find the suggestion of an alternative possibility for the participation of members in a democratic polity that is not predicated upon the separative dualisms of patriarchy. The major problem, however, is that women as a group have suffered precisely for this situation of living across the patriarchally divided realms.

OBSTACLES

If the project of feminist theory is to explore ways that women no longer have to suffer at the hands of patriarchy, we must ask the question: what are we to do about the particular situation that men have used women's "complicated" (in quotes because it is probably only complicated in the eyes of men in patriarchy) experience and motivations as reasons to exclude them from citizenship? One suggestion is looking for ways that feminists can continue to be these "integrated" selves,[17] and yet be more effective politically as these selves.[18] It is therefore important to look directly at some of the obstacles feminists face in acting out this alternative vision of citizenship that is grounded in these lessons gleaned from the experiences of many of the marginalized on their own terrain.

In order to help examine obstacles to being effective feminist citizens (in this case, effective as integrated actors), theorists must take seriously an epithet that feminists often dismiss out of hand: the cry that women's participation will cause the downfall of society. How many times have people heard such a statement, directly and indirectly, when women sought the right to vote, to sit on juries, to run for office, reproductive and sexual freedoms, economic equity/independence, and cultural recognition? In response, some feminists have sought to calm the fears of those in power by assuring them that feminist perspectives and demands are not really so radical. As an alternative, those concerned might carefully address the dynamic at work in this patriarchal response to a feminist view of citizenship so that we may understand more clearly the obstacles that confront women as they move toward more radical democratic possibilities.

A Two-Layered Response

In examining women's contributions to the discussion of participation as possibly distinct from canonical theories written by and for elite men, the analysis has thus far focused on the similarities between common views of citizenship that have excluded women and many minorities. To keep the theorizing practical, this exploration now needs to examine the challenges of incorporating women's contributions into patriarchal society through a more subtle analysis that addresses some of the differences between major democratic theories. The reason for this is that feminists find themselves hitting different sorts of walls of patriarchy in the course of their political organizing. Women suffer directly from the limitations in traditional theorizing on political motivation. Women long have been chastised for their attempts at political participation, and their demands for inclusion are often rebuffed. Why is it, however, that only sometimes the rationale for such exclusion is that women are *too interested,* as if women's political demands are more selfish than the everyday demands men make? At other times women are thwarted because their efforts are not taken seriously. In this second instance, women are seen as *too nice,* not cut out for the rough-and-tumble of interest politics. The women concerned are the same beings, the "integrated" beings described above. But sometimes the rationale for exclusion focuses on one side of their selves, at other times it focuses on the other characteristics. The reason for this is that although in patriarchy, by definition, women are oppressed and excluded, patriarchy has numerous faces. Thus, the challenges to effective feminist participation will take shape differently depending on the face of patriarchy that activists find themselves up against. Feminists must, therefore, more fully understand the dynamic with each face so that their motivations are no longer mistrusted and so that they may go about their work more effectively.

The following discussion focuses primarily on two democratic traditions, the Republican and the Liberal, due to their centrality in the (U.S.) American political mind and experience. Such a focus makes sense in light of Roelofs's (1992) work, which clarifies our schizophrenia as a nation. In contrast to the cleavage/consensus theorists, or those who claim either Liberalism or Republicanism as *the* philosophical legacy of our politics here in the United States, Roelofs argues that "Americans" are both social and liberal democrats, together and at odds simultaneously. If this is true, then the challenges feminists face, due to presumptions about their political motivations, in the pursuit of a more inclusive *and* transformative theory and practice of citizenship, will look different when women are up against Liberal expectations of citizenship than when they hit the Republican side of the "American" psyche. Thus, at this stage in the argument, the differences between the theories of citizenship found in the civic Republican tradition and that of Liberalism become significant.

Republican Obstacles to Feminist Enfranchisement

In answering the *why* question of politics, interests are a primary concern for the civic Republican tradition. The reason for this is that in this tradition, attention to needs is wedded to the fear of the destructive capacity of "power-over." Interests are understood as problematic, as selfish, because they are defined as needs + power-over. Interests are viewed as zero-sum entities; that is, satisfying those of some serves as a hindrance to the satisfaction of others' interests.

If individuals were each alone on an island, perhaps interests would not be problematic. But in the civic Republican tradition we are assumed to be beings of society. It is in society, where people are collected together, that these selfish selves who pursue their interests are problematic. Stemming from the civic Republican concern with virtue, the aspiration for society is that it will be civil/gentlemanly. In this tradition, philosophers are concerned with the common good and the difficult task of how to promote the public welfare. According to this democratic theory, the name of the individuals as one finds them in society is citizens. They are citizens in the incarnation of themselves as public selves who are members of a society that it is hoped will be civil.

There is a problem, then, between the people individuals are as private selves and the citizens that philosophers want them to be. As private selves they are passionate and (selfishly) interested. In both cases they are self-directed and self-concerned. As citizens it is hoped that they will be civic-minded, other-directed, and other-concerned. Ackelsberg sums up the project of citizenship from a perspective grounded in women's experience as how to act effectively in the political arena with a connective sense of self and other. She contrasts this to other understandings of the project of citizenship as "that of creating an allegiance to something *other* than the self" (1988, 303),[19] describing primarily the project found as envisioned within the civic Republican tradition.

In order to get personal individuals to be the public citizens whom these philosophers want, it is assumed that they will have to transcend their private selves. To do this, as these philosophers see it, they must rely on rational capacities and objective decision-making skills. The objective powers are seen as what can enable individuals to take into account the predicaments of others, as opposed to an interested natural tendency. A rational capacity is appealed to because interests in this tradition are linked to passions, to an emotional side that is seen as uncontrollable and irrational. The problem historically is that some individuals have been seen as essentially more capable of such disinterested action than others. Thus, due to how the *why* question is answered, certain groups such as women and many minorities have been excluded categorically from this definition of citizenship found at the core of the Republican tradition.

Marx provides an interesting alternative assessment of the situation. In *On the Jewish Question*, Marx writes: "Human emancipation will only be complete when the real, individual man has absorbed into himself the abstract citizen; when as an individual man, in his everyday life, in his work, and in his relationships, he has become a *species-being*; and when he has recognized and organized his own powers (*forces propres*) as *social* powers so that he no longer separates this social power from himself as *political* power" (in Tucker 1978, 46). Marx, like Republicans, notes a kind of separation between man and citizen, between the personal aspects of his everyday life and his group, or social, self. Republicans, however, accept this disconnection as real. If individuals are to be citizens in the realm of politics, then they cannot also be men. If the Republican preference is for citizens, then they have to transcend and leave behind their selves and motivations as men. As Ackelsberg notes, the project for Republicans is to get men to commit to something other than themselves. Marx's version differs significantly.

Although Marx notes this disconnection, he does so with a heavy heart as a man, and an activist's anger as a political being. For Marx this disconnection is not real, essential. Instead, the feeling that it exists is the result of alienation. Further, Marx understands alienation not as natural or as simply the existential reality of the human condition. For Marx, alienation is the problematic consequence of problematic social relations in capitalism that can and ought to be changed.

Marx's understanding also helps clarify certain aspects of the feminist view presented here. It has been a common feminist response that what needs to be done is to integrate the dichotomies of patriarchy. Marx helps illuminate why some feminists might think the project is one of integration. The dominant paradigm is one of separation. To Republicans, for example, the way to overcome the problem of separation is to transcend particular selves and civically become only social selves. Many feminists have also seen separation as a problem, but have rejected transcendence in favor of integration. This seems to be a better alternative, but still not quite on the mark. The pursuit of integration is a misguided goal in that it retains the patriarchal perspective that women are separated in the first place. It was argued above that women's experience is already integrated. Thus, the project cannot properly be understood as to integrate, but will be better seen instead as learning how to be more effective political actors as integrated beings.[20]

Marx can critically take notice of separation for the ruling class, and the hegemonic effect of such a paradigm on the working class. In Marx's view, such pressure to be separative is like a wrenching, a wrenching of our species-being from our being as individuals. One reading is that an element of essentialism may slip into Marx's thinking here, in that it appears he supposes our integrated selves to be the more natural selves, the way humans would be without oppression. One can empathize with the pain Marx seems to feel in the presence of this mechanism of oppression that would sever individual selves from group selves, private being and powers from social and political being and powers. Feminists do not, however, need to suggest that women's integrated selves are the more pure, unadulterated selves, but rather a model that some find more fulfilling and politically and philosophically preferable.

Finally, then, what does it mean to a Republican to claim that women's inclusion will ruin the body politic? If to patriarchy women are a muddle, then they include both connection and care for others (characteristics Republicans equate with a civically desirable altruism), as well as passion and interest (characteristics Republicans consider threatening). The Republican fear of letting women in on their own terms is that their passion/interests as political motivations would ruin the civic rationality of the public sphere. Republicans arrive at such a fear by abstracting out women's passions and interested approach from "the muddle" and taking women to task for that. However, although all private individuals have the problematic passions and interests, women are seen as *solely* passionate/interested, thus incapable of transcending this "part" of being.

Clarifying obstacles feminists will face in their work toward new conceptions and practices of political motivations, democratic membership and even citizenship in the presence of our Republican selves can help them to navigate their way beyond such obstacles. But what of the pressures from our Liberal selves?

Liberal Obstacles to Feminist Enfranchisement

Although Liberals make the claim that demands of inclusion from the margins will cause the "downfall of society" as often as Republicans, what they mean is significantly different. The place to begin this analysis is with what appears as a similarity between Republicanism and Liberalism. With respect to the *why* of politics, in both traditions, citizenship entails a rejection of the passions. In both traditions women and minorities known to be marginalized tend to be seen by elite men as too passionate, and therefore rejected from the world of enfranchised citizenship. What is important, however, is that passions and interests are treated similarly within the Republican tradition, but quite distinctly by Liberals.

Liberals, like Republicans, see interests as an aspect of man's condition in his precivic incarnation. For Liberals, like Republicans, interests are also based on needs, but with a noteworthy twist. As Liberalism emerges with capitalism, it is helpful to understand Liberalism's view of interests as a commodified abstraction of needs (Brettschneider 1996a). But Liberals do not see interests as negative, needing to be purged from the being of citizens. In fact, Liberalism is built upon the critique of what it views cynically as Republican utopianism. Liberalism finds interests so central to men's motivations that it deems naive and absurd the Republican expectation that they can be transcended. Instead, Liberalism bases itself on interest as the motivation of men, and builds a theory/system from that fact.

Liberalism can afford to do so, in contrast to Republicanism, because it separates passion from interest. Liberalism links its critique of passion with Republican concepts such as honor and virtue. These are irrational, or lead men to irrational actions. Interests, on the other hand, are seen by Liberals as calculable and rational.[21] Thus, for Liberals it is not the personal, acquisitive, or even selfish or self-centered nature of passion that is problematic, because interests are all of these things as well. Instead, what is problematic about passion for Liberals is the fact that one cannot securely make sense of and predict others' passions and plan to protect oneself in their presence.

Thus, insofar as Liberalism feels insecure around passion, it will feel insecure around women and minorities. Liberalism seeks to channel our passions into interests, enhancing our interested capacities and rewarding our interested behavior. Then, it might seem that Liberalism would do well to include women and minorities as citizens on its own terms, feeling more secure that these extra-passionate beings will now act more rationally and predictably. In fact, theorists have argued that, historically, this move to see self-interest as the main motivation in politics had democratizing effects.[22] But instead, Liberals make the "downfall of society" claim just as often as Republicans. Why? The answer to this question rests on another level of contradictions within a Liberalism that becomes invested not in what it perceives as women's too-passionate nature simply, but in the way that women's passion has been trained to be directed outward, toward others.

In what patriarchy perceives as the "muddle" of women, one must now look to what happens when the presumed motivational characteristics of connection and care assumed of women are abstracted out and fixated upon. The claim of "downfall of society" made by Liberals stems from patriarchy's complicated creation of women and minorities as caring and as caretakers, as soothers, nurturers, and responsible for the emotional work in relationships. To understand why this has become a problem, the Liberal view of society must be clarified.

Liberalism is a political system and philosophy predicated on an assumption of radically atomistic individual entities.[23] When these entities are considered capable of rationally acting on and to protect their interests, they are also accorded rights and are considered persons: people recognizable under the law. What kind of a society, a gathering of individuals, is possible with these atomistic, self-seeking beings? There is almost no social cohesion in a group understood as a heap, an aggregation of disparate self-interested persons. Within Liberalism, there is some conception of society, albeit a very weak and tenuous one, based on the strongest bond possible among these beings: what is almost misleadingly referred to as a common interest.

The contradiction of individual and society has long been a puzzlement of Liberalism. How could individuals understood as little sovereigns unto themselves commit to a social contract that would have them be the ultimate subjects? The closest thing to an answer available from within Liberalism begins with its claim that by each doing what he wants (pursuing unbridled selfish interests), all end up in a situation that no one wants (Hobbes characterizes it as a state of war of each against all). Everyone, therefore, has a common interest in keeping their separate selves from such extreme harm. This is how Hobbes arrives at a notion of society, established formally through a social contract, whereby the individuals erect a sovereign over them to keep them all in awe so that they stop killing each other. In Liberalism there is no conception of a common *good* such as is found in a Republican tradition. There is instead only an assumption of this selfish *interest* that is common to all men.

While some seem satisfied that this notion of a common interest is enough to constitute a conception of society, the view presented here is that it is so weak that one ought to remain skeptical. It is from a perspective generated from many women's and marginalized minorities' "integrated" situation that one can see more critically this tension in Liberalism for what it is. This assertion can be demonstrated through an analogy with a socialist feminist critique of the economic realm of Liberalism, capitalism.

Brilliant bourgeois economists have professed theories explaining how capitalism does/should work, pointing to such things as free markets, rational actors, supply and demand. Socialist feminists have shown us, however, that capitalism manages to function in practice not necessarily according to the explanations of these thinkers, but because the formal economy discussed by these theorists is supported by a vast pool of unpaid and underpaid labor performed by women and disempowered minorities. For example, if the domestic chores and child care duties of so many women in the United States were to be monetarily remunerated, the (U.S.) American economy would simply collapse. Thus, when patriarchy cries that feminists will ruin the economy and bring down the system, it is probably correct. When feminists demand equal pay (or pay at all) for equal work, they do threaten the stability of a system that has relied on a whole unacknowledged realm of women's activities without which that system would not survive.[24]

A parallel argument can be made on the level of politics. Despite the writing of Liberal political philosophers on how and why Liberalism can and should work, Liberals can probably hold society together only due to the whole unacknowledged realm of women's and many minorities' connection, self-sacrifice, caretaking, and nurturing work. The social ties between Liberal rights-bearing and hostile self-interest maximizers are too tenuous to actually keep a society intact. Because Liberals can acknowledge only these rights/interest-bearing persons as politically relevant, when women demand political enfranchisement, Liberals assume that women have to become these persons as well. If women did so, then there would be no one left to provide that unacknowledged buffer: the heart, warmth, and care in the competitive brutish world of Liberal society.[25] The Liberal claim that women's full inclusion would cause the downfall of society ought not to be dismissed. If women were fully enfranchised on Liberalism's terms, the last bit of glue holding Liberal society together would disintegrate.

Remember, again, that to a patriarchy that relies on separative dualisms, women as "integrated" beings are a "muddle." Specifically, they are characterized as being both, often fiercely, interested (which Liberals perceive as the proper basis for politics) as well as caring for others (which Liberals find confusing in formal politics). The Liberal fear of letting women play politics on Liberalism's terms, as solely self-interested rational actors, is that society would lose the underworld of care that actually holds it together. Liberals arrive at such a fear, like Republicans, although the terms are almost reversed, by abstracting out the side they find frightening and taking us to task for it.

Conclusion

Theorists have generated various responses to the *why* question in politics. As they play out in theories of citizenship, Republicans have historically leaned toward altruistic conceptions of honor, virtue, and the public good. Liberals have severely critiqued the Republican view and claimed self-interest to be the motivation for political participation. These two theories arrive at their conclusions by polarizing particulars and universals. In both cases, such polarizing has enabled these theories to justify marginalizing women as a group, and most minorities as well. In response, postmodernists have rejected theories that make use of these polarized categories. Instead of jettisoning all notions of universals, however, we can see that some of those working in a more multicultural framework have sought to articulate a dialectical relationship between universals and particulars. As critical as postmodernists are of the biases, those grounded in this alternative diversity-based framework have instead problematized the polarization by drawing on experiences and ideas of those on the margins.

What might it mean to theorize the *why* question in politics from the margins? In the context of this book, it has meant that in the struggle for democracy theorists must situate themselves on the terrain on which the marginalized in (U.S.) American society live their lives and create perspective. To be among those who are working to envision the democratic project from the ground of/with the historically disempowered is to revitalize democratic thought as both practicable and visionary.

Although democratic theorists have had a tendency to understand citizenship as *the* political relationship, it actually is a particular form of political relationship. Also, there is a connection between the fact that the experiences of women and that of numerous other marginalized groups have been dismissed as nonpolitical and that, traditionally, they also have been seen as outside of the boundaries of what is understood to constitute proper citizens. Thus, it has been helpful to explore the confluence between these theories of motivation, citizenship, definitions of politics, and the exclusion of women and other marginalized groups.

The hope expressed here is that redefining what counts as political, and then rethinking the relation between politics and other spheres, can enable democratic theorists to draw on the experiences of many of those on the margins in new ways in order to re-vision membership, and in particular citizenship due to its centrality in the history of Western democratic thought, as a political relationship.

The notion of an "integrated" model of citizenship drawn from experiences among marginalized communities holds much promise for a more transformatively inclusive politics. It has been argued that many communities' historically "integrated" experience provides a good model of being that democrats ought to protect and more effectively rely on in politics. It should also be clear, now that we have clarified certain obstacles, why attempts to abandon such a model will not work. Even if democratic activists wanted to and could abandon such a model, which side should be chosen as the basis in an argument about motivations that will lead to enfranchisement? They might choose the other-directed care to gain the favor of Republicans who appreciate some semblance of that behavior, but then they would not be taken seriously by Liberals. If democratic activists choose to engage politically on the basis of interests, Republicans will exclude them for being selfish. Working on patriarchy's terms to clarify the muddle, being one thing or the other, is a no-win situation. It seems that radical democrats might do well, therefore, to work at resisting the pressure to assimilate historically marginalized political selves to elite-patriarchal dichotomous models. Keeping in mind the external obstacles, it might be more empowering to go about the struggle for inclusion on "integrative" terms and see where this leads.

But where and how might it be possible to do so? How can we conceptualize the sites, and potential sites, of politics where such "integrative" activism may be effective? In Chapter Six we begin to address this question. In doing so we will find that we must again question the common Western understanding of politics as that which is engaged in by property-owning, heterosexual, Christian men. We will take the challenge this chapter has posed to Western distinctions between public and private and re-place it in a geographic understanding of the "where" question for new democratic theory.

6   Where: Multiple Publics

INTRODUCTION

WE HAVE now had an opportunity to look at some of the when, who, what, and why of diversity-based politics' potential contributions to new democratic theory. It is time that we address the question concerning where. Where do we see these newer, alternative, and potentially radical forms of politics taking place? What are their locations? What spaces might we need to attend to, imagine, open up, and/or create in order to facilitate a deeper engagement with democracy? How could attention to the geography, imaginative and physical, of politics enable more democratic modes of political praxis? How might an inquiry into the places of politics aid us in sorting through confusing facets of contemporary culture that appear contradictory? How might this inquiry aid us in acting more effectively in the face of these apparent confusions?

One of those sets of confusing apparent contradictions may be found in media portrayals of clusters of the populace such as young people and queer-identified people. Douglas Coupland (1991) is credited with coining the term "Generation X," used to name the generation of the U.S. populace born between 1961 and 1981.[1] In using the umbrella term *queer*, I mean to refer to segments of the population, some even overlapping, including: homosexuals as an historical category, bisexuals, gays, lesbians, transsexuals, transgendered people, or those sexual minorities cast in culture as sexual outlaws.[2] Depending on the level and scope of our analysis of these two clusters, we might emerge inclined toward cynicism and apathy, or we might develop clarity and insight and be inspired toward action. Developing robust, multifaceted, and nuanced theories of the public sphere and the potentially participatory political locations of a growing and changing civil society will be important if we

An earlier version of the argument in this chapter was originally prepared for delivery at the 1999 Annual Meeting of the Western Political Science Association, Seattle, Washington, March 1999.

are to walk the latter path to build on activism. My intention for this chapter is to offer the confusing portrait of the political standing of queers and Gen Xers today as an example, and then to present the basic contours of some of the issues and additional paradoxes in theorizing the public sphere that democratic activists and thinkers encounter as we work to clarify our analysis and act more effectively politically.

Queers and young people present a significant challenge to many political analysts and theorists. Sometimes queers and young people are considered frightening, much of the time simply confusing. Both groups have been portrayed as quintessentially apolitical. Like many youth eras, Generation X is considered individualistic, apathetic, and disaffected. Gen Xers distinctly have the lowest proportion of voters of any age group. Conservatives lament their lack of values, respect, and direction. The more progressive-minded write them off as alienated slackers. Lesbians, bisexuals, gays, transsexuals, transgendered people, and other sexual outlaws are considered "queer," generally deviant and not to be politically trusted. Queers are also a minority, the majority of whom do not identify as a group in their practice at the polls. Conservatives lambast their hedonistic lack of morals. In the old left they were seen as part of the potentially reactionary lumpen proletariat. Due to their apparent apathy, queers and Generation Xers have thus tended to share the slate of low esteem in political science analyses of various ideological slants. Are we, however, to accept at face value a media portrait of these groups as deviants and slackers?

This is far from the only portrait to be painted. Are there other vantage points from which to look at the political states of these two groups? In order to nudge ourselves along to another vantage point, let us recollect one of the long-standing insights of radical democrats. Radical democratic political theorists have long criticized the limitations of Liberalism's relegation of politics to the specific spheres of rights discourses, legal battles, and the legislative arena. Concrete change in these spheres can be extremely important. However, radical democratic theorists have said that any attempt at radical social transformation focused only in the political realm (if understood as consisting of elections or in a fight for equal rights granted in law) will necessarily be stymied. Political movement that does not reach deeper layers—attending to the fundamental relationships between members of a polity and their prejudices, fears, hopes, and aspirations—will not become a liberation movement.[3] Given the popular media portrayal of both youths and queers, is there something else going on with these groups that might actually be of interest to radical critics of Liberalism? Although both queers and Generation Xers are called apolitical and considered two of the groups with the least political clout (due to their "lack of involvement"), it is in the cross-pollination of these two groups that we find one of the most interesting examples of what critics of Liberalism would identify as the necessary arenas and conditions for radical political change.

That is why these groups at first appear to represent such a paradox. If we look again, we see that queers have also populated one of the most activist political movements of our time. In 1994 a million people took to the streets to commemorate the twenty-fifth anniversary of the Stonewall uprising with an international human rights march in front of the United Nations on First Avenue in New York City. More radical queers ran their own march up the traditional gay pride route on Fifth Avenue.[4] Queer politics is also one of the best examples currently of participatory democracy. In the early 1990s ACT UP weekly New York chapter meetings would gather six hundred activists. By the close of the decade Sex Panic weekly meetings took their place.

With the rise of queer activism we also see an increasingly public backlash. Although Bill Clinton was the first candidate to actively appeal to progay support in his run for presidency, one of his first publicized acts as new president was to back down on the issue of gays in the military. Due to the advances made by gay and lesbian civil rights groups toward the "right to marry" for same-sex couples, Congress launched the "protection of marriage" campaign, regarding a bill by that name that Clinton himself signed into law. In states such as Colorado and Oregon, activity to keep sexual orientation clauses out of the civil rights ordinances exposed virulent antigay sentiment. In 1997–98, when the people of Maine successfully passed a referendum to include a sexual orientation clause in their state civil rights bill, the Christian right organized in reaction and actually had the decision overturned. These are just a few examples. George W. Bush and his supporters continued to work against claims for equality made by sexual minorities and outlaws, still using the delegitimizing adjective "special" when referring to the struggle for equal rights (for example, straight folk have rights: GLBT folk who don't are asking for "special rights").

On the other hand, in this time of national and state attacks on gay civil rights and demonization of queer "lifestyles," we find an interesting general exception to this rule. Despite the persistence of antiqueer stereotypes, and high school slang epithets such as "you're so gay," young adults (ages eighteen to twenty-nine) as a group actually rate significantly lower than other groups on various measures of homophobia. People in this age range are more likely than those of any other age group to have friends and/or acquaintances who are queer. They are most likely to support gay-friendly candidates, to agree with gay-friendly policy propositions, and to explicitly support both general and specific civil rights for queer people. Additionally, according to polls taken, Generation Xers are more likely to be comfortable with public visibility of queer people and same-sex relationships than any other age group.[5]

Taking note of the upswing in queer-related politics and the queer-friendly tendencies among many U.S. youth, it may not be surprising to find that queer activist politics—from groups such as ACT UP, Queer Nation, and Lesbian Avengers to Sex Panic—tends to be a "younger people's" politics. Members of sexual minorities over forty sparked a mass movement for liberation and are certainly found firing up many local activist campaigns. There are, however, still quite palpable average age differentials between rank-and-file members of gay and lesbian legal defense teams or AIDS buddy systems and the other groups mentioned above such as Lesbian Avengers or Sex Panic. This is particularly the case with minority queer groups such as Jewish Activist Gays and Lesbians, Gay Asian and Pacific Islanders, and Lesbian Latinas. Further, as the percentage of national exit poll respondents identifying as gay has increased overall, the explicitly identified queer vote is a distinctly younger vote. According to the age categories noted, voters ages eighteen to twenty-four self-identified as gay or lesbian significantly more often than either baby boomers or more senior voters. In general, Generation Xers are more likely to identify as queer (or two-spirited homosexual, lesbian, bisexual, gay, transsexual, or transgendered) than generations before them.

Popular political events make this connection between politicized Gen Xers and queers that much clearer. The brutal set-up and murder of Matthew Shepherd mobilized high schools and college campuses across the country in a renewed effort to stand against homophobia and hate crimes. The "political funeral" for Shepherd, where signs were also for James Byrd (an African American man lynched in Texas) staged in New York City brought together three generations of queer activists. It was estimated that eight thousand people were involved at the height of the march on that October night (October 19, 1998). News reports noted that the police presence and violence, reminiscent of the outrageous police action at the Million Youth March in Harlem a mere few months earlier, was unusually high and particularly targeted at the younger queer activists. Many of the young queer activists had been wearing purple ribbons that night in protest of the violence against queer youth and at least one Internet report credited the youth there with "provid[ing] militant spirit for the marchers."[6]

Who was it again, who said that Generation X and homosexuals are apolitical? Analysts focus on the comparatively low voter turnout of both queers and young people, the decline in party identification, and the failure of these groups "to organize effectively to advocate for and advance their economic and other interests."[7] On the other hand, we find generally among both Generation Xers and queers a distinctively progressive orientation and a penchant for grassroots activist politics. Further, Smith's (1998) preliminary findings regarding queer activism suggest that many queers view their own activities as politically salient and specifically "important in advancing the overall political interests of LGB people." In this chapter I propose that in order to make any sense of this apparent paradox, we will need to attend to discussions of the public sphere in democratic theory. Locating new forms of democratic praxis is important if we are to understand them as, and draw on them in, potentially radical modes of politics. Attending to the spatial dimensions of politics allows us to ground what can be an otherwise all too abstract tendency in political theory. It will be in grounding our inquiry that we will be able to clarify what seem confusing in their abstractions. Given the specific set of paradoxes presented by looking at the relation between Generation X and queer politics, for example, we will find that we must also revise long-standing conceptions of the public sphere. I will thus further propose that the method we utilize to undertake such a revision will be to attend to lessons we can learn for a new democratic theory of the public sphere from queers, Generation Xers, and a host of other minority and historically marginalized groups themselves.[8]

After a brief note on the origins of the notion of the public in Western democratic theory, I will identify the modern distinction of the public sphere from the state, and then how contemporary diversity politics forces us to confront a multiplicity of public spheres. I offer a reminder that spatializing our analyses in democratic theory crosses boundaries of actual and imagined political locations, and then address some of the difficulties of negotiating both between multiple political spaces and within individual spheres.

AN HISTORICAL NOTE

It is the changing political landscape since the rise of 1960s social movements that contours the transfiguring political identities of both queers and Generation X. In exploring how we might go about a more inclusive process that recognizes us in our difference, diversity politics emerging from the margins over time has refocused discussion on the location of politics in democratic theory. According to thinkers such as Taylor (1994) and West (1993b), if identity is a central component of freedom and comes about through dialogue and cultural practices, then the space of that dialogue and of those complex cultural practices must be one in which we are recognized so that we do not become social beings in the context of inferiority. Drawing on the work of Arendt (1958) and Habermas (1989), many theorists committed to questions of oppression, including those in relation to identity communities, have added interesting ideas to debates about the public sphere. But first, we must lay some common groundwork and take note of the historical importance of the public sphere in Western democratic thinking.

Since ancient Athens, the notion of the need for a public space in which citizens can deliberate on matters of concern to them has been considered a benchmark of democracy. This public space has been understood as a known and accessible site in which politics can take place. In ancient Athens the polis was conceptually designated as such a place, and amphitheaters and other concrete spaces were built and utilized for discourse and decision making. Moving to a modern example in the U.S. context, one of the markers of tyranny for the colonists was the tricks played by the British in holding meetings that were unannounced and in out-of-the-way places. Cries for regular, public, and known sites for legislatures and courts to meet, and citizens to air grievances, have sparked revolutionary sentiment among populations from colonial U.S. and French democrats in the 1700s, to resistance to the Nazis in mid-twentieth-century Germany, and human rights work in contemporary Bosnia, El Salvador, and Cambodia. New democratic thinkers have taken the need for such a space seriously and, in light of the precarious situation of women and many minority groups, find that we must reassess the current dynamics within older public spaces, attend to the recognition and protection of certain developing precious public spaces, and also possibly look to the creation of new ones.

The concept of the polis bequeathed to modern Western democracies from ancient Athens, interpreted in modernity through a Roman version of the ideal central to its legal tradition, is based on reason and is separate from aspects of life considered private, or intimate. The process of private, or individual, concerns moving into the public space, where they can be aired and subject to the rational interplay of citizens' dynamic interpretations and actions—in a word, politics—has been referred to as "publicity."[9] The public sphere, as Habermas has rightly treated it, is an historical category. Its meaning and constitution shift over time in the context of changing concrete social, political, and economic relations. The public sphere as an outgrowth of civil society where "private citizens put reason to use" is an eighteenth-century European development that corresponds to the needs of the new middle, merchant class of emerging capitalism.[10]

In comparison to Aristotle's reverence for *the* polis, a conceptually singular political space that one might argue was appropriate for city-states such as Athens, the advent of large-scale nation-states and more recently the increasing attention to difference necessitate that we rephrase the very question "what is the location of democratic politics?" In light of contemporary diversity-based politics and the contradictions they seem to generate, we are more likely to find an answer to this question rooted in the formulation of a new question altogether. If we want to move beyond alienating "paradoxical views" of queers and Generation X, of women or Native Americans, as other examples, as somehow not politically active and astute in the face of their years of difficult political struggle, we must reconceptualize the very questions we frame—and that in turn, therefore, frame our explorations—in democratic theory. Today we are best off asking, what are the locations of democratic politics?[11] If we do not shift to the plural in this case, we are bound to a static conception that will leave us stumped in the face of various analyses that, for example, cast a generation as oscitant and yet which experience demonstrates has quite developed political values and a distinctly progressive ideological orientation. Looking at activist politics among a variety of marginalized groups, we find that what is significant about contemporary discussions of the public is explicitly its multiplicity. The first step in understanding and being able to practice this idea is to note the relationship between the state and the public sphere in two sets of revolutionary democratic moves: Liberal and socialist.

THE PUBLIC SPHERE AND THE STATE

In the history of what one might consider "the public sphere" in the West, one of the most significant achievements of the Liberal revolutions was the creation of a new public space distinct from what had been designated as the state. In the French ancien régime, for example, the king was equated with the state; King Louis XIV is famous for saying "*L'État c'est moi.*" This meant that for political activity to have efficacy, one had to have the attention of the king. In this structure, the space for "politics" was exceedingly narrow. In the U.S. case, after much bloodshed and debate, the framers of the Constitution set up a large legislature, and explicitly rejected proposals that would have had the presidency more closely resemble a monarch. In England, and later in continental Western Europe, Liberals created parliaments, bodies outside the king's chambers, which were also to serve as more democratic fora by giving the new middle class a legitimate site in which to engage in politics, thereby expanding the political now to include more than the aristocratic elite.[12]

As Habermas put it, "The bourgeois idea of the law-based state, namely, the binding of all state activity to a system of norms legitimated by public opinion (a system that had no gaps, if possible), already aimed at abolishing the state as an instrument of domination altogether"(1989, 82).[13] However, issues problematic for more radical democrats eventually became apparent from developments particular to these Liberal democratic examples. Despite a Liberal definition of the public sphere as open and inclusive, the sphere created by the newly politicized bourgeoisie never was either.[14] Activist and philosopher during the revolutionary period in France, Olympe de Gouges, wrote, "Oh, women, women! When will you cease to be blind? What advantage have you received from the Revolution?" Grounding the new public sphere in "reason" served as "a two-edged sword which, even as it may deliver us from the fear of unthinking nature, also permits the misuse of this nature against half of humanity."[15] With Liberal success in the (U.S.)

American and French Revolutions, the new middle class consolidated its position and developed its own hegemonic modes of power. The new public space of the legislative branch, designed to defend and promote the developing interests of the bourgeoisie, eventually became equated with "the" public space.[16] Legislatures, which at one point in history represented spaces beyond the historical political space of the state, have now come to be identified with the state themselves.[17] We must continue the move away from understanding politics as oriented solely toward the state. A new democratic politics, in the U.S. example seeking to enfranchise groups beyond a white, heterosexual, Christian, male, middle aged, and middle class, demands a reassessment of parliamentary politics as the sole legitimate site of politics.[18]

We see that the trouble with equating the public with the state was itself a stimulus for Liberal democratic revolutions of the eighteenth century. And yet, Liberalism has come to fold the newly empowered public space of the legislature into its own state structure. In this process it has also failed to adequately create new arenas to serve the—even original Liberal—function of an open public space necessary in a democracy. It is in part in response to this failure that those committed to democratic ideals seek to reattend to the notion and revitalization of public space. As U.S. multicultural visions grow out of developments also in the historical left, however, we need to look at the legacy of leftist experiments with the public sphere.

Contemporary multicultural visions in large part have been inspired by lessons learned from the failures of the Liberal projects as well as the Soviet experiment. Fraser (1997), for example, discusses the importance of the need for acknowledgment and enhancement of the public sphere in the failures of the Soviet experiment to produce an actual socialist democracy as well. In the course of the socialist democratic revolution in the Soviet case, the liberatory promise of the state also came to be confounded with the public sphere as an arena in which serious discourse can take place. What came about in this instance was an authoritarian structure, rather than participatory democracy. Rather than smashing the state and replacing it with a critical collective apparatus of the working class, as one could argue Marx had called for,[19] actual communist revolutions failed to empower the public with *political*—critical, publicly dialogic, and therefore effective—powers.

As Scott discusses infrapolitics, or micro forms of everyday resistance, in the Third World, he understands politics as being composed of "the many battles to roll back constraints and exercise some power over, or create some space within the institutions and social relationships that dominate our lives" (1985, 9–10). In the politically crucial and pivotal period of the 1950s, people in the United States faced a particularly deep challenge to democracy. In the aftermath of World War II, as Liberalism was beginning to change shape, the nation was struggling to emerge from the darkness of the Red scare, and progressives were struggling to get their bearings in light of the news of Stalin's inhumanities. It is in this context that a new mode of democratic politics begins to develop. It is often community-based, with a grounding significantly below state-level politics. Many of the communities of that period hit hardest by the Holocaust, blacklisting, and segregation begin to revitalize progressive activism. New forms of mass democratic politics themselves intended and effected a reopening of public spaces for working out more democratic relations in (U.S.) American public life at large as well as within specific subspheres.[20] Out of the new forms of community-based activism emerging at this time, we can find a demand that the public sphere now be understood in terms of the public spaces necessary for movements to develop and take root. These new modes of politics grounded in often community-based movements are also experiments in intracommunity decision making, debate, and the struggle with identities and multiple representations of the self for the self. In the larger national arena, the development of these numerous movements must be understood as lines in a web of what has traditionally been understood monolithically, if not statically, as the public sphere.

Public Sphere(s)

New democratic theory from the margins, attending to multiple pathways of power and to how power works in relation to individuals as members of identity communities, is complicating the idea of the public space by decentralizing it. Mainline political theories, even democratic theories, tend not to be able to account for the current dynamism and creative tensions within, experienced by, and stimulating subaltern[21] communities and layers of society such as we see occurring within the youth generation simply called "X" or the intricate weave of various lesbian, bisexual, gay, transsexual, and transgendered communities. The grand narratives historically have reflected the experiences of hegemonic elites. This situation plays out in the concrete manifestations of those narratives, what counts as the public sphere as one among them. If we are to look to a more democratic view of where people, including minorities and the historically marginalized, are engaging in the political processes significant to their lives, we might best respond to Phelan's (1994) call to us, instead, to "get specific." We must move from an exploration of one universalized public sphere to many specific public spaces.[22] We must examine more closely communities and associations as locations of politics, as spaces where people come together to identify their selves, their needs, and their aspirations and to devise strategies to have these acknowledged and fulfilled.

It will only be in attending to the space(s) of politics understood in this way that we will be able to fully appreciate political activism from the margins. For example, in *Race Rebels*, Kelley discusses the significant historical example in which community benevolent associations and secret societies "constituted the organizational structures through which washerwomen waged a citywide strike in 1881" (1994, 38). If it is our interest to make possible public political actions where the disenfranchised will have access and agency—such as strikes, demonstrations, and boycotts—eventuating social change, then we must look at the dynamics and processes of these communities and community organizations through a political lens.[23]

We thus must confront another important apparent paradox of the spatial dimensions of politics. One interesting facet we learn is that oftentimes spaces created out of oppression have also been and can be used by communities for internally empowering ends. For example, due to the clearly discriminatory practices of Black-white racial segregation, many democratically minded activists, thinkers, and lawyers since the 1950s worked hard to effect an integration of different races at least in schools and other public places. Interestingly enough, this model has also been explicitly used against other minorities in the United States and its territories. Further, as discussed in previous chapters, with the development of identity politics, which drew on new ideas about how to attain equality, the idea was revived across many minority communities—including segments of the African American community—that simply integrating into majority cultures and spheres (especially but not only while so much of the work of recognition remains to be done) is not the only or always the best choice.[24] Communities also often need their own distinct spaces in order to develop political skills and visions. Despite the racist logic of U.S. policies that refused to integrate remaining Native Americans within U.S.-occupied lands, Native American tribes and contemporary political movements usually seek to keep their space and governance outside U.S. jurisdiction. Many African Americans, as a different example, realized that certain spaces created for communal gathering, expression, and development, often created under the duress of racist policies of apartheid, ought to be honored and not simply cast away. Baker explains that "without romanticizing or minimizing the brutal realities of America's deep-south apartheid, it is still possible to acknowledge that racial segregation in the United States both necessitated and gave birth to a remarkable black southern public sphere" (1994, 19).[25] Historically, African Americans often turned the racist segregation of Jim Crow into congregational spaces, as places to create, and to feel a space of power. Among other sites, Baker offers an example of jails, criminality, and incarceration that were "transformed into a public arena for black justice and freedom" (1994, 14–16). Kelley writes that "congregation can also be a dangerous thing. While Jim Crow ordinances ensured that churches, bars, social clubs, barber shops, beauty salons, even alleys, would remain 'black' space, segregation gave African Americans a place to hide, a place to plan" (1994, 51). This is why it is common for whites to close down these spaces. A similar assessment could be made of gay bars, as with the harassment of abortion clinics, Planned Parenthood guidance centers, women's peace encampments, and so on.

Numerous minority ethnic and sexual communities originally forced to live in ghettos or neighborhoods separate from majority ethnic and sexual groups due to racism and anti-Semitism, homophobia, and specific discriminatory housing policies have also utilized the neighborhood for developing community, inventing and celebrating customs, and developing political clout. Due to the discomfort and often peril experienced by different kinds of queers in heterosexual establishments, towns, streets, and services where heterosexuality is expected and enforced, many gather in and move to special areas known to be gay or gay-friendly. In these new spaces it is common for queers to develop social services to meet the various needs of their communities such as activist groups and local councils, aids buddy systems and gay/lesbian health centers, abuse or hate crimes hotlines, barter networks, and merchant organizations. American Jews who immigrated from Eastern Europe around the turn of the century, as another example, set up societies based on geographical locations from their towns in countries overseas. These developed into mutual aid societies that wove together immigrants in their new neighborhoods in the United States. These and other communal self-help organizations such as loan agencies, credit unions, and workmen's circles emerged as an intricate web providing much-needed social services to people in the neighborhoods in culturally specific ways. In addition to meeting social and cultural needs in the communities, they also facilitated rapid means of communication and were ready-made units for political organizing when particular issues arose. In the ensuing decades these webs of mutual aid societies found in Jewish and other minority ethnic and sexual neighborhoods became the subject of many fruitful intercommunal aid efforts. Not only can social services from one community help serve the needs of others, but communities newer to high levels of internal organization have often sought out each other and those with the benefit of experience for advice and consultation as they seek to utilize the lessons of community development practiced more or less successfully by other groups.[26]

From this communal and intercommunal base, we can understand the importance of public spaces and sort through the confusion of what appears at times to be their potential as radically democratic, other times or from another vantage point repressive, or even sometimes both at once.[27] In innumerable specific historical examples, public spaces have functioned as places for the varied masses to gather, develop, and exchange political critique. Theater, for example, whether it was in Shakespeare's day, Vaudeville, cabarets in interwar Germany, Augusto Boal's theater of the oppressed in South America, or guerrilla theater in our contemporary city streets, has often been reclaimed from high society by the marginalized as a radically creative space. The notion of free and open public parks has been a favorite topic for democratic proponents of the need for public spaces. Average folk, politicos, and hippies have declared vacant lots "people's parks" since at least the 1960s. Local communities have at times turned ravaged urban plots into gardens. New playgrounds for children have been designed to open their imaginations, senses, and physical capacities. Parks have been used as areas for classes to interact, whether it is for men in soccer games or mothers with children.

We can also see, however, a deeper level of critique even of these oft applauded public spaces. Most open public spaces are in fact only "so" open. Only recently might we find women able to utilize the multicultural potential of a public park to cross class, cultural, and race boundaries through sports. The sex/gender tyranny of who is free to bring their children, and what kind of children are free to play, in a local park still most likely excludes lesbian, transgendered, and single mothers, children beyond a single normative gender, and certain kinds of fathers. Generation Xers are often all too accustomed to police harassment for simply constituting the public of public spaces—even more so if they are racial/ethnic minorities. Kelley notes that "contrary to the experiences of white workers, for whom public space eventually became a kind of 'democratic space' where people of different class backgrounds shared city theatres, public conveyances, streets, and parks, for black people white dominated public space was vigilantly undemocratic and potentially dangerous" (1994, 56).

This is one of the reasons, however, that public spaces have also been the sites of explicit resistance. Public spaces are often the most charged sites of minority and marginalized opposition to the prevailing power structures. The point of a radical critique of our so-called democratic spaces is that many of them are actually predicated on inequality. This is why minorities and marginalized groups often direct their actions here.[28] The history of African American civil rights in the United States bears this out. African Americans have targeted "public" buses, commercial lunch counters, and "public" drinking fountains as sites for resistance. Eruptions among the populace in Watts, in Los Angeles after the Rodney King trial, in the streets and parks of cities, towns, and college campuses from coast to coast time and again demonstrate that from a radical democratic perspective, the function of the public space is to serve as a place to challenge hegemonic power dynamics. In a critical democratic conception, *the public space is a space for those among the public to be challenged themselves.*

The bombing in Atlanta during the 1996 Olympics stimulated many discussions even within the mainstream media regarding the precariousness of public spaces as open spaces. This event sparked wide-scale exploration of the notion that open public spaces are the least policed and often, therefore, the sites of unrest and even violence. The bombing confused many commentators because there were many public cries for more strict policing of the site while others claimed more policing would negate the very point of an open public space. These tensions are at the heart of what makes a public space special. Democratic processes ought not necessarily to aim at "solving" them, but rather at revitalizing the public sphere more by explicitly problematizing these tensions.

Other reasons to use public spaces for political activity involve the anonymity of such spaces and their tendency not to be policed as much as, for example, places where most people work.[29] On a work site individuals are often watched closely and political agitation more easily jeopardizes people's jobs. Kelley writes, "in public spaces of the city, the anonymity and sheer numbers of the crowd, whose movement was not directed by the discipline of work (and was therefore unpredictable), required more vigilance and violence to maintain order. Although arrests and beatings were always a possibility, so was escape. Thus, for black workers, public spaces both embodied the most repressive, violent aspect of race and gender oppression, and, ironically, afforded more opportunities than the workplace itself to engage in acts of resistance" (1994, 75). Kelley's description of public spaces' benefit of anonymity for blacks coincides with a central benefit for queers and Generation Xers as well. Young people are famous for their talents creating zines (small, independent magazines that do not need corporate backing or involve much overhead), using the free space of the Internet, and throwing raves (roaming parties) in public spaces. The shifting subgroups of queers have long created clubs, bars, coffeehouses, bookstores, and political and communal organizations and utilized public spaces such as parks, streets, designated areas of a town, and beaches in order to have spaces to gather with others, meet their needs, experiment with freedom, and organize politically. That these spaces are distinct from work sites for the vast majority of queers and Generation Xers has been essential to their development as places of exploration and community. In particular, political statements and demonstrations many queers would find impossible, terrifying, or simply too dangerous to engage in at work, they increasingly find possible, exhilarating, and empowering to perform in public and in the intricately connected network of civic associations and popular gathering places.[30]

Public spaces often embody contradictory dynamics, as these are the spaces where the less well-off are found, these are some of the spaces where the less well-off encounter certain aspects of discrimination, and thus also the spaces most often prone to mass instances of rebellion. Since the 1970s feminists have been launching "Take Back the Night" marches and rallies to reclaim the public spaces—streets, parks, plazas—

to which they have effectively been denied access by the threat of rape and assault. The popularity of gay pride parades, outdoor celebrations, and events grows out of just such a dynamic as well. The repressive state of so many public spaces, where sexual norms are policed by average fellow citizens, makes such spaces ripe for challenges. In towns and parks across the country, and increasingly around the globe, a summer day or week is claimed by local queers and allies as "gay pride." Down a central street or in a main park an array of people, organizations, lifestyles, and fantasies will jubilate and display themselves for themselves, for each other, and for all—from the most mundane and conservative to the most outrageous and provoking. At least in these places for this one time of year, the communities of feminists and queers in their diversity will claim liberatory space in exactly the locations where they, at other times, all too often suffer repression and violence.

In comparison to privately owned spaces of elites, those of the working class often use buses and subways because (whether ecologically desirable or not) they cannot afford private cars, tolls, taxis, or limousines. Those of the working class and the un/underemployed often congregate in the streets, on corners, stoops, and parks because they cannot afford private clubs. It will also be in these places that repression is noticed, and conversation toward strategizing can take place. For example, Kelley assesses the interesting fact that African American women have used public transportation as sites of resistance, more so than African American men. Kelley notes that "black women outnumbered black men in the number of incidents of resistance on buses and streetcars" (1994, 67). He situates the action taken by Rosa Parks in the civil rights era not as a singular incident or as a pawn for civil rights organizations, but as part of a long tradition of Black women fighting Jim Crow on public transportation, such as the well-known Sojourner Truth, and Ida B. Wells-Barnett, as well as numerous such instances of challenge by women who are not nationally known. Kelley explains that due to the gendered aspects of a societal racial division of labor, Black women used public transportation more frequently than did Black men.[31] Black women often had to suffer numerous indignities and dangers on public transportation in addition to sitting at the back of buses, or not knowing if they would always be scolded for sitting where they chose. Sometimes bus drivers would not pick up a Black woman, or make the appropriate stop to let her off, or they might harass individual women traveling during off-hours. Public spaces are some of the spaces where those with different relationships to power come into contact and interact. It is also in these spaces, then, that the indignities of inequality and power differentials will be practiced and experienced. We must also, therefore, look to these spaces for their potential as sites of resistance and empowerment.

THE SPATIAL IMAGINARY AND MOVEMENT POLITICS

We ought also to take note of the notion of locations in the imaginations of marginalized groups and how even an imaginary geography of community and power may help organize potential political energies of different groups. Referring to Songhay traders from Niger on the streets of Harlem, Coombe and Stoller write that a few of these migrants "accept the fact that the 'Africa' African Americans 'need' is not the Africa they know" (1994, 265). Imagined communities also have long been of concern for radical democrats. Marx explicitly critiqued the illusory community created for the bourgeoisie under capitalism. Critics of narrow nationalism caution us to be wary of the rhetoric and concrete effects of imagined nationhood, unity in an invented and glorified past, and redemption through violence and xenophobia. In the contemporary United States, insightful critiques are being developed of the dangers in imagined communities of gated and guarded spaces to live, work, engage in commerce, and enjoy entertainment.[32]

All of these are significant tendencies to be wary of. The quest for community that drives many in radical politics must be approached with self-critical caution as well as energizing vision. This does not mean, however, that any imaginative space is necessarily reactionary. On the contrary, creativity and invention are key to finding our way out of material conditions that have been repressive and exploitative.[33] Even the best analytic critique and pragmatic examination benefits from insight and inspiration. In addition, it is at times only with our imaginations that we can envision alternatives to the present and historical circumstances. For example, early in the development of 1960s radical Chicana/o political movement an imaginary homeland served as a mechanism for many in the community to develop ideas about what an ethical, un-occupied community could be. Commenting on this phenomenon, Gutiérrez writes that "Equally important to the young Chicano radicals was the construction of a moral community that was largely imagined as spatial and territorial. Aztla'n, the legendary homeland of the Aztecs, was advanced as the territory Chicanos hoped to repossess someday" (1993, 46). Imagining Aztla'n "out there" aided many in the movement to connect to aspirations and critique deep within their material experiences in the current political system.[34]

It is often out of the fantasies of a small group of people that new concrete spaces to experiment with democratic relations emerge. In a manner similar to anarchist ideas and practices, people often create cooperatives for living, laundry, day care, housing, health care, various businesses, schools, and so on in order to fill a need in their own lives which turns out to be a need in many people's lives. Many communities set up week-long or weekend camps, havurot (fellowships), and gatherings that are not intended as flights from the everyday. Instead these are places to be connected and rejuvenated, as they become creative spaces where people can learn to live deep lessons of democratic relations so that they may engage in them in the everyday as well. The political struggles for those involved in the Michigan Womyn's Music Festival, or the Seneca Falls Women's Peace Encampment suggest the intensity of people's desires to experience actually living in formerly imagined communal spaces and testing democratic processes with all the pain, disappointment, excitement, transformations, inclusion and exclusion along the way.[35]

Which communities are imagined and which are "real" is also not a straightforward fact. Critics of identity politics at times rely on the phenomenon that "identity communities" no longer live together geographically. To some this suggests that the community does not "really" exist. What is real, however, operates on many different levels, often at once. Many of the most important liberation struggles globally are waged by diasporic communities: Tibetan, Jewish, Palestinian, and Armenian, to name but a few examples. Domestically, local politics has been a primary location of progressive social change, but movement building beyond the local is also necessary. Linking up local chapters of larger organizations and gaining sustenance for one's local work through connection to others around the map is essential for fundamental and wide-ranging social change. Individuals might live in states, rural areas, and on campuses with only one or two other members of their affinity group, but feel deeply connected to the larger phenomenon. It is the connection in both directions—when local individuals or groups bring in reinforcements from the broader community to help in a particular campaign or educational work, and when movements draw together many specific communities from around the country to make a mass demonstration—from the everyday of the local to the imagined yet real of the national or global that has made much of progressive social change possible.

In this we might find yet another paradox in the history of the public sphere. It is often enough in the politics of what "does not yet fully exist" that we find the creation and/or recognition of counterpublic spheres on the margins whose purpose is to push hard for democratic change.[36] Long at the heart of modern notions of the public sphere we find this dynamic of assuming the public capable of democratic engagement, of populating the political public sphere. And yet, the purpose of the public sphere is to enable that very same public to be a political public.[37] We must think of politics in a democratic space that is at the same time a space contoured for the struggle to become democratic.[38] Struggling with this dialectic is the only way to make sense of the historical development of multiple publics and the enfranchisement of marginalized populations. One day women/slaves/homosexuals are without civil rights; the next day a state passes a law or the federal government passes a constitutional amendment that changes this condition. Seeing the potential of an open space within a closed one, or as a specific example of a rights-bearing individual in a disenfranchised one, is a necessary element in imagining and creating change. It is particularly important with respect to generational politics. If we assume Generation X to be irresponsible and retrograde, what can we expect from these people in creating a democratic future? If we expose and enhance the progressive aspects of the political orientations among Gen Xers today, we build on a democratic potential in the present as we set ourselves up toward democratic aspirations for the future.[39]

INTERSECTING SPHERES

The intersection of these multiple spheres is itself another level of politics toward which we also must turn our attention. Coalitions and other locations where individuals and select communities directly cross paths are public spaces of a specific sort, requiring examination and analysis for their potential contributions to larger or more complex democratic sites.[40] It is not only that there are multiple spheres that are distinct and periodically come into contact. Each of us, often daily, moves through numerous spheres. Neither spheres nor individuals are unitary and thickly bounded. Spheres and people often overlap, interact, mutually constitute, and filter in and out of each other. How we consider such interventions and crossings, how we ourselves handle being part of numerous spheres and moving through different ones, are matters for examination by democratic theorists interested in heightening the democratic potential of the spatial dimensions of politics.

A new phenomenon experienced more broadly among Generation Xers than previous youth generations, due to the slow but steady success of integration efforts, involves the multilayered spatial politics between minority and majority youth, particularly in school contexts. White students in majority white high schools and universities often "criticize" minority students for "sticking together" or sitting together for meals in their schools' cafeterias. These "critiques" are often made defensively in discussions of diversity and racism. At moments when majority students are asked to look at their own responsibility for marginalizing minorities, they often first attempt to deflect attention from themselves. They argue that minority students segregate themselves, do not want to be integrated into school traditions and customs, and themselves practice exclusion. In response to the confusions created by such deflections, let us think about West's notion of multicontextualism. In any particular day most of these minority students will pass through numerous spaces: some where they are outsiders, some where they are viciously othered, some where there is a rather benign ignorance, some where they are not minorities at all. Students move in and out of various contexts that are charged differently politically, each with its own potential for any combination of exclusion, inclusion, empowerment, disempowerment. Students occupy numerous contexts daily with roommates, in dormitory group bathrooms, in different classroom settings, sports teams, political groups, the school orchestra, at their work-study job in the registrar's office, the cafeterias, local stores, at the movies. Taking time to eat lunch with other African Americans might be one of the only times during a day that an African American student can experience the relief and potential empowerment of not being a minority or being with this community. Further, majority students who are privileged with usually not even noticing that they spend most of their time with others much like themselves ought to look at their own lives on campus and ask if they are creating and/or entering spaces to be with people different from themselves.

On a broader level, we can also see how the welfare office, the courts, the immigration office, legislatures, labor unions, interest groups, universities, grant makers, media, and others all interweave to make manifest the notion of public spaces for discourse. Are you a presence in these arenas? Do you feel able to raise your voice in these and have it heard and respected? How does having a voice or not in one of these spaces effect, enhance, diminish, and/or alter one's participation in others? In what ways must we be "different people" when we cross through these spaces? What different parts of our selves, skills, knowledges, and languages must we work to access, build, suppress, or leave outside any of these? In what ways do and can our power relationships generate that which we bring in or leave out? In what ways does bringing in and leaving out different skills enlarge or decrease our agency and potential for solidarity? How fluent are we in moving from one framework to another? How do different modes of power enhance that fluency or stifle it? What of "the Songhay vendor in Harlem, [who] for example, negotiates his sales in a multiplicity of jural landscapes. He parlays his place on the sidewalk with other West African traders using Islamic precepts of propriety, he expresses his sense of entitlement to local business associations, and arbitrates terms of supply with Asian wholesalers in Chinatown. He also masters a new vernacular of race, politics and property to articulate solidarity with local residents, who may see him (because of the Asian goods he sells) as but a black mask for yet another invasion of Asian capital into the African American community" (Coombe and Stoller 1994, 254). The authors write that "[t]o understand informal economic activity in the late twentieth century it is necessary to move beyond concepts of legal pluralism to consider the means by which an interjuridical consciousness is forged."

Looking at the politics of intersecting spheres through a frame of shifting lingual sites, in her chapter "How to Tame a Wild Tongue" in *Borderlands/La Frontera* (1987), Anzaldua writes poignantly of Chicano/a Spanish and the many languages Chicano/as speak. On one level, she writes, "I remember being caught speaking Spanish at recess—that was good for three licks on the knuckles with a sharp ruler. I remember being sent to the corner of the classroom for 'talking back' to the Anglo teacher when all I was trying to do was tell her how to pronounce my name. If you want to be American, speak 'American' " (53). But the point is that "America" is made up of innumerable spaces demanding we speak innumerable languages. Addressing another context, in Anzaldua's case, this means that other times when she speaks English she is accused of being a cultural traitor by various Latina/os.

Further, she describes the place of Chicano/a Spanish: "For a people who are neither Spanish nor live in a country in which Spanish is the first language; for a people who live in a country in which English is the reigning tongue but who are not Anglo; for a people who cannot entirely identify with either standard (formal, Castillian) Spanish nor standard English, what recourse is left to them but to create their own language? A language which they can connect their identity to, one capable of communicating the realities and values true to themselves—a language with terms that are neither español ni inglés, but both. We speak a patois, a forked tongue, a variation of two languages" (55).

But even as groups often need a language to communicate among themselves, no group has only one language. At the same time she writes of the need for a common, secret language, Anzaldua also writes: "And because we are a complex, heterogeneous people, we speak many languages" (55). Her listing of these languages is powerful:

1. Standard English
2. Working class and slang English
3. Standard Spanish
4. Standard Mexican Spanish
5. North Mexican Spanish dialect
6. Chicano Spanish (Texas, New Mexico, Arizona, and California have regional variations)
7. Tex-Mex
8. Pachuco (called caló)

Anzaldua goes on to describe the distinct spaces where she uses different languages. Some of these overlap; some instances are confusing. Each space calls on a different aspect of herself, different abilities, differently situated power dynamics. In her home, at school, with friends, in the media, at work, in politics there are different languages or dialects and each is politically charged.

As another example, an Iraqi Jew born and raised as a citizen of the United States might know, recognize, or relate to phrases in Arabic, Hebrew, Aramaic, Judeo-Arabic, Yiddish, Ladino, and English. In any of these she may or may not be fluent in reading, writing, or speaking an educated version, slang, working class or regional dialects. At home she may speak Arabic, with cousins who came through Turkey some Ladino, in synagogue Hebrew and Aramaic for prayers and Judeo-Arabic among congregants, English at the motor vehicle bureau, Yiddish phrases at a meeting of a national Jewish organization. Constitutive of her gender and depending on her class, education, immigrant status, sexual orientation, religious knowledge, age, and health, let alone self-esteem and individual capacities, she may be more or less able to communicate in any one of these languages in any one of these spaces and able to move in and out of them as the spheres themselves merge—or as she simply walks across the hall in her apartment building. In each case defining the power relationships, the political histories, and the potential for mutuality, equality, recognition, and respect will help clarify the fluency level and adaptive capacity important for that individual's dignity, agency, generosity, and solidarity in any given context and political situation.

Sometimes the intersection of spaces creates complex layers of exclusion. Community-based politics can often create confusions for those who identify with movement aims, but themselves are not members of a specific community. An Anglo man in North Dakota who supports Native American rights and wants to work to end racism and repression against Native Americans can at times be perplexed about his proper place in local social justice movements. There are also times when certain minorities themselves move into areas of hegemony among the marginalized. Some Latinas have at times felt it necessary to call attention to the dominance of African American womanists in spaces created by and creating room for women of color. Jewish feminists have often been caught in the middle between minority and majority politics, being a distinct minority and historically labeled racially dark, but having in the United States communal access to certain modes of privilege similar to those of some majorities. The confusing question for many in Los Angeles during the riots following Rodney King's trial was, who was victim and who oppressor—or in what ways: African American and Latina/o residents and rioters, Korean residents and merchants, Anglo police, and/or average white residents? The exclusions that are at times created in the intersection of spheres and communities can often be extremely detrimental to progressive movement.[41]

The fact that we each occupy multiple places in a power hierarchy, however,[42] can also stimulate much insight and generate much-needed coalitional activism. The crossed spaces reflect and create an interrelation between oppressions. Crossed spaces also, therefore, often reflect and create interrelated struggles to fight oppressions. The spaces where spheres overlap can be interesting and stimulate particular discourses. It is in these spaces that new forms of community, consciousness, and activism also often arise. These are the fraught spaces where Chicanas might merge their insights from Mexican American communities and feminist movement. These are the explosive spaces where gay Pacific Islanders combine culture and experiences from their heritage in the Pacific Islands with urban mainland queer politics. Progressive Jewish activist organizations have often struggled with the complications and strengths of their situation as a progressive presence in the world of American Jewish organizations and a Jewish presence in multicultural and other progressive communities they share and coalitions of which they are a part. These spaces that present difficulty also have the potential for radical creativity.[43]

DEMOCRATIC STRUGGLING WITHIN SPHERES

In expanding the traditional notions of the public sphere, and in the acknowledgment and creation of new ones, activists and thinkers have been challenged to apply new lessons of democracy, multiplicity, and change to their analyses of specific groups, identities, and identity communities. Rethinking the location(s) of politics enables us to focus on questions of democracy at multiple levels in society, and not only in the traditionally centralized public sphere. Even as democrats learn alternatives to oligarchy and majoritarianism from the concrete experiences within the political processes of many subaltern communities, disenfranchised members of those same communities are trying to reapply them internally in order to push the boundaries of democratic praxis within these microlocations. In the following chapter we will look at questions concerning issues of in-group representation: who speaks for Generation X, queers, Native Americans? At this point, however, we must address some theoretical aspects of communities in terms of their being political spaces below the level of the national public sphere.

Dean writes that "the discursive spheres within civil society can and must be subject to democratic norms" (1996, 97). Interestingly enough, however, democratic theorists seem to have had a difficult time conceptualizing groups, movements, and communities as political spaces in the multiplicity that many members and activists experience them and from which they often learn their lessons of diversity, solidarity, responsibility, and democratic transformations. For example, across a spectrum of Liberals, communitarians, and postmodern critics we will find a similarly unitary view of communities and groups that effects their theorizing the spatial dimensions of politics. Pluralism, as a first example, may be mistaking a deep sense of cohesion—experienced within many groups active in the political arena that emerge and exist with the internal ties of communities or movements—for unanimity. Drawing on the Liberal understanding of the individual self as a universal being, atomistic and unencumbered by social ties,[44] pluralism treats groups as isolated, and rather monolithic and unchanging. In response to this development within Liberalism, a body of literature often referred to under the broad label communitarianism is emerging that *situates* the self. However, some of these communitarians display a tendency to envision communities as places spared the difficulties of diversity, debate, and politics. Additionally, there is a certain inadequacy common to postmodern critiques of communitarians for their own assumptions of group sameness. Because these thinkers seem to accept the undialectical view of community, their critical response is to abandon the concept rather than to problematize it.

It is important to look at this problem closely, as it is not only about groups themselves, but reflects the very problem of shifting to the plural when thinking about the concept of the public more broadly. Diversity politics suggests that in order to more fully engage democratic praxes, we must translate historic notions of the public sphere into decentralized, often community based, practices of multiple and overlapping publics. Until we can grasp multiplicity and change within the specific spheres, we will be unable to theorize multiplicity and change within democratic discourse on the public sphere itself. In this section, therefore, we will take a critical look at each of the major ideological approaches to theorizing community—Liberal, communitarian, and postmodern—as part of developing multilayered and more fully contoured theories of the public sphere, its role, limitations, and potential in democratic practices.

Liberalism

Some critics have suggested that in the way that Liberalism has developed, it has actually ended up without a "public" at all. In the version of Liberalism most common today, pluralism, the closest dynamic to resemble a public tends to be the competitive struggle between interest groups.[45] Disch's view is, however, that to the degree that "interest group competition is the mechanism through which fair decision making is institutionalized, there is no 'public' in pluralism. Further, the vast disparities of informational and financial resources that prevail in this society make interest group competition neither inclusive nor heterogenous" (1994, 217).

Instead of the public, many Liberal theorists have preferred a notion of civil society, where emphasis on private associations is taken to satisfy the democratic requirement of spaces for an active citizenry. When viewed from the margins, above we challenged this view of "private associations" as not politically charged. In this instance the Liberal predilection for such a view nicely avoids the difficulties of politics, particularities, and struggle. Volunteers populate this sphere, not activists. Those who keep the church soup kitchen running or the neighborhood watch operating are "just" doing their private religious or their particularized civic duty. In the United States, volunteers seem to be less fiery and therefore less threatening.[46] It is a world where specific interests are allowed and therefore must be seen as separate from the political realm proper, which either (in the republican example) must operate in the general, or (in the pluralist example) must maintain neutrality and therefore stand above this particular privatized world of affinity groups.[47]

This relates directly to the common Liberal understanding of groups and communities.[48] Because they view each individual as an unattached atom, completely in charge of an individual life plan, Liberals consider group identifications as external to, or nonconstitutive of, the authentic self. Membership, in this scheme, is incidental and instrumental.[49] As long as we agree with group policies and get our needs met, we may be part of a group. As long as its members agree, a group exists. Groups' representations themselves are not seen as made up of numerous, often conflicting and usually shifting, viewpoints. Needs are not seen as developing through political and discursive processes over time, multiple and frequently contradictory. To the degree that Liberal analysts note disagreement and conflict within communities and groups, they cease to see the community or group. Group identity is taken to mean sameness, so that fissures in the seamless whole spell disaster, and connote dissolution.[50] "The incompleteness of liberal theory affects action and understanding, leaving people with motives too weak to protect communities, models too meager to assist efforts in creating and maintaining communities."[51]

In response to this tendency in Liberalism, multiculturalists have drawn on a rich tradition of communitarian writing that situates us as developed in and through our membership in multiple communities.[52] Despite the differences among them, communitarians assert the social nature of individual identity and affirm commitments based on the experience of internal ties between specially designated groups.[53] Communitarians suggest that many people live (and others aspire to live) as members of communities, rather than merely as isolated individuals heaped together to form society. Communitarians critique Liberalism on this basis and have been developing alternative theories of human existence, motivation, and aspirations based on the special concept of "community."

Communitarianism

Multiculturalist-communitarian theory has helped us conceive of the multiplicity of society on a nation-state level. At this point there is much literature focused on reconceptualizing the oneness of "America" in terms of the manyness of our communal affiliations.[54] Although multicultural theorists have benefited tremendously from the insights of communitarianism, some have also suffered from its shortcomings. Despite much work to re-vision the sameness of our national identity in terms of the difference of our subcommunal experiences, multiculturalists have at times not taken these lessons further into their understandings of these subcommunities themselves. Some efforts toward multiculturalism stop with superficial renderings of our communities, essentializing the community based on one or another characteristic.[55]

For example, some communitarians fall into the habit of reifying the unit of the community itself, solidifying it into a static entity. Community is understood as a bounded entity exhibiting a homogeneous consensus.[56] When contemplating community, some have a tendency to abandon a presumption of politics, contestation, discourse, debate—in short, the communal grappling that accompanies identity formation and actual living in history.[57] Communitarian theorists as different as Habermas, Barber, Sandel, and MacIntyre have, at times, exhibited this tendency.[58] They have been criticized on this point by theorists writing from both Liberal and postmodernist perspectives.[59]

We see that there seems to be a strangely similar preoccupation with sameness between the Liberals from the group theory perspective and some communitarians, which ignores or actually stifles the reality and contribution of difference. In Chapter Two we traced the problem for contemporary Liberals back to Hobbes's idea of compleasance: natural law prescribes that each strive to accommodate himself to the rest and those who remain different will be cast out of society. We can now trace a similar problem for contemporary communitarians back to Rousseau. Rousseau's conceptualization of the general will, and the expectations of politics and society necessary in order to create it, informs the thought of many contemporary communitarian theorists. But Rousseau himself forbids group identification in a manner that is similar to the way that the Liberal James Madison[60] sought to break the violence of faction. Rousseau told us that the common interest to be expounded as the general will must rise above particular interests (1973, 185). Rousseau wrote in *The Social Contract* that "the particular will tends, by its very nature, to partiality, while the general will tends toward equality" (1973, 182). In this vision previously discussed in Chapter Five, revived by some contemporary communitarians, we must transcend these particulars, the substance of our difference, if we are to achieve community. This, however, is the exact problem multiculturalism on a national level was designed to overcome.

Despite the communitarian grounding, affirming the socially embedded self, these theories may, at times, revive undialectical assumptions of community. From a dialectical perspective, communitarians go one step further than Liberals in their commitment to acknowledging connection (as opposed to the atomism of Liberal thinking). However, it may be that part of problem of this aspect of communitarianism stems from forgetting to see phenomena as also—and always—changing. As will be discussed below, communities and movements exist, by definition, historically. On the surface, at least, communitarian theorists refer to this. But when situating the self, it is possible that some thinkers are situating that self only in terms of connection in an actual or imagined spatial dimension, without including the dimension of time (situating us historically). The problem here is that when we do not look at things in history, in their concrete life over time, we tend to see only static and simplistic caricatures. A more dialectical view shows that as soon as "we consider things in their motion," moving through time, we are forced to see them with all of their contradictions and internal multiplicity.[61]

What is interesting is that there are also those who are doing more postmodern critical theory who seem to accept this characterization of the homogeneity of community assumed by some of the Liberal and communitarian theorists they themselves critique. Although they criticize the urge for sameness, they do not problematize it. Thus, they not only reject communitarian theory on this basis, but reject community itself. In the next section I will look at two examples of this kind of theory and suggest that these thinkers draw a false empirical conclusion from what I agree with as an appropriate critique of theory. Community, both lived and aspired to, has potential to be, and often already is for many members of various groupings, an important and liberating element of diversity-based democratic theory. The problem in this case lies not inherently in community, but in theorists' inability to keep the notions of difference and sameness in dialectical tension when theorizing community (as discussed in earlier chapters, creating other problems for democratic theory as well).

Postmodernism

The work of Iris Young provides an example of one conceptualization in which a theorist mistakes the implications in the critique of the assumption of homogeneity made by communitarians. In the early sections of *Justice and the Politics of Difference*, for example, Young makes clear that we need to remember the existence of groups when talking about justice. Many of the groups she actually refers to are commonly known as communities, such as Jews and African Americans, and are not merely groups understood in the pluralist mode as interest groups—such as the National Rifle Association or the wheat growers' lobby. Young not only reminds us that the broader national body politic is composed of many subcommunities, but that as individuals we are each members of various subcommunities. For example, one may be Native-American, particularly Acoma Pueblo, a two-spirited woman, and so on. In the beginning of this chapter we noted the interesting overlap between youth politics and queer politics. Conversely, most Generation Xers are probably more comfortable with sexual desires oriented toward members of the opposite sex, and many homosexuals and sexual outlaws are well over forty. We must remember not to essentialize groups, and to affirm the difference within them.

In this style Young rises to a multiculturalist call to struggle dialectically with difference and sameness. Young's understanding of commu-nities, when treated directly, is thus surprising in the context of her the-ory as a whole. Young not only critiques certain community *theorists* such as Habermas, but extends that critique to community *itself* based on the assumption that community essentially represents an urge to homogeneity. In her chapter on community, the author somehow loses her otherwise keen ability to keep unity and difference in constant ten-sion, existing simultaneously. Young speaks eloquently in the language of difference and then abandons it at its most crucial point—in the midst of a self-conscious unity. Young, therefore, seems to see community as negating difference. Where difference is recognized, she will not call the entity a community.

Young resists the notion of groupings as communities when she finds difference among members. Take, for example, the Korean American community. There is no doubt that there are many different types of Korean Americans, even Korean American subcommunities based on religious, regional, immigrant status, cultural, gender, sexual, class, or other experiences of a more general Korean American identity. There is no doubt that a particular person whose origins are Korean American may often feel that he or she has more in common with other particular (U.S) Americans who are not of Korean descent than with many particu-lar Korean Americans whom he or she knows. There is no doubt that many people who are of Korean descent, or may even identify themselves as Korean American, do not understand themselves as members of this phenomenon referred to as the Korean American community. This is sim-ilar to the observation that there are many women who are not woman-identified, or others who do not feel themselves as an integral part of that amorphous phenomenon called women's or the women's movement, homosexuals who do not identify with gay liberation, younger people who do not identify with being of "Generation X." But identifying these differences to show that there is no community is a mistake. It completely misses the lived experience of a reality, however hard to pin down, of such a thing as the Korean American community, for example.

Some comments by Nancy Fraser will demonstrate this point one step further. Fraser's work (like Young's) in general will prove helpful to many interested in thinking about democracy with an appreciation of communal difference. Fraser's work on the public sphere referred to in this chapter discusses a central aspect of diversity-based theory, which she suggests in terms of "multiple publics." No longer can we accept the dominance of a single hegemonic public space on the level of the nation-state. The author argues eloquently for affirming the many subspheres in the country in which we actually find politics taking place. Drawing much on Habermas, she is also critical of what she, like Young, sees as his tendency toward homogeneity.[62]

A problem with her work emerges, however, when the author then clearly distinguishes for the reader her understanding of a "public" and her understanding of a "community." In one article Fraser writes that she wants us "to consider replacing the homogenizing, ideological category of 'community' with the potentially more critical category of 'public' in the sense of a discursive arena for staging conflicts" (1997, 118). In another, oft cited, article on the public sphere, Fraser writes that "'[c]ommunity' suggests a bounded and fairly homogenous group, and it often connotes consensus. 'Public,' in contrast, emphasizes discursive interaction that is in principle unbounded and open-ended, and this in turn implies a plurality of perspectives. Thus, the idea of a public, better than that of a community, can accommodate internal differences, antagonisms, and debates" (1997, 97, n. 33).

On the one hand, however, we have already noted (as does Fraser herself) that most publics themselves and even the very concept of the public historically, have been quite exclusionary. Imminent critique (rather than idealized definitions) of the need to police the boundaries of supposedly open publics is fundamental for those who appreciate the liberatory potential of the notion and practices of public spheres. On the other hand, my own personal experience of communities, along with that of many others, has never been one of simple homogeneity and rarely of (at least simple) consensus. Although I do not intend to make an exhaustive assessment, the communities I know from experience as a member and from analysis as a scholar all exist through internal multiplicity and struggle. The boundaries that identify them are always both real and mythic, solid and permeable, understood and ever contested.

Readers will likely find helpful most of Fraser's discussion of publics, and it is certainly important to distinguish at times between communities and publics. Although communities are political, and in my experience exist in political process, that is not always the only level of focus needed to understand them. In addition, not all publics would be properly understood as communities. However, to cast the difference between them in terms of difference, politics, boundedness, and so on simply does not reflect the variety of actual communities and the multiplicity of actual publics. Much in this literature also overstates the glories of agonism.[63] Within our system of unequal power dynamics, agonistic or antagonistic relations do not inherently suggest transformation.[64] Democratic politics does not necessitate agonistic and conflictual relations over and against empathy, solidarity, and cooperation. In spatializing our theoretical engagements with democratic politics, we must avoid mapping our schematized conceptual frameworks neatly drawn in theory. Instead, as theorists, we must work to respect and attend to the differing needs of different locations grounded historically.[65] In attending to the spatial dimensions of politics, theorists may be reminded to situate their discussions. In doing so we are likely to find that different circumstances require different dynamics to best approximate democratic solutions or work through a particularly difficult impasse.

For example, given the tendency to glorify a simplistic notion of the public in contemporary democratic theory, we must remind ourselves again that many publics are not (or are plagued by dominant elements who do not want them to be) open and accommodating of difference. It is precisely in response to the fact that many publics are too closed—such as the broadest public spaces of the United States, many media, and most levels of government—that Fraser and others write of the benefits of open and multiple publics. On the other hand, to describe community as a totalitarian-style society in miniature is to miss its liberating aspects and potential, which have actually spurred the kind of theorizing these thinkers are doing in the first place. It is in large part the identity-based activism of communities of African Americans and other communities of color, women, queers, radical Gen Xers, and so on that has both stimulated and made possible the theories of diversity that the work of those such as Fraser and Young represent.[66] Thus, thinking that strictly dichotomizes notions of the *public* and ideas about *community* will tend to be unhelpful and problematic.[67] Further, such a utopian view of a public tends to reify actual publics, taking them out of real space and time.[68] A static view of a public misses the paradoxical dynamics that may turn even the most exemplary publics into restricted spaces, depriving them of their vibrancy and radical contestational capacities, or turn narrow spaces into participatory sites.[69]

History

It is especially at this point that including history in one's thinking becomes crucial. Without situating citizenship in its various spatial contexts we end up with static and unchanging theories and politics. Attending even to the spatial dimension of politics will, however, prove limiting if it is not done in the context of time also. Within her own framework of political analysis, which she refers to as Getting Specific, Phelan (who is generally favorably predisposed to postmodern critique) takes Foucault to task on exactly this point: she notes that Foucault does not "leave us with any categories or frameworks for understanding historical change."[70] We now turn to a discussion concerning how we might be able to use history to help keep theorizing community engaged in the dialectic of sameness and difference so that we may ultimately be able to do so in theoretical work on the public sphere as well.

Diversity theorists must address the need to see on a dual level when theorizing community. We must enhance our fluency in seeing on the level of sameness, similarity, or unity, on the one hand—and diversity, multiplicity, or difference on the other hand. In my own attempts to do so I have found that history becomes another fundamental characteristic to be held in constant dialectical tension when looking at community. Here I mean history on two levels. On one level we may think of the need for an historical perspective on our own part as scholars. On another level we may think of history in terms of the reality of actual communities: as central to the notion of community itself is a sense of history, or a being informed by/a living in history, and therefore a living through change.

In the example of the American Jewish community, one need not essentialize Jews to relate to a conception/life experience of the Jewish community. One does not need to see the Jewish community as many do, especially in the more well-known aspects of its political incarnation as the Jewish lobby, as having natural, unified, and unchanging needs or interests, in order to acknowledge the bonds of community, the historical situatedness, the meaning and identity of so many individual Jews who feel themselves to be a part of, and live their lives through, Jewish community.[71] Activists and communal leaders are able to promote multiculturalist aims within communities more effectively as they become conscious of the reality and history of dissent within their own community. Group studies and communal self-perceptions that treat communities ahistorically perceive a monolith. Activists and leaders will doubtless find it much harder to promote tolerance and diversity within this rubric. Including a sense of history in the analysis forces one to confront the political process of struggling among varying group identity conceptions, with helpful consequences not only to activists but also to scholars.[72]

An attention to history and the movement it suggests brings us as scholars directly into doing theory that struggles with sameness and difference. We must appreciate the way communities themselves tend to exist historically, with a sense (whether mythic or not) of their collective past, the forces that propel them and that they set in motion, and their perceived mission. (I do not wish to suggest, of course, that this experience is monolithic; rather, it is itself subject to the same dialectic of multiple vantage points.) Therefore, despite the approach by many scholars that attempts to see groups ahistorically, and to draw theoretical and empirical conclusions from that perspective, communities often experience *themselves* historically. Theory will thus need to attend this experience. When it does so I suggest theorists will find attention to history a helpful tool in keeping us constantly in the dialectic of unity and multiplicity. One is unlikely to find any issue, any set of priorities, any identity representation, any style of leadership, any particular internal set of power relations, or any specific mode of intracommunal relationship that has not changed somehow over the community's history. As each and all of these directly affect the spatial boundaries of communities, through an historical lens these boundaries are seen as inherently shifting and dynamic, their changing locations the result of politics as much as they signify the process of politics itself.

CONCLUSION

Sanders reprints a quote from a twenty-five-year-old gay man interviewed in the gay newsmagazine *The Advocate*: "Of party politics, [the man] snorts, 'Democratic, Republican. Coke, Pepsi. It all tastes the same.' " Sanders writes that "young people in the 1990s . . . are notoriously fickle and independent; they are not 'joiners,' and are much less inclined than older generations to inform themselves about political and social issues. It is fashionable among this generation to affect cynicism about politics, . . . when what is probably more often at work is an unwillingness to take the time or effort to acquaint themselves with the differences between parties and candidates" (1998, 2).

Sanders is concerned that the two groups least homophobic and most inclined to support gay-positive policies—Generation Xers and queers themselves—are also the least likely to engage in electoral politics. Conversely, the two groups most likely to vote—older people and conservative Christian evangelicals—are also "the most often hostile" to "gay/lesbian issues" (1998, 5). This is a serious concern, but it itself replicates a significant problem for Gen X and queer political agency and effectiveness. Sanders, like most political analysts, defines politics as government-related activities. Public collective action is then largely understood as party- and policy-affiliated action.

Queers and Gen Xers, like women and many minorities, are certainly rarely taken into account in policy fora. This is an important disadvantage that a country calling itself a democracy must change. It does not mean, however, that queers, Gen Xers, and most other marginalized groups do not engage in the political system, or that they have not long acted to promote their needs and affect justice. It also does not square with these groups' understanding of themselves as having political ideas and being political agents. What it does mean is that what is deemed fit for much political analysis does not reflect the political lives of most queer people, young people, women, and marginalized minority communities.

Discussed in the introduction to this chapter, Smith's research focuses on gay pride marches. Millions of queers and their allies have participated in these events. It is clear that pride marches alone will not eradicate homophobia and change the lives and prejudices of the populace, queer and straight. It is instructive, however, that the overwhelming majority of participants Smith interviewed consider these events politically salient. Smith also points out that the pride marches, which 88.7 percent of participants view as "important in advancing the overall political interests of LGB people," have not even been studied by political science analysts. Scott's insight clarifies the problem here. He writes that "so long as we confine our conceptions of the *political* to activity that is openly declared we are driven to conclude that subordinate groups essentially lack a political life or that what political life they do have is restricted to those exceptional moments of popular explosion. To do so is to miss the immense political terrain that lies between quiescence and revolt and that, for better or worse, is the political environment of subject classes. It is to focus on the visible coastline of politics and miss the continent that lies beyond" (1990, 199).

Queers and Gen Xers are not out in droves at voting booths each November. That so many *are* out dancing every week is looked down upon as evidence of their political quiescence. I would like to see more queer and youth presence in electoral politics. We must ask, however, are raves and gay or lesbian clubs social spaces only, devoid of any political meaning and lacking emancipatory power as sites of resistance? In writing of the political significance that dance halls, blues bars, and gospel churches have historically held for African Americans, Kelley writes that "for a working class whose days consisted of backbreaking wage work, low income, long hours, and pervasive racism, these social sites were more than relatively free spaces in which the grievances and dreams of an exploited class could be openly articulated. They enabled African-Americans to take back their bodies for their own pleasure rather than another's profit" (1994, 44). Although micro forms of resistance must become, or link up to, larger action if broad-based social transformation is to be possible, mass public transformation is impossible without these micro forms of politics. Drawing on the activism of diversity-based politics, democratic theorists must look to these subaltern sites, beyond the level of the state.

Trained as a geographer, Brown offers a radical, political analysis of AIDS-oriented gay health, activist, cultural, and civic organizations to challenge many ideas about actual and potential public spheres long discussed in political theory. Conversely, political theorists need to begin to address geographic conceptualizations of such public spaces if we are interested in responding to and supporting radical democratic politics. Perhaps we also need to look more closely at raves, clubs, and gay and lesbian churches and synagogues as political spaces. Policymakers and average gay men know quite clearly that bathhouses, for example, have been the sites of intense clashes with ideology and the state, as well as of communal destruction and liberation. Political analysts and theorists must respond to the multiplicity of these sites, on the numerous levels where the public engages in political action and resistance.

The long-held public-private distinction does not offer a sufficient analytical tool to examine the politics of communities and culture as practiced. It certainly does not help us to understand the politics of something as "cultural," yet constitutive of power struggles for many minorities, as dress. Is drag, for example, reactionary, or worse yet a wholesale flight from politics? If it has no political significance, then why has cross-dressing been the subject for public policies in many schools and cities? Why have those who cross-dress so often been responded to with violence? Drag has certainly been a point of much political debate, disappointment, and solidarity between various segments of queer and feminist communities, activists, and thinkers. If kids wearing jeans and long hair were beat up and turned away from employment in the 1960s and 1970s, what of the piercing and tattooing craze of youth today? Due to wartime fabric rationing, the War Production Board made zoot suits illegal in 1942. Kelley points out that Blacks who wore them were seen as anti-American. Homophobia and sexism combined to reinforce the notion that patriotism is a "man's" business. Racism was also operative in the white press, which called the Blacks who wore these "loud and flamboyant" suits "unpatriotic dandies." For a young Malcolm X, Kelley argues, the zoot suit "was a rejection of both American patriotism and Black petit bourgeois respectability" (1994, 166–72). If political theorists were to take the cue from geographers, we will find that in community dynamics and culture there are myriad "surfaces" on which politics is made and played out. As theorists we must develop multilayered analyses of the places of politics, the relations within them, and how they intersect if our work is to be relevant to people seeking democratic futures in their diverse situations.

But how might we be able to do so? Having sketched the when, who, what, why, and now where of an emerging democratic praxis, we will next turn our attention to some lessons democratic theorists might learn from the experiences, strategies, successes, and failures of marginalized groups in their concrete work to enact and enable justice. In this we will find a significant critique of popular Liberal and conservative views on the "how" question, and interesting alternatives.

7   How: Minoritizing and Majoritizing

INTRODUCTION

[D]emocracy is not seen as an unfolding historical reality, to be understood at each point in its evolution, but as an eternal absolute defined in terms of majority will. This abstract and pure conception is seen as a value to be upheld at all costs in all circumstances. The object of all government, for such pursuits, is the attainment of that value in preference to any other. That being the case, any instrumentalities of government that frustrate the attainment of that value must be suspect, if not downright evil.   —Judge Gibbons[1]

IT IS often difficult to engage in critical discussions of fundamental democratic principles. Basic questions of democratic praxis are often assumed to be easily answered, or thought to have been answered declaratively by the "founding fathers." Sometimes merely suggesting that we reopen the discussion can lead to charges of disloyalty and evil doings. What I treat in this book as the "how" question of democracy suffers such a fate no less than any other. The question "*how* ought we to go about enacting systems of governance by, for, and of the people?" now for the most part has a simple answer: majoritarianism. Decision making according to the will of the majority appeals to a certain sense of fairness, for why should the whole populace bow to the demands of the few, especially when the few may just be stubborn, acting like spoiled children or bullies in the playground? Ancient Greek elite philosophers such as Aristotle connected the dangers and instability related to democracy to its base in mob rule, rule by the majority class. Majoritarianism was thus a radical aspect of modern democratic revolutions. The colonists in what was to become the United States strove to break away from rule by a minority aristocratic regime. (U.S.) Americans have thus grown to

Earlier versions of the argument for this chapter were originally prepared for delivery at the 1997 Annual Meeting of the American Political Science Association, Washington, D.C., August 28–31, 1997, and the UNH-Political Science Colloquium 1997.

believe fervently in majoritarianism as the core of their democratic ideals.

This country has had, however, a number of shaky encounters with majority voting that might give us insight into some of its shortcomings and point toward more fulfilling alternatives. For a brief moment in the 2000 presidential election the country realized that our system was not as straightforward as many had thought. Vice President Al Gore and his running-mate Connecticut Senator Joseph Lieberman won the majority of the popular vote, but did not win the electoral college majority. Average citizens were outraged that the person they voted into office would not be declared the winner due to that little-understood institution called the electoral college. It was then made public that there had been a serious miscount in the state of Florida where, incidentally, the brother of the state's ostensible winner, Texas Governor George W. Bush, was serving as governor. A recount was ordered, further recounts were demanded, court battles ensued, the media was in a frenzy. The country was in an uproar. Both here and abroad our democratic process was called into question. Ultimately, however, the calls made for "fundamental reform of our antiquated system" by those with access to the major media amounted to little more than proposals to alter slightly our basic mechanisms of majority rule. Most national spokespersons expended much energy to quell "fears" of any change at all, and reassured us that our system was alive and well, our democracy invigorated from the national attention. They warned anyone aspiring to utilize the opportunities created by the 2000 presidential election fiasco to threaten our status quo that such challenges would not be tolerated.

So many citizens did find this response "reassuring." The idea "that American democracy means majority rule"[2] is thought to be so well accepted that, as Judge Gibbons put it, any challenge or suggested alternative to it "must be suspect, if not downright evil." In the United States children are taught this lesson from their earliest years. The rules of group decision making follow a simple majority showing. A teacher asks a classroom of first grade pupils how many would like the class to participate in the school fair. Some children raise their hands in favor, other children raise their hands against. The teacher deliberately counts each child and asks the students to count along. When counting, the students can practice their numbers. When counted, each student is acknowledged as contributing to the decision. The tally is in: fifteen in favor, twelve against. The choice is clear: the class will participate in the fair. The teacher has taught the class one of the most important civics lessons the children will have to learn. This is the way we make democratic decisions for a group.

Lani Guinier[3] relates a story of a conversation she had with her then four-year-old son, Nikolas. A *Sesame Street Magazine* exercise prompted readers to decide what game a group of children would play when it pictured four children with raised hands who wanted to play tag, while two children who wanted to play another game were pictured with their hands down. The children were asked to decide which game the children would play by counting those with their hands raised and comparing them to those with their hands drawn as down. But Nikolas told his mother that he thought the children ought to play two games. First they could play tag, and then the children who wanted to play a different game could get a turn to choose another game to play. According to even the quite progressive *Sesame Street* materials, Nikolas would have been "wrong." His mother, however, did not see things this way.

Increasingly, we are finding adults who are taking this currently unpopular position (even on *Sesame Street!*) publicly. We are finding some who are willing to face public doubt of their patriotism and morals. Specifically, many minorities and those attending to minority concerns have begun to question a democratic system organized structurally to guarantee that the majority always wins. United States Supreme Court Justice Brennan, in a dissenting opinion in *Goldman v. Weinberger*, 475 U.S. 503, 523–24 (1986), writes: "in pluralistic societies such as ours, institutions dominated by a majority are inevitably, if inadvertently, insensitive to the needs and values of minorities when these needs and values differ from those of the majority." It is thus now being argued that strict proponents of majoritarianism are being, rather than democratic, too often antidemocratic. A strict interpretation of majority rule as the foundational answer to the "how" question of democratic practice tends to serve and protect the interests of those already privileged.

Given the presumption of a constitutional commitment to majority rule as the operative mechanism of democracy, many consider this to be a founding principle and therefore attributed to James Madison. Madison, however, was neither a democrat nor a majoritarian. Interestingly enough, the reason for this is precisely because he sought to promote elite interests. In this chapter I will attempt to unscramble this confusion of politics, power, and principles. I will argue that democracy is not only "an unfolding reality" but one that is also best served in reference to, rather than "eternal absolutes," value commitments evaluated and designed to meet the specific needs of specific fora. We must remember why majoritarianism was at times considered a radical technique of democracy, and therefore, or perhaps even more importantly, that it is *a technique of democracy* and not to be simply equated with democracy itself. The practice must serve the principle, and if there are times when democracy will be better served by other means then we ought to employ those other means. In fact, popular rhetoric in the United States notwithstanding, democratic theorists have long questioned majority rule; and myriad institutions, governing bodies, groups, and organizations in democracies have long employed methods that run counter to the majoritarian principle specifically in the interest of promoting democratic egalitarianism.

In this chapter I present a critical analysis of the theoretical background on the idea of majority rule in the context of politics in the United States. Feminist principles and the writings of James Madison, John Stuart Mill, Lani Guinier, and John C. Calhoun will be discussed. I then look at some of the institutional consequences of such a theoretical legacy and debate. Contributions from marginalized and minority groups such as women, African Americans, Jews, and queers will be examined in a discussion of coalitions, minoritizing and majoritizing strategies, record keeping and inscribing the future in the present, consociationalism and (neo)corporatism, voting rights activism, representation and in-group democracy, and localizing issues. In doing so I hope to help stimulate new ideas about *how* we might best engage as a polity democratically, in different spaces, in different ways.

THEORETICAL BACKGROUND

To the average (U.S.) American, majority rule is as "American as apple pie." In the midst of the 2000 presidential election confusion, both camps could be heard appealing to the courts and media that we must protect our democracy, uphold the Constitution, respect the will of the people, and fairly decide who constituted the majority: Gore or Bush supporters. Even the more educated citizen will easily note the preponderance of Supreme Court decisions based on the assumption of majoritarianism. Many, thus, think that majority rule is a constitutional principle of U.S. democracy built into its structure since the founding period. It is important to note, however, that there is nothing constitutional that establishes majority rule in this way. As Supreme Court Chief Justice Burger has written, "There is nothing in the language of the Constitution, our history, or our cases that requires that a majority always prevails on every issue."[4] In addition, although new students of political science often seemed shocked with the news, James Madison was not a democrat.

In *Federalist Paper* 10 (1961) Madison tells us that he knows exactly what a democracy is . . . and he is not interested. What Madison puts forward is, instead, an argument for a republic. Though, again, most new students will not even know that there is a difference between democracies and republics, Madison knew the difference and his choice was clear. As he described in *Federalist Paper* 10, democracies are smaller, with more people participating and less guided by the rights of individual property. Republics can be larger, relying on representation of the people, and are better protectors of property. It is not only the fact that Madison stood for a more elitist system of representation that will interest those in search of new answers to the "how" question of democracy, but the spatial and temporal dimension of the discussion as well.

Madison can be confusing for contemporary (U.S.) Americans because (1) he was a thinker afraid of both minority rule and majority abuse; (2) he devised a system to protect minorities but used a version of majoritarianism to do so; and finally, (3) as mentioned above, none of this was in the service of democracy. His method is less straightforward, therefore, than it might first appear. One of the central benefits of a republic is that, due to its system of representation, it has the capacity to cover large geographical distances. This was essential to Madison as he knew that differences "are sown in the nature of man" and that the more diverse the geographical landscape, the more diverse the people. Madison thought that by structurally encouraging diversity, in a vast geographical area, that it would be almost impossible for any one idea or interest to be taken up by a majority. Although he designed the system to utilize a winner-take-all style of majority rule voting, the actual winning party would never be a true majority. The winning party would of necessity always be constituted by a temporary coalition of minorities. The temporal nature of this coalition was important. Due to the diversity structurally secured, Madison felt it was unlikely that any two issues would attract the same configuration of minorities for and against. Thus, afraid of the tyrannical potential of majorities and seeking to curb this development, Madison utilized a specific form of majority rule as a mechanism to prevent the formation and sustenance of majorities.

As we began to discuss in Chapter Two, many democratic theorists have found in this argument the basis for a kind of democracy understood as pluralist. On this score, the persuasiveness of Madison's theory for more contemporary democratic thinkers rests on (1) the assumption that there are numerous and shifting factional interests, and (2) the dimension of time. Each of us will find ourselves in the minority at some points, but not permanently. This form of democratic theory, utilizing majoritarianism, claims that no one group will persistently win political battles, nor will anyone lose so often that they are effectively disenfranchised.[5] In a pluralist society, basically a nation of myriad minority groups, your group might lose on this turn in politics, but the system remains fair, democratic, because it is sure that you will win in another turn. Losers are soothed by the promise of time.

Some have even updated this discussion into the language of what they see as multicultural politics.[6] Scholars have even read back into the First Amendment, the clauses on religion, and Supreme Court tests on the point to indicate that the founders established a system to promote and protect multiculturalism. These discussions can be confusing, as majoritarianism was long considered the mainstream principle and so critiqued by more radical democrats concerned with the fate of minorities. These particular voices reading multiculturalism back into the founding are also considered undemocratic though they run counter to traditional majoritarians and speak in the name of diversity. The discussion on Madison demonstrates, however, that one can *seem* to speak in the name of diversity in this way and still not be a democrat. Actually, from Madison's writings, we find that this might be considered the triumphant founding approach. How is this possible? It depends on whom you include in your conception of diversity.

THEORETICAL CRITIQUE

John Stuart Mill opens *On Liberty* with a discussion of the historical movement against tyranny. We are now gladly at the point, he writes, when "the rulers should be identified with the people, that their interest and will should be the interest and will of the nation." This seemed the crowning achievement for democracy as "[t]he nation did not need to be protected against its own will. There was no fear of its tyrannizing over itself." Despite Madison's carefully taken precautions against new forms of tyranny, history has a way of creating new problems even when long-sought goals have been achieved. Mill writes, "But, in political and philosophical theories as well as in persons, success discloses faults and infirmities which failure might have concealed from observation" (1984, 61).

Writing almost a century after the (U.S.) American and French Revolutions, Mill looks back on a Liberal democracy in practice, and must face some of the "faults and infirmities" that have transpired since the actualization of the grand theoretical proposal. He tells us that "self-government and the power of the people over themselves," have not exactly turned out to be true. In a government "of each by all the rest," he considers, "the will of the people, moreover, practically means the will of the most numerous or the most active *part* of the people—the majority, or those who succeed in making themselves accepted as the majority; the people, consequently, *may* desire to oppress a part of their number, and precautions are as much needed against this as against any other abuse of power" (1984,62). We find a similar wariness on the part of Tocqueville (1994) as well. Tocqueville was a Frenchman who came to the United States in the 1800s to study the new form of democracy developing in this country. He was impressed in many ways with what he saw. But he also noticed something unusual. In their own ways, majorities, majority opinion, and majority practices had so come to dominate U.S. culture that Tocqueville thought the U.S. form of democracy had created a form of majority tyranny previously unseen in any despotic form of government.

In the modern context of the United States, early in the development of the twentieth century pluralist conception, scholars such as Schattschneider (1960) took issue with the Madisonian formulation as a democratic formulation. He argued that there was an inherent class bias in understanding our system as made up of an array of groups competing in the political marketplace. Although the theory suggests that no one wins or loses in these battles all of the time, Schattschneider argued that in fact this was not the case. To look at this point in a different way, Feldman (1997) argues that what many consider our most prominent demo-

cratic example of pluralism is more a re-inscription of majority domination. The freedom of religion clauses found in the Bill of Rights,
Feldman demonstrates, merely served to bolster and protect the majority Christian hegemony, at the expense of non-Christian minorities.
What is often seen as the diversity protected by these clauses is merely
a multiplicity of groups belonging to the dominant Christian majority.
This insight resonates with the critique of other aspects of what some
might attribute to the "multiculturalism" of Madison.

The "difference" Madison is concerned about being able to engage is
different segments of the ruling class during his historical period.
Including those disenfranchised at his time, many still so, was not on
the agenda. Despite pleas to the contrary, women, slaves, indentured
servants, Native Americans, Jews, those without property, Hessians,
Russians, Lanjobbers, Catholics, and so on[7] were expressly excluded
from governance and the new system of rights. Radical democrats
working from a grounding in diversity politics have been developing
critiques of various aspects of the inegalitarian nature of majoritarianism based on the Madisonian model and exploring alternatives. Perhaps the most famous and careful of these is Lani Guinier.

Early in his first term, President Bill Clinton nominated Lani Guinier for
the position of civil rights enforcement chief. Not only was Guinier not
appointed, Clinton's nomination never even went through the channels of
a usual nomination. Instead, within a few months' time Clinton withdrew
his nomination. At the heart of the controversy, Guinier's legal writings
analyzed alternatives to a particular form of majoritarianism. In some of
her work, Guinier questioned the relationship between democratic values
and (U.S.) American-style one-person–one-vote, winner-take-all majority
rule. Detractors called the nominee crazy and simply un-American.
Guinier, on the other hand, pointed out that her ideas are quite "American." On the one hand, she reminds us that corporations utilize strategies
of block voting in order to protect stockholders. On the other hand, she
draws the connecting line straight from her ideas philosophically to
founding father James Madison and the U.S. Constitution through their
twentieth-century mainstream manifestations in voting rights activism,
Congressional legislation, Supreme Court cases, and Justice Department
decisions between 1969 and 1993 (therefore even under numerous Republican administrations).

What Guinier's central writings do not mention are the roots of her ideas in early second-wave feminist concerns with democratic praxis. The antidemocratic manifestations of Madisonian-style majoritarianism not only kept certain minorities disenfranchised, but women as a group for the most part as well. Women are technically a majority of the United States' population. Since Mill, however, we have seen that in this system, certain groups can "succeed in making themselves accepted as the majority" (1984, 62). Since Schattschneider we have seen that the ability to do so refers back to whether or not such groups are already empowered. Thus, it was actually early second-wave feminists who popularized the critique of this sort of majoritarianism within the workings of U.S. politics and clarified its relationship to identity-based oppression.

Characteristic of second-wave feminism was a fundamental concern with "doing what we know and knowing what we do." This insight was another way of naming attention to the relationship between democratic theory and practice. As components of this emphasis on "praxis," other ideas characteristic of this movement were "process" and often "consensus" attitudes and mechanisms that went along with the feminist meanings of process. Any honest contemporary scholarly critique of majoritarianism ought to point out its relationship to this major overturning of fundamental majoritarian assumptions. Here, majoritarianism was not only critiqued as antidemocratic, but myriad institutions were built by feminists under explicitly alternative terms.

The process orientation and development of consensus methods by early second-wave feminists were greatly influenced by meeting styles developed in the peace movement and in nonviolence groups. These styles drew significantly on the meeting process of the Quakers (Religious Society of Friends), used since the 1600s and put in writing as early as 1688.[8] This alternative decision-making structure emerged because feminists critiqued majoritarianism as inherently linked to adversarial patriarchal modes of domination where women were typically "out-voted, out-shouted and unheard" (Wheeler and Chinn 1984, viii). In many small groups women explored organizational and decision-making structures that aimed to be localized, efficient, and empowering. The structures themselves were developed to help encourage the participation of all members, to encourage criticism and self-criticism, to notice different voices (particularly those of the historically silenced), and to seek decisions acceptable to all. Experimenting with alternative decision-making structures was seen as one way to put into practice basic feminist values.

These alternative values included: nonviolence/creative peaceableness/ spontaneous pacifism, equality, community, and what the Quakers understood as simplicity, which often found its way into feminist circles as "checking-in," or care for intention toward self and others.

The fundamental commitments to flexibility, noncoercive interaction, creative problem-solving, sensitivity, care, and fairness were typically expressed in the feminist groups through the structural mechanisms of collectivity, consensus, and turn-taking. Also, sensitivities to the needs of the group meant that the specifics of context be taken into account in structuring any particular group.[9] These feminist aspects are more than similar to Guinier's commitments and suggestions through her high-level legal scholarship on voting rights and redistricting. Guinier's contributions to democratic praxis are based on the idea that in a racially divided society we cannot rely on majority rule as a useful democratic method. As the work of a self-conscious African American legal scholar, Guinier's conclusions thus share much of second-wave feminist insights, values, critiques, and goals concerning gender-based experiences with majority rule and its alternatives.

Guinier's (1994) controversial work shows that one of the central flaws in the founders' majoritarianism is that in a heterogenous society with relatively permanent minorities, certain groups will continuously end up on the outside. Our experiences in a country where minorities bear the brunt of the failures of Liberal democracy illuminate how the consequences of substituting *majoritarianism* for *democracy* are fatal. Replacing the principled goal of democracy with a particular strategy for running institutions has enabled—sometimes even well-meaning—people to use a culturally and historically specific procedural method for antidemocratic purposes: namely, the continued exclusion of many minorities. As the historical experiences of, for example, Jews or Japanese, Arab, Muslim, and African Americans bear out, majorities can consistently ignore the concerns of minorities through legal means when the technique of majoritarianism is substituted for the principle of democracy.

This is why understanding the work of Guinier in light of the theories of the nineteenth-century figure John C. Calhoun is not as strange as it might first appear. It is true that Guinier is an African American woman, whose mother is Jewish, working on civil rights issues. Calhoun was a southern white Christian working to protect the interests of the South and slave traders. I am afraid that some might even find it offensive to look at the two thinkers together. I hope, instead, to demonstrate that doing so might be constructive for contemporary diversity politics. Philosophy can often help us to find important lessons in perhaps unlikely places. I believe that through this comparison we can learn a lot about how Guinier's ideas might succeed or fail. Calhoun was also greatly troubled by the development of majoritarianism as a system that proved to be unfair and worked to develop methods to protect minorities. That this occurred for the express goal of protecting slavery should not blind us to the similarities between the power of his basic assumptions, his theoretical contributions, and the concrete suggestions he makes and those of contemporary thinkers such as Guinier.

Like the contemporary Guinier, Calhoun presented a critique of the tyranny inherent in the form of majority rule adopted in the early republic. Interestingly, Calhoun also sought to develop a system in which the interests of majorities and minorities might be more evenly balanced. Further, in a way similar to that of Guinier, Calhoun proposed methods whereby minorities could actually block actions from being taken when they found them abhorrent or fundamentally at odds with their interests. In fact, the particular veto-based mechanism to protect minority concerns, known from Calhoun as the doctrine of concurrent majority, strongly resembles Guinier's discussion of supermajority voting.

Calhoun wrote in *A Disquisition on Government* (1943) that he was proposing a provision "calculated to prevent any one interest or combination of interests from using the powers of government to aggrandize itself at the expense of others" (20). Most democratic thinkers would be interested in such a provision. What made Calhoun controversial is that the provision he proposed was "by dividing and distributing the powers of government, give to each division or interest, through its appropriate organ, either a concurrent voice in making and executing the laws or a veto on their execution" (20). Calhoun found that the essence of absolute authority was that a specific group could make decisions according to its own interests and impose them on the whole populace. As a supporter of constitutional government, Calhoun found compromise to be the foundation of a decision-making process that took into account various groups, concerns, and interests. His notion of the concurrent majority relied on a practice whereby all those with a stake in a decision would have a say in forming that decision and in vetoing, or stopping, any action deemed harmful. Interestingly, Calhoun did not see this method as divisive and cumbersome. Instead, by enfranchising all those involved in a decision in this manner, he thought that all would have a sincere common interest in finding a solution suitable enough to all parties concerned. His doctrine of concurrent majority was devised to prompt all groups to take others into account so as to help reach decisions acceptable to all in an efficient and fair manner when an item came onto the agenda.

Despite the fact that Calhoun was a political insider and member of the elite, he knew that his colleagues would find such ideas radical. The doctrine of concurrent majority fundamentally challenged the absolutism of our dominant system of majority rule. Guinier, as we know, was subject to vitriolic attacks for her ideas. Other contemporary thinkers involved in working with group-based politics to end oppression have been led down similar roads.[10] As many who work with feminist ideas of consensus are aware, the process of negotiation and compromise involved in coming to a decision on which all can at least basically agree (meaning no one will exercise a right to veto) is also meant to address how intensely an individual or group opposes a proposal and why. Consensus even in small groups does not need to presuppose that relations are harmonious and everyone is always gloriously happy with all decisions. Instead, it often just means that at least no one feels grievously harmed, unfairly thwarted, intolerably opposed, or the like.

Guinier is an important, if cautious, advocate for what she calls "supermajority voting." In her view, this is a mechanism whereby, "depending on the issue, different members of the voting body can 'veto' impending action" (1994, 16). It is added to her discussion of "cumulative voting" as an "exceptional remedy" (17) "modify[ing] winner-take-all majority rule to require that something more than a bare majority of voters must approve or concur before action is taken. As a uniform decisional rule, a supermajority empowers any numerically small but cohesive group of voters" (16). Calhoun explored like mechanisms in the Polish, British, and Roman constitutions and the Iroquois Confederacy in order to support his call for the doctrine of concurrent majority to be used in the United States. Guinier references Senatorial filibusters, Supreme Court decisions, and the actions of both President Reagan and President Bush to situate her suggestions within the normative framework of U.S. politics.

What might we learn from comparing this promoter of slavery and a civil rights lawyer? Let us look for a moment at the differential power context for each thinker and the power position of the constituency that serves to benefit from their divergent political aspirations. The "minority" Calhoun sought to serve was the Southern elite slave-holding interest. At his time, they were a minority influence in national government, but they were members of an elite class all the same. As members of the elite, Calhoun's constituency was already enfranchised with the presumption of its own importance. This political context is significant. Calhoun could engage in his project because he presumed his minority interest to be legitimate, and particularly legitimate in the context of the public struggles of U.S. politics of his day. One person/entity-one vote in a system with permanent majorities means that the votes of some will not matter. Assuming the legitimacy of his minority, however, of course Calhoun's minority should be given a voice that mattered in decision making and could not be drowned out simply because other voices had larger numbers.

The minorities with which Guinier is concerned occupy a very different place in the power hierarchies of her political context. Racial minorities are only barely enfranchised in formal ways. In the less formal power dynamics of our time, racial minorities are marginalized and disempowered. What if we in contemporary politics were to take racial and other marginalized minorities as seriously as Calhoun took his? What if we presumed their enfranchisement to the same degree that Calhoun presumed for the minority he cared about? In this case, perhaps our first assumptions would be inclusion and voice as well, rather than being stuck in procedures as we have found ourselves to be. If we assumed that the votes of marginalized minorities must matter, perhaps we would be open to alternative methods of decision making that would have those votes count. Thus, despite the complications of their contradictory political goals, Calhoun's ideas and the debates surrounding them are very useful for contemporary diversity theorists in the face of a persistent majoritarianism that consistently disenfranchises specific groups of citizens.

INSTITUTIONAL CONSEQUENCES

In the contemporary mode of diversity politics, numerous minority groups have added other ideas and experiences to this discussion. Working from the concrete demands of politics faced by marginalized minorities, these groups are exploring further biases of majority rule and testing alternatives. Let us look briefly at some examples.

Coalitions

In a majority rule system that favors those already in power, women and minorities have sought, of necessity, to recast the notion of coalition politics.[11] As set up, minorities and the historically marginalized cannot win on issues where alliances have achieved high levels of permanence. Although women, for example, are a majority of the population, they have always constituted a small minority of legislators. When women work for an issue of concern to them, be it fair pay for equal work or funding for breast cancer research, they must work with those who are not women. As a small minority of legislators, even if women's activist groups were to convince every single woman legislator to vote for a particular bill, this effort would not help very much. Women must develop alliances with different groups of men if they want to see legislation passed on their behalf. If this is the case for women, it is certainly the case for racial/ethnic/religious/sexual/gender minorities. If Latino/as want to develop bilingual education in the public schools, they must build relationships over time with other non-English-speaking minorities and even native English speakers who see the value of such curricular changes. Latina/os are a numerical minority in the country as a whole and they are also usually a minority on school boards and in local governing bodies. People with English as their first and only language are the distinct majority of U.S. citizens. Exploring an alternative to an English first and only policy will be impossible in this country if those who are multilingual work only as separate groups and without ties to some monolingual citizens. When looked at in this way, we find that coalition politics becomes a basic strategy of survival for many.

For marginalized groups, coalitions then come to take on a meaning different from the meaning that they have had traditionally in Western pluralist democracies among discrete competing, though basically already enfranchised, interest groups. In traditional democratic theory, separated selfish interests are assumed to motivate coalitions so that these formations are seen, as noted above, as inherently temporary. Coalition does not suggest solidarity, and individual selfish interest easily trumps coalition goals.[12] The forming, disbanding, and re-forming of coalitions is viewed as no more significant than the opening and closing of businesses for the capitalist concerned with profit rather than with the business itself, products/services, or personnel. Farming interests might work together with certain other interests when a free trade agreement with another country is being drafted. On an issue of gun control those that were in coalition before might find themselves on opposite sides of the negotiating table. It is taken as normal that today there is an alliance where tomorrow there is not.

For many minorities, however, where coalition with one another equals survival, difficult issues of solidarity, reciprocity, and mutual need are the fundamental premises of joint projects.[13] Coalitions among these groups are constantly being formed, disbanding, changing shape and direction. These shifting coalitions are often perceived by the group members themselves not as disjointed ventures, but as evolutions in the relationships within overall communities of affinity. Last year groups might have worked on issues of police brutality. Today the issue might be one of housing. Next year it might be welfare reform. Usually all these issues are being worked on at once. Minority racial groups are likely to see that they are directly affected in each case. Poor whites, as the largest racial group in the welfare system, face a primary risk. Some groups might get actively involved, some serve as supporters. This time, during a zoning battle, a local multiracial tenants group might volunteer its office to be the headquarters of operations. Next time, on a push for diversity education in the public schools, the tenants group merely shows up at demonstrations. Last year they helped organize neighborhood residents to sign a petition demanding a civilian review board on cases of police violence. In each instance they likely worked in coalition with numerous other small groups, and/or were active on behalf, of racial or national minorities, workers, parents and teachers, homeowners or renters.

It is also important to realize that these relationships over time among groups in tremendous need can also serve as sites of mutual hurt. If alliances among pluralist democrats are short, and serve whatever is deemed to be the current self-interest, so then are political memories. Among minorities that interweave in coalitions over time, memories can often be much longer and past choices remembered as betrayals of solidarity. Why didn't those community organizers join the coalition for multilanguage signs on the main street? Remember that we could not count on the X-solidarity committee when things got really heated. Back in 1999 the X-nationality restaurant workers union never came to a single meeting. Joe Smith talks about civil rights but refused to support the gay civil rights bill. The gentlemanly rules of temporary alliances—no hard feelings; business is business and politics is politics—rarely apply among the overworked small groups that minorities often work in. Thus, the nature of coalitions among marginalized groups suggests interesting alternatives to their role in mainstream politics, but also highlights certain inherent difficulties of coalition work for those seeking empowerment.

Minoritizing and Majoritizing Strategies

From among queer activists and thinkers we now have terms such as majoritizing and minoritizing to guide a critical political strategy, even when such a strategy is not based on specific working coalitions. A minoritizing strategy is one that relies on and reinforces the particular nature of an issue. In contrast, a majoritizing strategy might emphasize the universal aspects of a point, and seek to bring majorities or many different minorities into a campaign. To be a minority in our system using a minoritizing strategy often means certain failure/death. Conceptually, minorities often cannot approach their own concerns as if successful minority enfranchisement only benefits those specific groups.[14] We thus find many examples of specific minorities using majoritizing strategies, stressing that all people are affected by the matter affecting them, or that other minority interests will be served by joining with them.

Along these lines, some activists have argued that a more full definition of solidarity is necessary. They seek to increase public awareness so that each member of a society knows that what may appear to be separate oppressions are actually interwoven.[15] A related insight gleaned from the politics of the marginalized is the need to understand, deeply, that the oppression of one group is unjust not only with respect to that one group. The oppression of a group demonstrates to us all the systemic *capacity* for injustice. Everyone in such a system is, therefore, threatened when oppression is possible. This view switches the focus of what is often pity for specific oppressed groups to issues of justice structurally. It helps us to see that we all really are affected by (even another group's) oppression.

There are, of course, potential problems with this mode of thinking as well. Keppel (1995) discusses how, in working to get the *Brown* decision enforced, Kenneth Clark built a united front "by recasting the issues of racial injustice as 'an aspect of the larger issue of civil liberties,' arguing further that 'if the rights of Negroes can be abridged with impunity, the rights of all Americans are weakened. . . . This fact is unrelated to the positive or negative attitudes toward Negroes' " (121). In his writing on Lorraine Hansberry, however, Keppel looks at how this methodology risks obscuring the difficulties of the particulars. Casting *A Raisin in the Sun* not as a racial piece, for example, but as a universal social piece was a "compliment" that came to haunt the play. To say that the play was "beyond race," Keppel writes, "was a common mechanism by which white critics looked past the uncomfortable fact that *Raisin* was, among other things, part of a national discourse on race" (183–84).

In the context of more contemporary identity-politics, other activists and scholars have addressed similar challenges to some of the potential problems in the majoritizing method. For example, in examining antiracist activism among whites, bell hooks argues that majoritizing strategies that work by stimulating support through an appeal to feelings and personal experience can create false impressions of shared experiences and erode the principled, political bases of solidarity. In *Black Looks* (1992), hooks critiques some strategies in "unlearning racism" workshops for whites. At times the goal of such workshops is to get whites to see that they too are hurt by racism. This can be important. However, if this sort of education is not undertaken carefully and critically, it can end up glossing over differences between the hurt of majority whites and that of the marginalized. Hooks writes that "anti racist work that tries to get these individuals to see themselves as 'victimized' by racism in the hopes that this will act as an intervention is a misguided strategy." As an alternative she clarifies that "indeed we must be willing to acknowledge that individuals of great privilege who are in no way victimized are capable, *via* political choices, of working on behalf of the oppressed. Such solidarity does not need to be rooted in shared experience. It can be based on one's political and ethical understanding of racism and one's rejection of domination" (1992, 13–14).

We can look at another example of a majoritizing concept that, when practiced over time, highlighted certain limitations. Early in the development of a mass-based lesbian liberation movement, Adrienne Rich (1980) developed the theory of the Lesbian Continuum. The idea of placing lesbianism on a continuum, rather than as a separate way of being from heterosexual women, was appealing to many women of various sexual orientations. Rich's notion of a continuum suggested that women loving women be understood in a feminist spectrum of commitment to women and not only about sexuality or sex acts. Part of the power of this framework was the way in which it removed some false barriers between women across sexual differences and reduced the isolation of lesbians in the feminist movement. In critiquing how some have used Rich's notion, however, Phelan, has pointed out that, in fact, some have used the idea of the continuum in such a way that it has actually kept lesbians marginalized. Phelan (1989) points out that such a majoritizing strategy at times ends up with a continued focus on the majority, celebrating those now aligned with the oppressed. Although this might sound helpful, in concrete terms its effect has been to further marginalize the minority even within its own issue arena. In this case, rather than a focus, lesbians as women who love and identify with women become "one small part of the continuum" that some have taken as less important than those famous women who can now be placed on a lesbian continuum but who never called themselves lesbians or took the risks that lesbians take (1989, 169).

Thus, although justice claims for the disenfranchised are often criticized in popular politics as illegitimate "special" rights, democratic activists must be careful about simply using majoritizing justifications for demands. Clarifying both options, their possible strengths and weaknesses, can aid us in better choosing strategies that use minoritizing and majoritizing methods where appropriate.

Record Keeping and Inscribing the Future in the Present

What is known as *halacha*, or Jewish law, is primarily derived from an ancient compilation of texts called the Talmud.[16] What is interesting about the Talmud in the context of this discussion is that as the point of authority and mandate for law it is actually a compendium of arguments and interpretations. The opinions and debates between rabbis, who often actually lived centuries apart, over long stretches of history, are edited together on specific topics. What is considered law is taken from the judgments or rulings of a specific rabbi considered by a community in history as most authoritative. The methods of reading the texts that have developed over the centuries suggest how a scholar is to surmise which argument is the most convincing. The text itself usually does not make formal declarations of which principle or interpretation is correct over and against the others. A common mechanism utilized to challenge a concrete practice within a specific Jewish community is to look back to the Talmudic debate and argue that a different set of arguments would better apply in a case, or that a different Talmudic rabbi's interpretation sheds more insight into a particular dynamic. Although a community is able to encode laws pertinent to them for their time, the multivocal qualities of the text lend a certain fluidity to the legal process. This aspect of the text's character allows for later interpreters to reenter the debates and derive differing lessons from them.

A number of contemporary political philosophers have utilized these notions of time and record that we have in the Talmudic example in their explorations of alternatives for democratic praxis. Both Benhabib (1990) and Ackelsberg (1986), for instance, write of the need to include a conception that politics and change happen over time and that decisions are better understood in the context of application in the present and possible revisiting in a future context. If the reader recalls, the problem with a pluralist assumption of time is that losers are expected to accept their loss with the promise of fairness over time, which for certain groups never, or rarely, materializes. What Benhabib and Ackelsberg are talking about is a commitment to fairness and justice first in order that structures and decisions are seen as flexible so that they may be reviewed and revamped.

Related to this proposition is the idea of keeping multiple views on record for use in future revisiting. Barber (1984) has discussed how in Liberal democracy dissent and discussion are relegated to the time prior to decision making. He recommends record keeping so as to enable issues to remain on the public agenda. We can include here Honig's (1993) assertion that democratic politics ought to make use of its "remainders" to bolster resistance to oppressive authority. Disch (1994) takes up this discussion in her explication of publicity in the context of her reading of Hannah Arendt. Here she looks, for example, at the way in which the Supreme Court (although admittedly a problematic model for a democratic politics in other respects) keeps on record both multiple records within the majority ruling as well as a record of any number of minority opinions. This example comes as a demonstration of her argument for how a situated impartiality informs publicity by "prescribing disputation as the way to arrive at a decision and it requires that any decision be justified not as a resolution of conflict but as a position in a specific political context" (215). Recording various opinions within the majority helps avoid a "claim to a false mandate," as well as avoiding polemics and the tendency toward a "self-congratulatory pose that imputes unanimity to its allies" (216).

If we pause for a moment to compare this to a common source of a Liberal view, the differences become clearer. Hobbes writes, "And if the Representative consist of many men, the voyce of the greatest number, must be considered as the voyce of them all. For if the lesser number pronounce (for example) in the Affirmative, and the greater in the Negative, there will be Negatives more than enough to destroy the Affirmatives; and thereby the excesse of Negatives, standing uncontradicted, are the onely voyce the Representative hath. And a Representative of even number . . . whereby the contradictory voyces are oftentimes equall, is therefore oftentimes mute, and uncapable of Action" (1968, 221).

For Hobbes, the majority opinion is simply *the* opinion because it can overpower the minority in a power struggle. Further, diversity of opinion expressed in an equal number of dissenting opinions renders the group immobile—a condition much feared. In contrast, Disch skillfully demonstrates that the benefit of recording a dissenting opinion is that then it is understood that the minority opinion is not necessarily "wrong simply because it did not prevail in this particular instance: it can be cited for future challenges to the decision." In much the same way that Talmudic methodology mentioned above works, Disch then writes, "This respect for the decision-makers, manifest in any treatment of a decision as a precedent for future affirmation of the status quo and for future opposition, is crucial to inscribing plurality into the final record of a decision" (212).

Consociationalism and Corporatism

An interesting facet of this discussion thus far is how (U.S.) American it is, grounded in both the realities of our tremendous diversity and our deeply rooted ideological presumptions. In Liberal democratic thought the political process is understood in market terms, and the promises of majority rule are cast in terms similar to the promises of a capitalist economy.[17] There will be a free flow of competition between groups as there is between business interests. Further, Madison's version of majority rule that avoids majority tyranny works in much the same way as the invisible hand of capitalism. Through the constant fracturing of interests due to natural diversity, self-interest, and competition, if the government will just stay out of it, the system will take care of itself, ultimately working in the best interest of each competitor. Some democratic theorists in search of alternatives have thus been led to explore more formally organized approaches to the problem of minority-majority relations, as found at times in Europe and the Third World. Although terms used to describe often very different systems, scholars have called these more organized approaches consociationalism and corporatism.[18]

Political scientists in the field of comparative politics are probably more familiar with these terms than are political theorists and average U.S. activists. The term consociationalism was developed by Arend Lijphart to describe systems operating on the level of a nation-state with more formal national representation in their pluralist-style democracies. Segments of society are granted official representation in political organizations, decision-making processes, and often in budgeting. Groups would be granted a veto power to be used when a situation is deemed essential for the livelihood of their segment. Much of policy making and implementation regarding issues pertinent to a segment is left up to these semiautonomous organs. Lijphart's suggestion of consociationalism is meant to alleviate tensions in a highly diverse society by directly recognizing the subnational groupings and empowering them in a way that an individualist model and a simple majority-rule system cannot.[19]

Another model that comes from a study of comparative politics is that of corporatism. Again, this term has been used to describe a number of different political arrangements. A traditional definition of corporatism is a system through which interests are represented nationally through a stylized and hierarchical model. Membership in the interest groups is compulsory and the relations between interests are noncompetitive. Each interest is granted a monopoly representation by the state for which they agree to follow certain strictures or employ select controls on their members as deemed necessary by the state. Historically, poor and/or more authoritarian countries that relied on a corporatist model tended to strictly regulate the organization of interests. At times this form of corporatism characterized fascist and military-authoritarian states. Since World War II, however, a revised version of corporatism, often referred to as neocorporatism, has emerged in developed, industrialized nations with more abundant resources. Neocorporatism, as found in some Western European countries in the 1960s and 1970s, utilized a more open representational mechanism. The model was more inclusionary and participatory so that it served democratic regimes as well (Wiarda 1997, 118–19).

For U.S. thinkers who are concerned with the problems of our brand of majoritarianism when there are permanent minorities, these alternatives prove interesting. They have been employed in other countries where the linguistic, religious, regional, cultural, or racial bases of minorities renders their situations serious. Minority representation is formalized in the political process through various mechanisms, depending on the context, that incorporate groups as a whole as actors in national politics. What is interesting is that these same modes of cultural differences in the United States do not get conceived as incorporated group bases for representation. Our system resists group-based processes in contrast to individualist ones and finds formalizing such processes antidemocratic. In other nations with more social aspects in their history, whether feudal or socialist, group recognition and corporate planning in politics can be seen as a viable, and perfectly democratic, option. Certain countries in Western Europe, India, and Lebanon as well as—perhaps most interesting to (U.S.) Americans— Canada have all utilized any number of variations on this theme of formal incorporation of minorities for their protection and enhancing of their place in representational politics in some form.[20]

Given that many arrangements have been utilized in countries with widely divergent subnational populations, numerous examples of corporated strategies are in use around the globe. One mechanism might be that a certain percentage of seats in a parliament is guaranteed to parties representative of specific national groupings. An alternative to this would be where such a guarantee takes place in local elections, but not in national elections. If diversity is geographically based, then a federated system may be employed that allows significant autonomy to subnational governing bodies. Another example would be that different groups have designated ombudspersons within the governmental structure allowing them official access and voice to governors. What is common to these different examples is that subnational communities are recognized, legitimated as group entities, and enfranchised with formal powers of self-rule and/or advocacy.

Democratic theorists who have explored consociationalism and corporatism as alternatives to the failures of (U.S.) American majority rule have not, however, been able to wholly embrace these based on ways that they been concretely practiced. The (U.S.) American hesitancy with formal incorporation does have merit and finds its way into radical democratic critiques of consociational and (neo)corporatist systems. We must ask, for example: in the U.S. context, what groups are to be recognized as corporated bodies? On what basis and who is to decide? Not surprisingly, what we often find in existing corporated systems is that the more marginalized groups are, the less likely they are to be organized and recognized in the political structure. How will the groups be represented and in whose voice? Often these systems end up looking more like power negotiations between particular elites than democratic safeguards for marginalized minorities.[21] For the U.S. context, the strength of the corporated models is that they take diversity issues seriously and find it incumbent on democratic politics to develop responsible modes of group-based representation. However, voting rights advocates in the United States, as an example, have had problems similar to those mentioned in consociationalism and (neo)corporatism even in this more decentralized avenue of corporated representation attempted in the United States.

Voting Rights Activism

The fundamental issue stimulating the phases of civil rights activism in formal political terms has been how to ensure qualitative representation. Much of this work focused on the electoral process. There are commonly understood to be three generations of this form of voting rights activism in the United States. The first phase of this movement may be seen in terms of suffrage in and of itself. The second phase of work in this area of civil rights included efforts to represent individuals from marginalized groups among those in government and elected office. What some see as a third phase of voting rights work involves how to actually have group ideas, interests, concerns, and aspirations represented in the course of politics and decision making. Let us look briefly at the strengths and weaknesses of these three stages as aspects of a strategy designed to address issues of minority visibility and enfranchisement.

The vote has been understood in Liberal democracy as *the* mechanism of representation. What is at issue here is that one's voice contributes to a collective debate in a way that matters. When privileged groups (whether it was men for women, whites for Blacks, or British representatives for the colonists) said to the masses, we will represent you, the masses cried that this was not true representation and that they wanted to speak for themselves. When an individual or group is denied the basic right to vote, democracy is diminished. The first phase of voting rights activism for groups denied suffrage, therefore, has been to eliminate legal barriers to voting. However, suffrage in the United States, for example for women and Americans of African descent, became only the first step in this process.[22]

Activists soon realized that if their elected bodies did not look like them demographically, they were not truly representative. Even the 1965 Voting Rights Act and amendments that focused on protecting the actual act of voting, as important as they were, were not enough. In response to the possibility of African Americans actually having a say through the vote in the South, many local elections were redesigned to ensure that those elected to office remained white. Thus, the second-generation focus on combating structural barriers to the election of minority representatives was important. When the actual issue is, however, how to ensure that minorities will have a voice that matters in governance and decision making, electing individual legislators also came to be seen as not enough.

Entrenched white supremacy has proven tenacious. The first wave of action succeeded in securing the fundamental right to vote for (U.S.) Americans of African descent. The second wave of voting rights activism was somewhat successful in getting minorities elected into office. However, when minority and marginalized *candidates* win elections, they tend to become minority and marginalized *legislators*—not only in terms of their race/ethnicity, sexuality, and/or gender nationally, but also in terms of their identity and goals in these legislatures. The very problem with minorities in a majoritarian system is that they are minorities. Even if our governing bodies actually did reflect the population demographically so that more minority faces were seen in the halls of government and minority opinions were on the register, their concerns could still easily be dismissed in the legal and proper functioning of a winner-take-all majority-rule democracy.

What is worse is that in the meantime (hardly a period with even demographic representation) we often already find a backlash. Affirmative action policies that have succeeded in slowly changing the makeup of the appointed government staff are being targeted for reversal. There is also backlash against content-based representation in our elected bodies. For example, scholars have discussed what they call the assembly backlash hypothesis, which refers to "the idea that districting plans that increase the number of black legislators may nevertheless produce legislative assemblies less receptive to black interests. The hypothesis maintains that by packing minority voters into a few districts, racial gerrymanders increase the likelihood that the state's remaining districts will elect representatives hostile to minority interests" (Eisgruber 1997, 347–48).

Further, Madison's promise of how to avoid tyranny rested, in part, on the establishment of a representative republic with a large population and covering a large geographical area. In a system of proportional representation, it is understood that the intense interests of the many in the population will get diluted when transferred to the representative. Madison argued on such grounds purposely to prevent parochialism from affecting government power. However, over the years the nation grew increasingly enormous. This means that, thanks to our representational structure, many minorities, such as Muslims, Jews, and Native Americans, would find themselves out of representation altogether if it were based demographically. The corporated strategies of voting rights and affirmative action advocates have been important for large marginalized groups and minorities such as African Americans, women as a group, and even to some extent Latina/os and Asian Americans. These same strategies also include dangerous aspects for these and other smaller communities.

Representation and In-Group Democracy

The second wave of voting rights activism has been important. This mode included moves toward block voting, redistricting, and for some the power of a veto as possible alternatives to the equation of democracy with individualist and "color-blind" majoritarianism when such a method turns out to be antidemocratic. The second wave of voting rights activism also generated attention to more entrenched problems within our democracy. Despite common fears in the United States of these challenges to majoritarianism, a deeper problem with corporated identity-based alternatives involves the complexities of identity and representation themselves. Guinier faced much criticism for her use of the concept "authentic" in arguing for further minority representation. How do we know a proposal or policy would actually represent the diverse members of any minority group? Though much of the criticism of Guinier was misguided, we must work with the complicated, multiple, and often contradictory nature of the identity groups that we are seeking to represent more fully.[23]

We do not want to make the mistake of ascribing unified, a priori interests to groups, ignoring the "how" of diversity and political processes within them. This is precisely the problem nationally that we are trying to avoid. Subcommunities in the United States have often noted that members of their own group who claim to represent them have not been brought to the fore through democratic means. Elite aspects of minority interests are more easily brought to the floor of broader public spaces than are those of the marginalized within subcommunities.[24] As discussed with respect to the "where" question, these lessons of diversity that we have been learning from this emerging diversity-based democratic theory are needed for analysis of the "how" question within subcommunities as well.[25] Critical discussions of in-group democracy are necessary to figure out how we push forward with analysis of, and proposals and strategies for, corporated forms of democratic politics appropriate to political styles in the United States.

In order to explore issues of in-group democracy within subcommunities, we will also need to hone our skills of analysis without looking to formal mechanisms of the state. Minority communities may live in a geographically defined area, but they are just as likely not to. We thus cannot always rely on geographical mechanisms of group process such as town meetings. What are some extrageographical, and yet still democratic, methods of finding the pulse of a community? Communities do not generally have formal memberships, like citizenship, to declare who can participate in group processes such as elections. Who can claim to participate in group dialogue and what sorts of elections are meaningful for subnational minority groups? Groups do not usually have a single authoritative body, such as a government or church fathers, to speak on their behalf. How does someone come to be an authoritative speaker on behalf of the needs, aspirations, and concerns of any particular community?

As we work on these and other issues of representation and in-group democracy we will need to be attentive to the historical moment in which issues arise. We will need to assess clearly the processes and practices of groups, their interactions, and also the larger political climate. Here again within communities and groups, theory must stay in touch with politics. Ultimately, it is politics that is important because it will often be through active democratic participation over time that we will find ways through an all too possible elitism within subcommunities as well.[26]

Localizing

We must explore further multiple levels of representation, drawing on the lessons of a politics of recognition, and how to allow for the fact that, depending on the issue and arena, representation may look different. To add to the discussion of Chapter Six in the context of the *how* of democratic praxis, part of the strength of a more localized, rather than universalist, approach to democracy is that it can address different sorts of concerns with mechanisms appropriate to the issue and arena. For example, decisions made democratically as to how a community can best cope with the problem of hate speech that may be suitable in the relatively secure and defined environment of a college campus may not make sense in other environments.[27] Actions taken to address discrimination affirmatively might well look different in groups of various sizes, in corporations, or in different branches of government. Second-wave feminist attention to process as a radical experiment with democracy addressed the need for a localized strategy. Guinier's work also emphasizes the context and arena. She makes specific recommendations for political solutions to the problems of achieving democratic fair play depending on the local context (1994, 14) and sometimes discusses what she refers to as "exceptional remedies . . . in the context of a particular case" (17).

Context-dependent rules can seem abhorrent to a certain understanding of Liberal democracy whose strength has often been in its precept of universal laws and their application. The variegated structures of feudalism that applied different understandings of humanity and rights depending on class and family heritage were certainly oppressive. Contemporary radical democrats have no need for an unreconstructed notion of proportionate equality, but universal concepts that cannot take difference into account have been similarly problematic. In monarchies and tyrannical governments principles and methods were often decided on whims. Liberalism sought the assurance of generalized principles and laws. With this legacy, however, we also often get stuck not being able to respond to an arena or an issue on its own terms for fear of setting precedents. Interestingly enough, on the topic of majoritarianism and its alternatives, as the above discussion demonstrates, we already employ different mechanisms in different contexts in the United States. Continuing to look at examples in different arenas—often traditional and venerated institutions such as the Supreme Court, local politics, and corporations as well as alternative grassroots groups—may enable us to loosen the hold of majoritarianism in other areas when it is found to be counterproductive to a democratic vision based on fair play.

CONCLUSION

As we engage with the "how" question, of how to get on together in a democracy based on the experiences and insights from the margins, we find that we must reevaluate concepts that are currently seen as core facets of Western democratic thought. Majority rule, for example, comes in many forms that might be employed democratically to enhance diversity and fair play. Historically majoritarianism was an important step in the move toward functioning democracies. Unfortunately, however, this method has also been used to thwart democratic praxis. Those on the margins, including disenfranchised minorities and, interestingly enough, women, have shouldered the major burden of this democratic lapse. By remembering that majoritarianism is not the principle, but a technique in service to a principle, we can, hopefully, continue exploring mechanisms appropriate to the context in the application of democratic principles.

This is a helpful point on which to bring our discussion to a close. The United States represents itself as a democracy. More, it likes to fashion itself as the most democratic nation, the country with the most advanced ideas about what constitutes democratic practices. But how often do defenders of the status quo tell us "like it or leave it" when we question whether we are really on the right track here. How often do you encounter only defensiveness when you challenge others to live up to their democratic aspirations? Knee-jerk responses conjure the most-antidemocratic horrors and suggest that they only happen "over there." Here, in *America*, we may not be perfect, but we are still the best, the leader of the free world.

If we are to be our best, here or anywhere, we must continually critically engage with our history, our ideas, our social structures. We have said that democratic spaces are those in which the practices of communities may be challenged to be the most democratic they can be. If this is so, then we must commit ourselves to open, honest, caring self-inquiry. We must also ask: who populates such spaces? Can we gain a greater understanding of the complex issues of enfranchisement from the perspectives of those most in need? Can we navigate successfully between the yearnings of individuals and their mutually constituted and ever changing group affiliations? What are the different individuals and groups after in democracy, and how can we develop institutions that enable each and all to understand and articulate their visions? In what ways can our democracy allow different individuals and groups to participate in politics effectively without demanding assimilation to elite manners? Can we learn lessons for democratic politics from the knowledges gained over time in various spheres by ordinary and extra-ordinary people? How can we put any of these knowledges into action?

We must look to the margins. Democratic theory is a grand tradition with a rich history . . . but it has also been all too limited. Let us not be afraid to critically engage the great works. Let us muster the courage to let diversity inform our democratic experiments.

In this book we have looked at what it might mean to develop a democratic polity that is not only more inclusive of specific individuals and groups, but also of some of the particular ideological and cultural contributions of the newly included. At this point the discussion should enable us to ask new sorts of questions. What does it mean to theorize democracy from the margins of society? Can we learn to listen to each other and to those historically disenfranchised? Can we commit to making the participation of democratically inclined, marginalized communities matter among the amplified voices of the already powerful? Many minorities are likely to remain minorities. Must they be punished, overlooked, exoticized, patronized, unheard, exploited, and systemically marginalized for being so? Can we find ways to recognize, name, and challenge the primacy of elite modes and perspectives? Are we bold enough and committed enough to democratic praxis to pursue alternatives informed by the ideas and practices of the historically marginalized? How can we continue to stop the crushing realities of economic, spiritual, and cultural deprivation all too common in our so-called democratic system? Will we be able to design paths to equality that do not deny the difference of minorities and majorities, that empower all in new ways as we go along? Can we acknowledge that our solutions will be temporary without diminishing their importance to us in our day?

These are heady questions. I hope that this book has helped articulate the significance of the inquiry. I hope that it has helped clarify the terms being introduced into the discussion from the margins. As activists and concerned participants we need to think through the lessons we can learn from our own successes and failures, from our partial victories and the complicated implications of our contributions to new democratic praxis. Political theory must ground itself in the concrete practices of politics over time, and it must speak to the actors as well. It has been my hope throughout that theory can assist us in the strenuous and scary business of taking ourselves seriously, in the humbling and exhilarating work we do for justice.

Notes

Notes to Chapter 1

1. See for example the discussion in Jacobs and Landau 1966, 17, 20, 24–25; Anderson 1995, 83.

2. Rothman and Lichter 1982, 16.

3. Numerous different kinds of politics go by the label multiculturalism. In referring to this term my intention is not to solidify the diverse strands of movement and thought at work in radical politics, but to keep the theoretical account, and thus the terminology, grounded in what is happening in different settings of activist politics. Further, the aim of this book is not to theorize "identity politics" or "multiculturalism" necessarily, but to theorize from these strands of politics to see what they might have to contribute to a new, radical democratic theory. Given that "multiculturalism" is also often criticized, readers might find helpful certain attempts to delineate divergent conceptualizations of multiculturalism. See for example Fraser 1997, McClaren 1997, and Michaels 1995.

4. See hooks and West (1991, particularly chapter six) for their critical discussion of how to approach such issues as mass distribution and consumerism and their relation to internalized victimization and narrow nationalism.

5. See for example Cross 1991, 138, and Stack's 1974 contribution to a new mode of scholarship on African Americans that does not pathologize this community.

6. As much of this new form of democratic theory is critical of the canon of Western thought, it is important to note that some remind us that even thinkers as representative as John Stuart Mill state that "neglected interests" not merely be tolerated but "encouraged and countenanced." See Green 1992 on this point and also Susan James 1992.

7. This tendency stimulates Berlin's critique of paternalism. He writes, "to manipulate men, to propel them towards goals which you—the social reformer—see, but they may not, is to deny their human essence, to treat them as objects without wills of their own, and therefore to degrade them" (1969, 137).

8. On "cyborgs" see Haraway 1991; on "needs" see Fraser 1986; on "minoritizing and majoritizing" see Sedgewick 1990; and on "mestiza" see Anzaldua 1987.

9. See for example, Gould 1988, James 1992, Mouffe 1992, and Young 1987. Having said this, we must be careful not to assume that those marginalized have nothing to do with the constitution of citizenship. On the contrary, Spelman writes, "In a well-ordered city-state, women and slaves are not parts of the polis, but they are the conditions of it" (1988, 38).

10. I am indebted to Wendy Lee-Lampshire for the development of my thoughts in this section.

11. Although I would not consider this a standpoint exactly, in part because it is so multiply situated itself, my choices are indebted to the *debates* concerning standpoint epistemology. Early empowering presentations of standpoint demonstrated that the marginalized position of oppressed groups contributes to a different vantage point from hegemonic truths, which can provide us all with new insights, understandings, and strategies to overcome oppression (hooks 1984 ; Hartsock 1983). There was a potential in early feminist standpoint theories, however, to assume a unity of women's experience, for example, suggesting *a* truth from women's situation and an unproblematized acceptance of gender as a category that was criticized particularly from the postmodern perspective (Narayan 1989; Flax 1993; Butler 1990; Riley 1988). Others are working in an epistemological grounding that both presupposes, and seeks to further clarify, a more situated standpoint that is historically, culturally, and locally diverse (Fisher and Davis 1993; Haraway 1991; Harding 1986 and 1991; Hill Collins 1990; Sedgewick 1990).

12. See, for example, Aufderheide 1992, Berman 1989, Berman, 1992, Bernstein 1994, Brown 1995, Butler 1990, Grant 1993, Kymlicka 1995, Phelan 1989, Nicholson and Seidman 1995, Schlesinger 1992, West 1993a, and the commentary in Taylor 1994.

13. Some examples of compelling critiques in this genre may be found in Dean 1996; Brown 1995; Fraser 1997; and Benhabib, Butler, Cornell, and Fraser 1994.

14. Throughout this work I will utilize the term Liberal in the technical sense employed in political philosophy as articulated by early modern thinkers in Britain such as Thomas Hobbes and John Locke in the 1600s and developed since.

15. See for example Dean 1996.

16. Personal communication October 17, 1996.

17. See Johnson Reagon's important contribution to Smith, ed. "Coalition Politics: Turning the Century" (1983, 356–69). For additional grapplings with the notion of home see Levitt 1997 and Brettschneider 1997.

18. I am indebted here to Waskow's 1978 notion of wrestling.

19. Despite the views of critics such as Stanley Crouch, many point to Toni Morrison's appeal in these terms for example.

20. Thanks to Lisa Disch for articulating her understanding of the project as such. Further, in response to the potential for commodification of the relationship between diversity and enchantment—as it can easily be "channeled into the thrall of shopping"—Jane Bennet writes: "But alternative deployments of the new remain available even to slaves of fashion. The new still has the power to heighten your sense of interdependency and interconnection with the morphings escaping in the wake of the current configuration of your identity; it still can open a window into occluded lines of alliance, affiliation, and identification; it still can reconfigure political discourse in surprising and productive ways" (1998, 8).

NOTES TO CHAPTER 2

1. A few radical foreign reporters sent news of the events leading up to, of, and following the 1905 and 1917 Russian Revolutions. In March 1919, John Reed, one of these observers, published in English a full-length firsthand account of the 1917 Bolshevik Revolution with a brief foreword by Lenin. *Ten Days That Shook the World* was received as an exciting, partisan, and hopeful "masterpiece." For example, Reed reported Trotsky's speech declaring that the Provisional Government "no longer existed" and telling the mass of people crammed into the meeting of the Petrograd Soviet that they were now "going to try an experiment unique in history" (1967, 86). Within four months of its publication, the book had gone into its fourth printing and subsequently went through numerous editions and many translations. In light of the discussion of this chapter, it is fascinating to compare the edition published by Random House in 1960, edited and introduced by Bertram Wolfe, with the International Publishers edition of 1967 with an introduction by John Howard Lawson. Wolfe's edition from a major press reflects a more cold war perspective characteristic of the 1950s. Lawson's edition from a small left-wing press is indicative of the growing capacity of older people on the left to begin speaking again after the fall of McCarthy and of their endeavors to connect with young activists of the 1960s.

2. Reed reports the program of the revolution as published at the time in the Bolshevik press in Petrograd:

All power to the Soviets—both in the capital and in the provinces.
Immediate truce on all fronts. An honest peace between peoples.
Landlord estates—without compensation—to the peasants.
Workers' control over industrial production.
A faithfully and honestly elected Constituent Assembly. (1967, 30–31)

Despite the significant differences between groups on the left (more significant in Russia than abroad), most of the left in the United States enthusiastically supported this early program.

3. Less well-known than its 1950s incarnation, but setting the stage for McCarthy's actions, this Red scare followed World War I and began to heat up in 1919 with Attorney General A. Mitchell Palmer at the helm and J. Edgar Hoover in charge of Mitchell's new General Intelligence Division of the Justice Department. This new arm of the government opened files on hundreds of thousands of U.S. citizens and residents said to be radicals. Using the 1917 Espionage Act, the Trading with the Enemy Act, and the 1918 Sedition Act, socialists, anarchists and other "subversives" were targeted with the backing of the Supreme Court. When Charles Schenck, for example, was charged with violating the Espionage Act of 1917 for disseminating pamphlets resisting the draft during World War I, he took the case to the Supreme Court on the grounds the act violated free speech. In *Schenck v. United States* (1919) the Court defended the government use of such on the basis of "clear and present danger." Throughout the year raids were conducted, a thousand arrests were made in New York City

alone, documents were seized, aliens were rounded up in cities throughout the country, and the Great Steel Strike was squelched. In January 1920 Hoover and Palmer organized the "Palmer Raids," in which more than ten thousand people were arrested at once in thirty cities from coast to coast.

4. The Smith Act is the popular name for the Nationality Act of 1940. By 1939 Frank Murphey, U.S. Attorney General, had begun a campaign against espionage, sabotage, and subversion. Within the year over seventy bills had been introduced into Congress targeting aliens. A main impetus for the Smith Act was to seek to "maintain the national racial mix as of 1920." The act included an English-language provision, and predicated the right to become a naturalized citizen upon racial origins (white persons, persons of African descent and descendants of races indigenous to the Western Hemisphere—plus Filipino/as who served in the U.S. armed forces). Interestingly enough, the act also provided for the reinstatement of a woman's citizenship lost before 1922 due to marriage to an alien if the marriage had been terminated. (Before this, female U.S. citizens actually lost their citizenship status if they married non-U.S. citizens.) Following the Red scare, the act was amended so that it would not discriminate on the basis of race, sex, or marital status, and no longer barred naturalization to persons based on their beliefs.

5. In 1889, not long after Puerto Rico had gained independence from Spain, the United States took control of the territory. In the 1930s, Albizu Campos, a leader in the Puerto Rican independence movement, was sent to prison. In 1947, after a decade in prison, Campos returned to Puerto Rico and helped organize the independence-oriented Nationalist Party. The following year students went on strike in support of Campos (after he was barred from presenting the party program). These actions prompted the U.S. application of the Smith Act. (Note: this occurred before 1951, when the United States made Puerto Rico a commonwealth).

6. Penalties ensued if one was deemed to be influenced by the Communist Party, including limitations on speech, prohibition of naturalization, and denial of a passport (or use of one if already secured) for U.S. citizens. Further, the act actually suggested the Tule Lake camp as a designated site for an internment camp for "subversives." Tule Lake was one of the concentration camps used to intern Japanese residents and Japanese Americans during World War II.

7. The House Select Committee on UnAmerican Activities was established in 1938 and was soon made into a standing committee.

8. Anderson (1995, 15) notes that FBI Director J. Edgar Hoover's 1958 book *Masters of Deceit* sold over two million copies. On this period see also Caute 1978, Miller and Nowak 1977, and Schultz and Schultz 1989 for interesting autobiographical accounts.

9. See for example Horne 1986 and Rothman and Lichter 1982. Locally, there were other examples of Red scare hysteria, also in large part fueled by racism and anti-Semitism. For example, as Svonkin discusses, in 1949 New York State passed the Feinberg Law, which "barred members of the Communist Party and related organizations from employment in the public schools." In

New York City a high percentage of teachers in public schools were Jewish women, and the teachers' union was largely Jewish. Ultimately, "every one of the New York City school teachers dismissed for political reasons during the postwar Red scare was Jewish" (1997, 131).

10. On these points see Rothman and Lichter 1982,100 and Horne 1986.

11. On these issues see Horne 1986 and Rothman and Lichter 1982. Interestingly enough, the Frankfurt School, developing a line of Marxism more in line with what would become the new left, was also largely Jewish: for example, Horkheimer, Marcuse, Benjamin, Fromm, and Adorno (as half) were all Jewish. Some of these men were also major figures of the academic wing of Jewish and other minority community's civil rights organizations.(Svonkin 1997)

12. In 1950 Du Bois organized activities in the Peace Information Center, which sponsored the Stockholm Peace Appeal. This appeal was a petition to outlaw "atomic weapons as instruments of intimidation and mass murder." Ten million people in France, sixty million people in China, one hundred fifteen million in the Soviet Union, one and a half million in the United States, as well as those in other countries, signed the document. When the petition came under attack from the HUAC, those U.S. citizens who had signed the document were labeled traitors. (See Horne 1986, 126–33 and passim for this section.)

13. In spring 1968 a reformist section of the Czechoslovakian Communist Party—initiated by professionals, scientists, intellectuals and artists—ousted hard-liners and began instituting various democratic reforms. Progressives in the United States felt a strong affinity for these developments. By this time, when the Soviet military invaded Czechoslovakia and crushed the movement, the mass of U.S. progressives had distanced themselves from ties to the USSR and saw the two events of state repression in Chicago and Prague as connected. (See Anderson 1995, 224; Zeman 1969; Journalist 1970)

14. Having stated this in the context of Soviet influence, one could still argue that the U.S. left maintained a certain fascination with socialism, displayed primarily in idealization of China's and Cuba's revolutions. Many U.S. radicals since the 1960s had a long-distance love affair with the images and writings of Mao, Fidel, and especially the macho-mythic Che Guevara. See also Rothman and Lichter 1982, 19 and 102; and the films and books that became classics for this period, such as *A Rebel without a Cause*, Goodman's 1956 *Growing Up Absurd*, and Salinger's 1964 *A Catcher in the Rye*.

15. For a comparative look at students protests at this time see Altbach and Lipset 1969.

16. In addition to the inhuman "three-fifths compromise" between the Northern and Southern states declaring African slaves to be three-fifths of a person, John Adams responded to his wife Abigail Adams' plea to "Remember the Ladies" and include them in the new Code of Laws by declaring his fear of the potential cry of equality from all subordinates such as children and students, apprentices, Indians, Negroes and other undesirable elements such as "Tories, Landjobbers, Trimmers, Bigots, Canadians . . . Hanoverians, Hessians, Russians, Irish Roman Catholicks [sic], [and] Scotch Renegadoes" (reprinted in Scott

and Scott 1982, 54). As a comment on class, Madison notes that "the most common and durable source of factions has been the verious [sic] and unequal distribution of property" between those who hold and those who are without it (1961, 79). For a discussion of the "uneasy encounter" of Jews in early U.S. history, see Hertzberg 1989.

17. See Roelofs's (1992) discussion of a history of related consensus-cleavage debates in (U.S.) American democratic thought. As another example, Rogin characterizes the distinctive feature of (U.S.) American multiculturalism as "racial division and ethnic incorporation" (1996, 2).

18. For some interesting essays on European ethnicity in the United States, see Walch 1994. For a look at the emerging field of critical white studies, see Delgado and Stefancic 1997.

19. The text from *Leviathan* runs as follows: "Every man strive to accomodate himselfe to the rest. For the understanding whereof, we may consider, that there is in mens aptnesse to Society; a diversity of nature, rising from their diversity of Affections; not unlike to that we see in stones brought together for building of an AEdifice. For as that stone which by asperity, and irregularity of Figure, takes more room from others, than it selfe fills; and for the hardnesse, cannot be easily made plain, and thereby hindereth the building, is by the builders cast away as unprofitable, and Nature will strive to retain those things which to himselfe are superfluous, and to others necessary; and for the stubbornness of his Passions, cannot be corrected, is to be left, or cast out of Society, as combersome thereunto" (1968, 209).

20. Representations of "melting pots" came to be used in widely differing contexts. At the Ford Motor Company at the time, Henry Ford set up a school to teach English to his immigrant employees and required attendance. The commencement consisted of a ceremony simulating a melting pot where graduates of the program walked down a "gangplank" from their "immigrant ship," dressed in "national costumes" and carrying "bulky baggage," into Ford's "melting pot." The teachers "stirred the contents" of the pot with "long ladles" and as the "pot boiled over" the men came over the surface dressed in "American clothes" and waving American flags (see Zunz 1982, 311–12). In film, *The King of Jazz* also used a "melting pot finale," stirring an enormous pot, though as Rogin points out, African and Caribbean Americans were not included (1996, 140–41).

21. See Kraver 1999, and the introduction to Brettschneider 1996b for more detailed analyses of this period and the changes it spurred.

22. See the essays in Reed 1997.

23. That Americans of African descent were usually excluded from the possibilities of the melting pot form of assimilationism did not mean that many of this community did not aspire to such inclusion. Langston Hughes and other less well-known African Americans understood, or attempted to place, Blacks within the "American immigrant mosaic." See Keppel 1995 and Dyson 1995 for interesting and critical discussion.

24. It was only after the slowdown of Chinese immigration due to the 1882

act that the first major wave of Japanese immigration began. As Barringer, Gardner, and Levin (1995, 22–28) point out, despite the increasing exclusion of Chinese, cheap labor was still needed. The influx of Japanese people to the United States then stirred its own racist response and the passage of many antialien laws, culminating in the National Origins Act. As in the previous example, the continued need for cheap labor created by the slowdown of Japanese immigration was filled by a wave of Filipino immigrants (not excluded under the National Origins Act as were other Asians because the United States had annexed the Philippines).

25. Although we will address the treatment of Japanese in the United States during wartime below, it is important to note here that Japanese immigrants to the United States could not become citizens until 1952. (Nagata 1993)

26. Rogin 1996, 56; Allen 1994; Curtis 1971.

27. Defining U.S. American identity against the portrayal of natives as "savage" is as much true as Baldwin's famous insight that "no one was white before he/she came to America. Everyone who got here, and paid the price of the ticket, the price was to become white" (1963). On becoming white and race as a social construction, see for example: Roediger 1994, Kaye/Kantrowitz 1992, and Brodkin 1998.

28. By the later 1800s, a widespread campaign had been launched to forcibly remove (if they did not go upon request) Native children from their homes and tribes and take them to one of the various school systems run by the U.S. Bureau of Indian Affairs or explicitly Christian groups. Conditions tended to be poor. The curricula taught Christian American subjects, demanded English only, and employed degrading images of Native American culture. The children were often punished, including physical punishment (which for girls also often meant sexual abuse), emotional abuse, and tranquilizers (especially for those who demanded their rights to return home, use their Native names, speak native dialects or practice cultural/religious rituals and traditions). (See for example: Hoxie 1984, Beuf 1977). Forced sterilization of Native women, as with other marginalized minority women, constituted another manifestation of the genocide/assimilation approach that continues to be a significant problem for Native and many minority women today.

29. See also Bell 1984 for an historical discussion.

30. See (1971) chapter III, "Subjects and Citizens," especially his comments on 439–40. In *Mein Kampf* Hitler makes numerous other references to the great example of "American union" as well. See also Rogin's discussion (1996, 64).

31. For further reading see for example: Gesensway and Roseman 1987, Hatamiya 1993, Nagata 1993, Nishimoto 1995, Okihiro 1996.

32. See Michaels 1995, Phillips (1993, chapter eight), Sandel 1984, Barringer, Gardner, and Levin (1995, chapter one), and Walzer, "What Does It Mean to Be an 'American'?" in Brettschneider (1996b, 267–86).

33. For a more critical indictment of pluralism see Michaels 1995.

34. See Svonkin 1997, 5.

35. Dahl's book was one of three—by other respected political scientists—published from the same large study of the city of New Haven. The other two also looked at such leadership questions and were seen as "complementing" Dahl's volume. Polsby's work, for example, also "state[d] the need for a new pluralist theory of community power." See Dahl's 1961 preface, p. vi.

36. See, for example, the discussion in Manley 1983.

37. See, for example, Brettschneider 1996a, 1996b, Svonkin 1997, Waskow 1983, Prell 1989, Kaye/Kantrowitz 1992, Brodkin 1998.

38. See Seidman's 1997 argument.

39. See, for example, Cruikshank 1992, Duberman 1993, Faderman 1991, Marcus 1992, Weiss and Schiller 1988.

40. See Butler 1990, Feinberg 1998, Califia 1997.

41. On these developments see, for example, Wagenheim and Wagenheim 1996, Cordasco and Bucchioni 1973, and Bloomfield 1985.

42. For some interesting reading see Crow Dog 1991, Jaimes 1992, Allen 1986, and Peltier's piece, "War against the American Nation," 213–29 in Schultz and Schultz 1989.

43. For more information see, for example, Asian Women United of California, 1989, Espiritu 1992, and Barringer, Gardner, and Levin 1995.

44. An 1874 bill regulating food production was the first consumer rights–related bill passed by Congress. Upton Sinclair's popular book *The Jungle* catalyzed early-twentieth-century advocacy that was not to become a widespread movement until the New Deal ushered in a second phase of consumer rights legislation. The Red scare made continuing support for New Deal legislation difficult, and dangerous for many groups, while all activities criticizing big business were labeled communist. Consumer rights does not become a feasible public issue again until the post-McCarthy 1960s. On consumer rights–related issues see, for example, Feldman 1976, Brobeck 1990, Nader 1965.

45. Despite much activity, and numerous follow-up laws, over twenty years after the passage of the 1968 FHA, studies show that discrimination in the banking sector had not been reduced, and by 1991 disparities between whites and Blacks had actually increased. Examination of discriminatory lending policies is important, particularly in the context of contemporary diversity politics. Many issues multicultural activists support are defeated with the justification that the United States cannot guarantee equality of outcome, but merely equality of opportunities. The capitalist influence in U.S. democratic thought suggests that if everyone leaves the starting line in the race of life on equal terms, the fact that there are winners and losers does not reflect inequalities in the system. Radical democrats argue that concern for where individuals fall in the "game" *is* a matter of justice. But the issue of discrimination in lending is, more clearly than many other issues, actually an "opportunity" issue that becomes an "outcome" issue.

For some related reading, see Squires 1992.

46. See Hawes 1991, especially chapter eight.

Notes to Chapter 3

1. The categories and their names I use here are those used by the newspaper (October 28, 1997).

2. Thanks to Lisa Disch for pushing me to think further about the relationship between political valence and agency.

3. Remember, however, that Aristotle thought that democracy had the potential to be the very worst form of government, the most unstable and subject to a tyranny of the masses. We revisit this notion as revived by framer of the United States Constitution James Madison in Chapter Seven.

4. See Lukes 1986 for his work on power that extends beyond traditional understandings within politics, and particularly Lugones' and Spelman's 1983 situation of such a discussion within more recent diversity conceptualizations and concerns.

5. See, for example, Hertzberg 1968, and for a critical feminist discussion Levitt 1997.

6. The literature here is extensive. Some examples are Asian Women United 1989, Bell 1987 and 1992, Brettschneider 1996a, 1996b, Cordova 1983, Gooding-Williams 1993, Jaimes 1992, Jordan 1994, Minow 1990, Moraga 1983, Vaid 1996, West 1993a, 1993b, and Williams 1991.

7. As discussed in Chapter Two. Bentley (1908) was one of the first to make this shift, while Truman (1951) and later Dahl (beginning with *Who Governs?* 1961) are credited for the midcentury and 1960s turn. See Manley's 1983 discussion of this with respect to Marx.

8. See, for example, Phelan's 1989 well argued perspective on this point coming out of lesbian politics, and Castillo 1980 (and Gutiérrez 1993 for a summary of some of the literature) on the Chicana critique of the Chicano movement in the United States at this time. See Almaguer 1987 and Saragoza 1987 for critical reflections on Chicano historiography.

9. Malinche is the name given to the historical/mythical figure Malintzin Tenepal, who served as a translator and adviser to Cortez, the Spanish conqueror of Mexico. She was also his mistress. It is said that it was due to her that the indigenous people of Mexico became a mixed race with the "white" Spanish conquerors. Although therefore seen as the mother of the mestizo/a people, historically she has been blamed for selling out her people. *Malinche* is usually used as an extremely negative, anti-Chicana slur. Numerous contemporary Chicana feminists have sought to reclaim Malintzin's legacy for a new feminist political vision. See, for example, Moraga 1983 and Anzaldua 1987.

10. Patricia Hill Collins' work is a good example of this. Such is also the mission of the academic journal *Race, Gender and Class*. Gutiérrez 1993 gives a history of Chicana feminist cultural production that assumed the centrality of this intersectionality (54). See Lerner 1997, chapter 1, on these developments.

11. I use Adrienne Rich's term here. Audre Lorde is one of the early activist/thinkers to provide us with such insights. Kaye/Kantrowitz 1992 does this kind of work very well also. In the area of philosophy, Spelman 1988 and But-

ler 1990 were significant contributors to this line of thinking. See also my critique of some of this material focused primarily on Spelman in Brettschneider 2001. As brilliant as Butler is, however, I find her extremely important discussion of performativity at times too overstated, suggesting the unreality of identity. That there might not be a subject behind the performance, that identity is a social construction, does not necessarily make it any less meaningful for living communities. I will deal with such issues subsequently in this chapter; on this point, however, see Kaufman-Osborn 1997 for an appreciative and well developed critique.

12. Some examples are Hall 1990, Walzer in Brettschneider 1996b, Alarcón in Anzaldua 1990, and Bhabha 1990.

13. Hewitt 1992.

14. E.g., Seif 1999, Narayan 1997a.

15. Yiddish, for example, is a language of Hebrew and middle German, Ladino of Hebrew and Spanish; what is called in English Judeo-Arabic is of Hebrew and certain Arabic dialects.

16. See for example Du Bois 1903, Saucedo 1996, Collins 1991, and Baldwin 1963.

17. Lorde 1984, 138, and see Zack 1995.

18. For examples of critical race and other identity theories see for example Allen 1986, Allison 1994, Anzaldua 1987, Anzaldua and Moraga 1982, Matsuda et al. 1993, Boyarin and Boyarin 1997, hooks 1989, and West 1993a, 1993b, as well as Phelan 1989, who explicitly works with postmodern theories.

19. See, for example, Christian 1990, Di Stefano and Hartsock in Nicholson 1990, and the work of Michael Dyson.

20. For further discussion see for example Butler 1990, Grant 1993, Phelan 1994.

21. This view is critiqued explicitly in Brown 1995.

22. As yet another perspective, Kaufman-Osborn is critical of this turn against the subject as actually retaining a problematic hint of Cartesianism (1997, 120).

23. When I refer to particular groups here, I fully intend to connote the communities in their diversity. I do not mean merely "normative" members of discrete communities, for example, but rather members of certain racial, class, or gender groupings.

24. This is why we find that what "postmodernism" means in certain communities is a rejection of modernism, but one that is taken to mean also a new openness to (transformed?) premodern ideas from those communities' histories. Some interesting examples on such a view are Anzaldua 1987 and Kepnes 1996.

25. See, for example, Boswell 1994.

26. See, for example, Lerner's 1997 discussion of this point.

27. The creation of a proletariat (as opposed to a peasantry or other historical forms of the poor) and the development of communism in eighteenth century Europe as identities are taking root in the politics of modernism, mark a shift in "class" as an identity signifier.

28. Although in this specific section I am exploring the ways that postmodernism and post-1960s multiculturalism are rather distinct philosophical orientations, I cite them together here in terms of historical context.

29. Some examples from various identity communities may be found in Plaskow 1991, Gutiérrez 1993, and Collins 1990.

30. The literature here abounds. Some examples on this point are found in Tate 1983, 91; Collins 1991; Belenky et al. 1986; Gilligan 1982; Kaye/Kantrowitz and Klepfisz 1986, Beck 1984, Heshel 1983, Plaskow 1991, Falk 1996, and Brettschneider 1996a, 1996b.

31. Young (1990) is helpful on this point. Phelan (1994) offers a wonderful discussion of "coming" out as lesbian as also a process of be-coming. Stuart Hall (1990) writes of both being and becoming. As a more extreme example, Asante (1988) writes that Afrocentricity is as much about rediscovering a lost connection as it is also about self-consciously creating and reconstructing. See also bell hooks 1992.

32. As bell hooks (1992, 20) sees this, "loving blackness as a political resistance transforms our ways of looking and being, and thus creates the conditions necessary for us to move against the forces of domination and death and reclaim black life."

33. As much work has been done problematizing core identity categories, showing how over history in the West Blackness, sex, and heterosexuality have been created, I will not restate these theses. Some interesting examples of how, over time, these designations were created and how different groups would thus move in and out of the hated classifications are: on how immigrant groups to the United States such as Jews and the Irish had to become white, see Curtis 1971, Rogin 1996, Brodkin 1998; on how Mexicans in the United States were sometimes seen as white and other times seen as colored, see Horne 1995, 29; on how sex, and the fact that only two sexes are designated, and heterosexuality are cultural creations not true universally, see Edgerton 1964, Fausto-Sterling 1993, and postmodern contributions such as that by Butler 1990; and for an explicit treatment of how class affected these movements, see Roediger 1994.

34. See, for example, hooks 1989, 42; Walker 1983, 36; Cannon 1988.

35. Although as postmodernists will warn us, we should be careful in our reconstructions, many minority communities need the postmodern-style fracturing of hegemonic discourse as they also need their work of repair. See for examples Anzaldua and Moraga 1982, Allen 1986, Kepnes 1996, Zerubavel 1995, Espiritu 1992.

36. See also Lange 1998; Collins 1991; Lugones and Spelman 1983. Kaufman-Osborn also hints at this in his critique of post-modernism's insistence on language over experience 1997, 118.

37. An excellent example of such an engagement may be found in Anzaldua 1987.

Notes to Chapter 4

1. See Young's description of cultural imperialism for a similar concept. Young explains cultural imperialism as "the paradox that the dominant meanings

of society render the particular perspective of one's own group invisible at the same time that they might stereotype the group and mark it as other" (1990, 58–59).

2. This explains, for example, the popularity of such later works as Goodman's 1956 *Growing Up Absurd* as a U.S. more popular interpretation of European existentialist philosophy. Young white middle-class men being prepared for their roles as cogs in the bourgeois machine lose all individuality, spontaneity, and authenticity.

3. Bell hooks (1992, 5) quotes this from Pratibha Parmar.

4. Sandra Harding asserts "the right to define the categories through which one is to see the world and to be seen by it is a fundamental political right" (1991, 252). Taylor puts it thus: "Due recognition is not just a courtesy but a vital human need" (1994, 26). See also Honneth (1992 and 1995).

5. Fraser finds that "[t]he 'struggle for recognition' is fast becoming the paradigmatic form of political conflict in the late twentieth century" (1997, 11).

6. For some feminist reconstructions of additional concepts common in Western political theory, see the essays in Hirschmann and Di Stefano 1996.

7. Others might understand it as does Berlin, who wrote: "The lack of freedom about which men or groups complain amounts, as often as not, to the lack of proper recognition" (1969, 155).

8. This excerpt is reprinted in Zinn (1990, 1).

9. Further "well-meaning" yet offensive efforts to include non-Christians in Christmas fun include "Christmas around the world" displays such as putting icons supposedly representing various cultures and other religions as decorations on a Christmas tree. These efforts to be "inclusive" are actually more insidious forms of cultural imperialism: participants in the festivities feel good about their "openness," yet come to think of "diversity" as just different kinds of Christmas, while many of these other cultures/religions have no Christian tradition at all (not being Christian). Some feminist communities have followed their own form of such assimilationism, holding "winter solstice" events which turn out to be not much more than Christmas celebrations with women's artistic touches. One who is hesitant to participate runs the risk of being labeled unfeminist. (By naming some winter solstice events as disingenuous masks, I do not at all mean to say that all honors of the solstices are thinly veiled multiculturalism on an entrenched Christian base.)

10. I draw on Butler's 1990 conception of performativity in this explanation of recognition and identity formation.

11. On a related note, see Benjamin (1988, 197).

12. Hawkesworth 1997. See also Fanon 1967 and Tronto (1993, 120–122).

13. See, for example, Burke 1969 for a traditional view and Kristol 1983 for a neo-conservative view.

14. The literature here is extensive; some representative examples are Walzer 1970, Pateman 1979, Hirschmann 1992 and Green 1986.

15. In her characteristically clear analytic style, Fraser (1997, chapter one) responds to what she finds are "unnuanced" accounts of the rise in the tendency to place demands for recognition in the central place that demands for redistri-

bution held under socialism. Instead she wants to develop a "'critical' theory of recognition" by proposing a set of analytic distinctions, which she acknowledges do not necessarily correspond to the concrete situation of groups in contemporary politics. Although readers will likely find Fraser's chapter a helpful tool, her own uncharacteristic (in this and later chapters) decoupling of theory from actual politics limits the strength of her warnings, analysis, and suggestions. Instead, what Fraser must present as essentialized categories in order to establish her neat and analytically nuanced model, I view as a possible trajectory of a certain mode of concrete political thinking and practice. Despite the lack of historical specificity, to the degree that specific individuals, organizations, and representations of "multiculturalism" (which she negatively distinguishes from her positive "deconstruction") proceed along this trajectory today, Fraser's conceptualization should prove helpful in understanding what is problematic and why. It is the argument here that if one mode is a possible trajectory, then there are also other modes that tend to follow different paths. It is these other forms of recognition demands emerging out of politics, and not out of the brilliant minds of neat theorists, that concern me for their potential contribution to radical democracy.

16. Fraser (1997, chapter one) is clear, however, on some of the potentially reactionary backlash that may occur with her characterization of the reformist mode.

17. Fraser characterizes certain groups or issues as economic as opposed to cultural, and offers a critique, though she rarely cites examples of whose work is as limited as she suggests. Here I seek to let some writers she might have in mind speak to the issue.

18. In *Race Matters*, for example, Cornel West criticizes the Liberal notion that the introduction of more government programs can solve racial problems. This line of thinking actually is implicit in the problem of Liberalism's version of racial oppression precisely in that it focuses "solely on the economic dimension" (1993b, 4–5). According to West, a democratic socialist and critical race theorist, looking only at economic solutions to even economic problems, will not attend to the multilayered forms of oppression and exploitation operating in our racist system.

19. Molefi Asante is an example of one who is often criticized as overly culturally based, some would say to the point of nationalism. However, Asante argues clearly that "[e]conomic freedom must always be connected to political and cultural freedom else freedom does not truly exist. . . . Furthermore, political power or state power without cultural and economic power is also meaningless for liberation" (1988, 9).

20. Fraser (1997, 6). Fraser writes: "My larger aim is *to connect* two political problematics that are currently dissociated from each other, for only by *integrating* recognition and redistribution can we arrive at a framework that is adequate to the demands of our age" (1997, 12) [italics mine]. Again, my argument is that where we find some actions and representations, or the possible trajectory in this direction, we will want to be clear about redirecting demands for

recognition toward a politics of redistribution. However, for the most part, Fraser needs only to "integrate" and aim at "connecting" the two because she purposely distinguishes them for purely analytic purposes. This does not mean that everyone else has severed the two and find themselves with the same aim. See for example Scott 1985 and Du Bois 1935.

21. Given political history, Berlin's fears and critiques are well placed. This does not mean, however, that a politics of recognition necessitates authoritarianism, oligarchy, or rude treatment by "our own" group or our acceptance of such conduct. This is precisely why we must engage in a critical politics of recognition based on a conception of "our own" group as diverse and committed also to justice in intragroup dynamics.

22. See Spelman 1988, Davis 1981, Moraga 1983, and Anzaldua 1987 for examples of such grappling.

23. It is only by getting beyond this distributive paradigm that justice could begin to respond to Berlin's assessment of demands. He suggests: "What oppressed classes or nationalities, as a rule, demand is neither simply unhampered liberty of action for their members, nor, above everything, equality of social or economic opportunities, still less assignment of place in a frictionless, organic state devised by a rational lawgiver. What they want, as often as not, is simply recognition (of their class or nation, colour or race) as an independent source of human activity, as an entity with a will of its own, intending to act in accordance with it (whether it is good or legitimate, or not) and not to be ruled, educated, guided, with however light a hand, as being not quite fully human, and therefore not quite fully free" (1969, 156–57).

24. The call to eliminate *any* wage differential at all has not been practiced in even most communist and advanced socialist countries such as Cuba, the former Soviet Union, or the early state of Israel.

25. Class struggle here is not simply a matter of economics, but involves (like other issues of oppression) differences in perspectives and differently situated knowledges. Arguments such as Fraser's, which cast class beyond categories of difference and thus not needing a politics of recognition, can therefore be too limited. It may well be that socialists work to abolish the category of class. This very fact, in addition to the democratic insights that would guide the strategy and the rebuilding of such a classless society, are grounded in the unique position of workers in capitalism and their demands. The working class, even in the most traditional reading of Marx, is not making an assimilationist claim (one where a recognition of difference will not be necessary). They are not asking to be let into the capitalist system so they can be capitalists themselves. They are working to overthrow the very system of capitalism from the bottom up. To argue that difference has no place here does not make much sense. A Marxist view of a class-based revolution is perhaps the clearest example of an oppressed group making demands from its standpoint of exploitation and seeking to put in place an entire system based on its situated vision of democracy.

26. See Honneth 1995 for an argument that subsumes distribution under the banner of recognition.

27. Hawkesworth also cites Tronto (1993, 157–80) on this point. Elsewhere in this same piece she makes an interesting point that relates her discussion of equality to the discussion above regarding privileged irresponsibility (1997, 6). She writes "The doctrine of equal opportunity combined with a faith in education as the avenue of upward social mobility suggest that the grounds for hierarchy is merit. Moreover, the initial assumption of human equality sustains the belief that one's place in the meritocracy reflects only the morally meritorious differences of hard work and initiative. Thus, the assumption of equality reinforces the myth of personal responsibility for individual success or failure."

28. See Fraser (1997, especially chapter seven) for an example of this interpretation. Theoretical accounts such as this portray an impasse. Because activists do not necessarily tend to think of themselves as at an impasse, the theoretical account must be revised to relate to diversity-based politics.

29. Marx clearly saw through such illusory claims, as he warns in such texts as *On the Jewish Question*. As Taylor notes, "[w]here the politics of universal dignity fought for forms of nondiscrimination that were quite 'blind' to the ways in which citizens differ, the politics of difference often redefines nondiscrimination as requiring that we make these distinctions the basis of differential treatment" (1994, 39). Similarly, in discussing her interpretation of publicity in Arendt Disch applies Minow's analysis of the 1993 Supreme Court decision in *Shaw v. Reno* regarding gerrymandering of electoral districts according to racial considerations. In this examination Disch argues for a situated impartiality that would "situate the principles of rights and equality in the context of existing power relations." In contrast to the abstract appeal to color blindness made in the majority opinion, the opinions written by judges in the minority "also make explicit the consequences their arguments will have for perpetuating or for transforming existing racially patterned inequities in the distribution of electoral power." (See discussion in 1994, 212–15.)

30. Young's 1990 chapter on affirmative action is particularly interesting in light of this interpretation of equality.

31. For an application of some of these ideas to the reworking of privacy rights see Eisenstein's "Equalizing Privacy and Specifying Equality" (in Hirschmann and Di Stefano 1996, 181–92).

32. In *The Manifesto of the Communist Party*, in Tucker (1978, 419).

33. Isaiah Berlin might suggest that such accounts confuse freedom and equality, but this is probably because he is focusing on "individual" or "personal" freedom rather than what he calls "other kinds" of freedom such as "social or economic" as his definition (1969, 125). The point here is that many on the margins are talking about these "other kinds" of freedom, so we must hear what they are saying. In this argument, in contrast to Berlin, we might remember Marx's comments in *The German Ideology* that "only in community [with others has each] individual the means of cultivating his gifts in all directions; only in the community, therefore, is personal freedom possible" (in Tucker 1978, 197).

34. The classic text here, again, is Berlin's 1969 essay "Two Concepts of Liberty," though he is far from the first to look at freedom this way and is explicitly

drawing on and differentiating himself from T. H. Green—particularly his "On the Different Senses of 'Freedom' As Applied to Will and to the Moral Progress of Man" (1986, 228–50). Because he is so often cited but nearly as often misused, we must note that Berlin himself uses the two senses as follows: the negative sense is involved in the answer to the question "What is the area within which the subject—a person or group of persons—is or should be left to do or be what he is able to do or be, without interference by other persons?" and the second, the positive sense, is involved in the answer to the question "What, or who, is the source of control or interference that can determine someone to do, or be, this rather than that?" (1969, 121–12). The following discussion owes much, particularly, to Berlin, though I will explicitly use the two concepts of liberty slightly differently. This is because the questions for radical democrats have shifted somewhat, and especially because I will include yet a third concept, which Berlin himself would think a mistake but will help us clarify the ideas related to a potentially critical politics of recognition coming from the margins.

35. Hirschmann's essay "Revisioning Freedom: Relationship, Context, and the Politics of Empowerment" (in Hirschmann and Di Stefano, 1996, 51–74) is one of the few discussions of freedom recently to address Berlin's famous essay directly. Of interest for readers is that Hirschmann does so critically, questioning whether his is part of a "masculinist theory of freedom" whereby both "positive" and "negative" freedom have been used in the history of Western political thought against women, people of color, and the poor. She suggests, therefore, that we "need to rethink what we mean by freedom" (55), a process she begins by looking at the contexts of equality, relationships, and material experience—contexts which, due to their currency in democratic discourses from the margins more generally, will be addressed below.

36. See in particular Berlin's essay "Two Concepts of Liberty" (1969, 118–72) and Green's essay "On the Different Senses of 'Freedom' As Applied to Will and to the Moral Progress of Man" (1986, 228–50).

37. The difference between its current employment in a critical politics of recognition and the positive freedom of which Berlin is likely to be so disapproving is that Berlin visions the "social 'whole' " as "imposing its collective, or 'organic', single will upon its recalcitrant 'members' " (132), or as one that "ignores the actual wishes of men or societies" (133). When this occurs it is certainly unacceptable. However, again, there is nothing inherent in group-based notions of freedom necessitating that individuals always be pitted against the overarching will of the whole, or that activists accept any notion of a unitary or organic community in the first place.

38. And finally, we can note that Berlin would likely say that this additional concept of freedom *with* is merely a desire for fraternity that is confused with social freedom. He writes: "The desire for recognition is a desire for something different: for union, closer understanding, integration of interests, a life of common dependence and common sacrifice. It is only the confusion of desire for liberty with this profound and universal craving for status and understanding, further confounded by being identified with the notion of social self-direction,

where the self to be liberated is no longer the individual but the 'social whole', that makes it possible for men, while submitting to the authority of oligarches or dictators, to claim that this in some sense liberates them" (158).

This is indeed a danger. A critical politics of recognition may, however, contribute to democratic capacities to identify and struggle against these instances. Such a politics is possible in that many find—as another trajectory that Berlin does not highlight—that the community also has the potential to empower and strengthen individual vision, direction, and agency. This is what those now suggesting a third concept of freedom *with* intend to bring forth from their experiences in community for a new democratic politics. In addition to his fear of how this plays out in dictatorship, Berlin is also well aware of its important role in democracies (see 144 as well as his quite public support of progressive Zionism).

39. We could see Bennet's notion itself as a version of Berlin's discussion of a "positive doctrine of liberation by reason," which despite its appearance in some totalitarian creeds is also found at the heart of many democratic practices. Although we might say that debates about just what is im/possible often motivate radical politics, Berlin anticipates these newer multicultural views when he writes: "Knowledge liberates not only by offering us more open possibilities amongst which we can make our choice, but by preserving us from the frustration of attempting the impossible" (1969, 144).

40. See John Stuart Mill's argument in *On Liberty* (1984).

41. See on this point Plaskow 1991 and Bickford 1996.

NOTES TO CHAPTER 5

1. She also clarifies why it can be problematic to refer to citizen-workers, as has been common in democratic theory: many women, particularly illegal immigrants, are not official workers. Where voting and work are traditionally argued as what entitles one to the benefits of social standing, dignity, and rights of citizenship, Narayan wants to be able to extend these regardless of whether individuals vote here or work for pay in the official labor market.

2. See, for example, Gould 1988, James 1992, Mouffe 1992, Young 1987. Having said this, we must be careful not to assume that those marginalized have nothing to do with the constitution of citizenship. On the contrary, Spelman writes, "In a well-ordered city-state, women and slaves are not parts of the polis, but they are the conditions of it" (1988, 38).

3. I rely on Young's 1990 typology of oppression here.

4. See Spelman 1988; Grant 1993; Scott in Butler and Scott 1992, 22–40; Flax 1993; Fuss 1989; Phelan 1989, 1994.

5. I appreciate Martin's 1994 response to the potential silencing effect caused by the many critiques of essentialism. We must be careful, but not stop our work.

6. See, for example, Choderow 1978, Rich 1986, Ruddick 1989, Pateman

1992. For critical responses see Grimshaw 1986, Ferguson, Zita, and Addelson 1982, Joseph and Lewis 1981, Dietz 1985, Hill Collins 1990, Spelman 1988, the critical symposium on Choderow in *Signs* (1981; vol. 6, no. 3), commentary in Trebilcot 1983, Phelan 1989, and Rich 1980.

7. The literature here is extensive. Some important contributions can be found in Allen 1986, Choderow 1978, Crow Dog 1991, Joseph and Lewis 1981, Trebilcot 1983, Stack 1974, Hill Collins 1990, hooks 1984, Hong Kingston 1976, Rich 1986, Ruddick 1989, Arnup 1995 and Gutiérrez's 1993 summary of some of the main literature from the view of the revolutionary daughters in the Chicana movements.

8. Spelman (1988, 97–99) draws on the writings of certain women of color in developing her critique of Choderow's limitations (a tendency to separate and hierarchically order gender-based and other oppressions as they affect mothering and its reproduction). I believe my formulation does not negate what are important contributions of Choderow's work, but pushes them as we analyze women's experiences in families when we think of diverse groups of women and the interplay of oppressions. In addition, although Spelman's critique of Choderow's focus on women's affective ties is appropriate in that it implies a sort of "woman-bonding" beyond the family unaffected by differences among women (110–11), it still seems to me appropriate to highlight the creation of women *in* the familial sphere as in affective ties, although characteristics such as love often play out differently, especially across communities (97–100).

9. The literature here is extensive as well. Some examples are diLeonardo 1984, Vecchio 1989, Deutsch 1987, Yanagisako 1985, Stack 1974, Gilkes 1988.

10. Some have understood this phenomenon in terms of a kind of "lesbian continuum" among women (e.g., Frye 1988, Lorde 1984, Rich 1980, Raymond 1986, and Daly 1978). Others have taken issue with this notion (e.g., Ferguson, Zita, and Addelson 1982, Phelan 1989).

11. Raymond 1986, Friedman 1993, Ackelsberg 1983, Hill Collins 1990.

12. Discussed in Stahl Weinberg (1989, 113).

13. See West and Blumberg 1990, Hyman 1980, Harzig 1989, Milkman 1985, Hill Collins 1990.

14. Krasniewicz 1992, McDonnell 1994, Edwards 1990. Speaking of urban contexts, Ackelsberg writes that women "live in a context of webs of relationships, informal and formal, which structure their patterns of interaction, give meaning and order to their lives, and may well be crucial factors affecting the development of their political consciousness" (1984, 251).

15. Ackelsberg 1988, 300; McAllister 1988; Stahl Weinberg 1992; Simke 1989; Chafe 1977; Smelser 1968; Rothman and Lichter 1982.

16. Fisher 1993, Gilligan 1982, Tronto 1993, Benhabib 1987. For critical discussion, see Grimshaw 1986, Flanagan 1982, and Auerbach, et al. 1985.

17. I do not really mean to be saying "integrated" here. This could be a term that, when being generous, patriarchy might call women for living across its separated realms. At other times the patriarchal labels might be "confused," "muddled," or "incompetent." In either case, labels that suggest bringing

together parts, judged positively or negatively, are generated from a patriarchal perspective that sees these as separated parts in the first place.

18. I realize that others might well prefer a route to more effective participation by altering some aspects of my characterization of women's experience. Among the many possible reasons, one I find most challenging reminds us that "women's ways" have been constructed under patriarchy; they are not "natural" to women but are an effect of oppression. Why would I want us to stay as we are under these circumstances? As inadequate as it might be for some readers, my first answer is that I find this "integrated" or more holistic experiential mode personally fulfilling and reasonable. Also, politically, noting the primacy of connection, interest, passion, and care in the lives of women, we can make sense of women's political activities as citizens. Finally, philosophically, women's lives may offer us a vision of citizenship that does not need to repress or transcend these characteristics, but suggests possibilities for citizenship as more broadly maintaining the tensions within the dialectic (rather than choosing sides or overcoming what appear to be contradictions in need of soothing).

19. Although her article is largely a critique of Liberalism, this description is more apt for what is referred to here as Republicanism.

20. For example, Boxer and Quataert's 1987 *Connecting Spheres* suggests not "to connect" but that the spheres have long been connected. But others have interpreted the challenge of feminist politics within patriarchy as being to forge connections "out in the patriarchal" world. This has led to a response by some feminists who fear "doing away with the distinctions between public and private" or "blurring the lines" (with the emphasis on the verb) and who want to maintain the separateness. See Dietz's 1985 critique for example, and in Phelan 1989. The point being argued here is that this perspective makes sense only in response to a view of the feminist project as "integrating," not acting more effectively "as integrated."

21. For example, see Holmes and others in Mansbridge 1990, Hirschmann 1977, Pomper 1992.

22. Holmes (in Mansbridge 1990, 284) writes, "At the end of the sixteenth century, Richard Hooker summarized traditional thinking with his claim that the common people are motivate by self-interest, while religious and political elites are motivated by virtue and devotion to the common good. Viewed in this context, the postulate of universal self-interest appears as a subversive doctrine, designed to remove all flattering obscurity about the motives of kings, aristocrats, and priests. . . . To say that *all* individuals were motivated by self-interest was to universalize the status of the common man."

23. Thanks to H. Mark Roelofs for his understandings of Liberal society, which I draw on in this section.

24. Thus, as long as it took Congress to pass the Pay Equity Act, since the idea was put on the agenda in 1943 with the War Labor Board, this went as far as stipulating equal pay for identical work. As significant as this law can be, its use remains limited in terms of actual wage differentials. Not only is compliance a problem, but given the gendering of so many job categories, the more far-

reaching conceptualization would be equal pay for comparable worth. The difficulty in getting such laws passed does have to do with how far-reaching such a stipulation would be.

25. Marx claimed that this was the role of religion. He was probably correct, though he left unexamined that this is the role of women and numerous minorities in bourgeois society as well (see the introduction to *Contribution to the Critique of Hegel's* Philosophy of Right in Tucker 1978, 54).

NOTES TO CHAPTER 6

1. Stemming from the former 1960s baby boomers' inability to cede substantive terrain to a new generation, the generic name given to today's youth is also meant to reflect the internalization of the late capitalist existential condition. *Generation X* refers to an orientation in the world, supposedly brought on by the disappointments with the failures of the previous generation to effect the revolution they claimed to be making, leaving the country that much more alienated. With the promises of their predecessors unfulfilled, Generation X is cast as responding with apathy, with antipathy to promises, goals, commitments, and stability. A generation raised on MTV and sound bites, we have no attention span. With Reagan's censorship of the invasion of Grenada, Bush's planned reporting of the Gulf War, and corporate programming in classrooms, Generation X is said to have lost/be losing the capacity to distinguish between fact and myth, publicity that promotes a critical public and that which purposively manipulates ideological signs in order to sell things (products, bodies, values, fears). Although I agree that this description is in some senses reflective of certain currents in popular culture, the following discussion also calls such a characterization into question.

2. I am also aware that any number of people that I include here in the term *queer* may not identify with the term. As the following discussion points to, both claiming the name queer and using it as an umbrella term are also largely actions that are themselves products of generational politics and experiences. There are many good reasons to reject the term queer; for example, an historical tendency to eclipse the politics, desires, and struggles of women under a supposedly (though due to sexist bias not usually) gender-inclusive linguistic and conceptual category, as well as possibly denying the significant specificity of any individual group under the overarching label or the tensions between the groups. Having said this, by the 1990s (and still today) "queer" politics had taken on a life of its own with enough cross-group coalition work and powerful activist name recognition that (while appreciating the reservations of others) I will use this term here.

3. Marx's point in *On the Jewish Question* regards the problem of a minority community's demands for political rights in the context of an economic system based on exploitation. Commenting on the failures of Reconstruction, in *The Souls of Black Folk* Du Bois (1903) notes that the ballot and even constitutional

amendments are not the same as an organizational structure and overturning bigotry. An argument on behalf of youth and queers in politics would be new, to say the least, to each of these thinkers.

4. These marches in celebration of gay pride began in the summer of 1970 in New York City's Greenwich Village to mark the 1969 Stonewall uprising. Smith reports that by 1998 such marches "were planned for 116 U.S. locations in 47 states and territories. Globally, pride marches were also scheduled in 15 locations in 5 provinces in Canada, 11 locations in 7 countries in Latin America, 49 sites in 19 countries in Europe, and 12 locations in Africa, Asia, Australia and New Zealand" (1998, 3).

5. See Sanders's 1998 presentation of much interesting data.

6. See, for example, reports posted on Leslie Feinberg's transgenderwarrior web site (October 20–29, 1998) and Kifner's (1998) report in the *New York Times*.

7. I owe a great debt to Sanders (1998) for helping me to conceptualize this apparent paradox and for his research and data presentation. However, Sanders's problem is the discrepancy between the proportion of the population and the political involvement of queers and youth. He finds this a problem specifically due to the progressive orientation of youth toward queers and queer issues. But Sanders remains stuck in a definition of politics as predominantly voting, and of political involvement primarily limited to the governmental arena. On the one hand, he would refer to youth as political "non-entities" (due to voter turnout); on the other, he states clearly the progressive ideological orientation, the more open and inclusive lifestyles, and the finding that Generation X makes its electoral choices according to actual issues more than to party/media hype (7). It is my contention that for those such as Sanders who seek to bolster the political efficacy of queers, Generation X, and a more radical democratic agenda, we need to recognize politics and potential agency for change in a way that brings together both facets of Sanders's research. Attending to the locations of politics will help us to do so.

8. Dean (1996, 75) "calls on us to challenge exclusionary notions of citizenship that fail to account for the variety of types of political action" and look to forms of politics that will further commit "us to the expansion of opportunities for democratic participation." In heeding her call, reviving and revising discussions of the public sphere will help us to make sense of the apparent contradiction of apathetic groups that can also be understood as highly active, as well as find ways to enhance democratic participation. See also Held 1986, especially chapter 9, for his discussion of a principle of democratic autonomy.

9. "Only in the light of the public sphere did that which existed become revealed, did everything become visible to all. In the discussion among citizens issues were made topical and took on shape" (Habermas 1989, 4; see also Arendt 1958; for a gender-critical view of this public/private distinction in Western philosophy see Elshtain 1981). Habermas's metaphor of the public sphere as the place of light, and therefore rational, is no coincidence in the racialized history of Western elite constructions of the public sphere as light in contrast to the darkness of all (people, ideas, and emotions) from which it desperately must be separated.

10. And thus the ideal of the public sphere for Western modernism differs from the original Greek. Habermas notes: "With the rise of a sphere of the social, over whose regulation public opinion battled with public power, the theme of the modern (in contrast to the ancient) public sphere shifted from the properly political tasks of a citizenry acting in common (i.e., administration of law as regards internal affairs and military survival as regards external affairs) to the more properly civic tasks of a society engaged in a critical public debate (i.e., the protection of a commercial economy)" (1989, 52).

11. In contemporary diversity politics, discussions of what political theorists might have historically referred to in terms of publicity, the public, the public sphere or space, the polis, and so on, might also be framed in the language of place, surfaces, locations, and the like. Some trained in political theory situate their examinations of these matters within the discourse of civil society, rather than that of the public sphere. Here I do not intend to privilege one discourse or argue for any specific geography of politics. I am interested in articulating the contours of newly spatialized conceptualizations of radical democratic praxis and its potentialities emerging from and in the service of historically marginalized populations.

12. The specific processes differed to some degree in each distinct country (e.g., in England the development of the Parliament happened in a more evolutionary manner; in France change was due to revolution. These material differences in history slightly altered the course of specific new public spheres out of civil society). Further, in addition to the parliament, Habermas at times mentions the development of the judiciary and the role of legal codification in his discussion of the emergence of the bourgeois public sphere as distinct from a hitherto state-related space for politics in the feudal system.

13. Numerous points of critique have been made against elite Western political theory's interpretation of the public sphere(see for example the essays in Calhoun 1992); for an historical understanding of this interpretation, see the detailed and influential discussion of a highly stylized version of the structural transformation of the bourgeois public sphere in Habermas 1989.

14. Habermas notes that "[t]he public sphere of civil society stood or fell with the principle of universal access. A public sphere from which specific groups would be *eo ipso* excluded was less than merely incomplete; it was not a public sphere at all" (1989, 85). The irony of Liberalism's triumph is that it failed before it could ever succeed. See Landes 1980 and Fauré 1991 for important work describing how the development of the bourgeois "public" sphere necessitated *removing* women, in large part from the upper classes, from public spaces they had already inhabited.

15. Citation from Gouges (see Fauré 1991, 112) and comment in Fauré 1991, 112. In addition to the many women writing and politically active in France at this time (there are English translations of much of Germaine de Stael's work; see also Marso 1999 for new work on Stael), similar critiques of the new Liberal revolutions and their claim to be "open" came from other women around Europe—in Holland Etta Palm d'Aelders (see Fauré) or in England such as

Mary Wollstonecraft (see her own works)—and even wives of the U.S. founding fathers (see, for example, the documents compiled by Scott and Scott 1982).

16. Critically articulating the power dynamics in this historical process was paramount to Marx's project. In particular, he utilized a critique of Hegel's conceptions of civil society and the state in order to demonstrate the contradictions in assuming the liberal formula that "[t]he *legislature* is the power to organize the universal" ("Critique of Hegel's Doctrine of the State" in Marx 1975, 117). For Marx, the civil society of the legislature was a fiction, the bourgeois public sphere an illusion, and public opinion a matter of false consciousness.

17. Habermas also comments on this contradiction: "From the very start, indeed, the parliament was rent by the contradiction of being an institution opposing all political authority and yet established as an 'authority' itself" (1989, 233).

18. Dean specifies that her interests in the "ideal of reflective solidarity and the struggles for recognition key to identity politics direct us away from a politics centered on the state" (1996, 75). See also Landes 1980, Sphere Collective 1995, Brown 1997, and Evans and Boyte 1992. Fraser writes that recognizing the gender and racial coding of publicity and privacy highlights "inadequacies of the liberal theory of the public sphere . . . it is not adequate to analyze these categories as supports for and challenges to state power exclusively. Rather, we need also to understand the ways in which discursive privatization supports the 'private' power of bosses over workers, husbands over wives, and whites over blacks. Publicity, then, is not only a weapon against state tyranny, as its bourgeois originators and current Eastern European exponents assume. It is also potentially a weapon against the extrastate power of capital, employers, supervisors, husbands, and fathers, among others" (1997, 116). Given the importance of Fraser's argument, we must also contextualize her point more historically: some nineteenth-century Liberals (who also happen to have been white-male-fathers-husbands-capitalists) such as Mill and Tocqueville were already then also concerned with the need for democratic publicity that attends to extrastate tyrannies.

19. See, for example, Marx's "The Critique of the Gotha Program" in Tucker (1978).

20. In *The Work of Democracy*, for example, Keppel states declaratively that "Americans have yet to fully understand the general significance of the civil rights movement as a rejuvenator of American public life after the fall of Joseph McCarthy" (1995, 236). Branch 1988, Gregory 1994, and Baker 1994 write about this period as "creat[ing] a new black *publicness*," "making visible this sphere, and expanding the black public's expression," "produc[ing] a new black American publicity," "creat[ing] a new space of black freedom" and "transform[ing] the invisible deprivations of black day-to-day life into a national *scene*," "politicization of existing public arenas," and a proliferation of public arenas where power relations are contested.

21. The term *subaltern communities* has come into use to describe communities below the national level that present alternative viewpoints and ways of life to the hegemonic, or prevailing, mode.

22. Dean suggests that the "spaces and possibilities for a democratic politics of difference and solidarity can be found in a revitalized civil society, a civil society conceived not in terms of an opposition between public and private spheres but as a variety of interconnecting discursive spheres" (1996, 75). Keane 1988 discusses what he refers to as a "plurality of democratic public spheres" in which different groups participate if they want to.

23. Gregory concludes his article on the changing shape of Black public spaces in Corona Queens: "If we are to change this society, we must learn much more about the church basements, hotel meeting rooms and other public arenas where we do politics, and indeed, where politics does us" (1994, 164). See also Robbins 1993 and Baker 1994.

24. Kymlicka reminds us that "*Brown's* formula for racial justice has also been invoked against the rights of American Indians, native Hawaiians, and the rights of national minorities in international law" (1995, 59). In addition, Baker writes that "since Jamestown in 1619, notions of black separatism . . . and community empowerment have always coexisted with other orientations in the black public sphere" (1994, 26).

25. See Austin for a view of "the black public sphere [that] should be where blacks are at the center of a universe of markets and audiences that integrate white and other nonblacks into arenas controlled by blacks, rather than the other way around" (1994, 245).

26. See Austin 1994, and Dekro and Gold in Brettschneider 1996b.

27. In Fraser's article on the Thomas-Hill hearings, which analyzes the raced and gendered power dynamics in drawing the line between public and private, she writes: "it is not correct to view publicity as always and unambiguously an instrument of empowerment and emancipation. For members of subordinate groups, it will always be a matter of balancing the potential political uses of publicity against the dangers of loss of privacy" (1997, 116).

28. See Austin 1994 for a discussion of the politics of commodification *and* cooperation, alienation *and* resistance of Black consumption and commerce constituting/effected by the stereotypes with currency in the U.S. public, with a look to the role of how Black youth and gay male cultures push boundaries.

29. Brown notes that "changes in locations themselves can contribute to or inhibit the emergence of citizenship in social relations not previously considered 'political' " (1997, 15). Changes in location can also enhance or diminish the very possibilities of acts of political resistance.

30. See Brown 1997 for an analysis of ACT UP's strategy of engaging in "highly theatrical disruption of public spaces" designed to attract media—meaning mass—attention "by transgressing cultural codes of what is acceptable behavior in a public space. ACT UP *spatially* hijacks cultural attitudes (relating to AIDS, disease, welfare, and sexuality) with irony and places them into heavily coded, unfamiliar contexts" (1997, 62). Lesbian "kiss-ins," the very naming of Sex Panic, and the life as show of what is now the institution of Wigstock, all rely on such strategies. This grows out of the campier feminist demonstrations over the years (e.g., those of Karen Findley) or the public pranks staged by the

Yippees (e.g., those of Abbie Hoffman). But it is also this element of camp, or self-conscious flamboyant irony, that distinguishes many queer uses of the public space from much of civil rights *and* Black Power uses historically.

31. Black men in this period tended to work within the neighborhoods where they lived and thus more often walked to work. Jobs available for Black women, such as domestic labor for white families who lived in different neighborhoods, tended to necessitate a longer and arduous commute on public transportation.

32. See Freie 1998, for example.

33. On this use of the imaginary and the Black public sphere, see Baker 1994, and Appadurai "Disjuncture and Difference in the Global Cultural Economy," in Robbins 1993, 269–95. See also Buber 1949.

34. See also Anzaldua 1997. African, Jewish, Irish, Armenian, Kurdish, Palestinian, and other Arab Americans have often used "Africa," "Israel," "a free Ireland," "Armenia," "Kurdistan," and "Palestine" in similar fashion. These imagined homelands can inspire narrow nationalism and reactionary imaginary communities, and they can provide frameworks for radical democratic imaginations and institution building. In each case, the reality of various movements might involve some of each tendency. The imperative for thinkers and actors is to be aware of each and maximize the open, dynamic, and democratic potential.

35. Weiss and Friedman eds. 1995, Krasniewicz 1992. It was largely for this reason that Marx criticized those he termed "critical utopian socialists." Despite their useful scathing critique of society, Marx criticized movements seeking to build small egalitarian-communitarian societies within capitalist ones as not properly materially grounded. He thought these efforts avoided class agitation and were thus not revolutionary. Anarchists have a different understanding of the potential of such experiments. These are not necessarily intended as an *alternative* to other forms of political action, but as simultaneous *additions* wherein we can learn to become democratic citizens. This theme will be addressed below.

36. In their introduction to the special issue of *Public Culture* on the Black public sphere, the editors write: "the good life is not only a matter of fair shares and popular wares. The good life is an effect of a Black public sphere that does not yet fully exist. It is always living with tradition, struggling with the future" (Appadurai et al. 1994, xiv).

37. Habermas characterizes the position of the public in Kant's conception as "ambiguous." He writes: "Being, on the one hand, under tutelage and still in need of enlightenment, it yet constituted itself, on the other hand, as a public already claiming the maturity of people capable of enlightenment" (1989 105). Later he writes declaratively that today "the public sphere has to be 'made' " (1989, 201).

38. Brown writes: "Place and situation are sets of social relations that are perpetually 'becoming' " (1997,190).

39. Sanders 1998 introduces some of the debate on interpreting the long-term effects of generational politics in terms of gay/lesbian politics.

40. See, for example, Zack 1995 and Abelman and Lie 1995. In this section I will primarily focus on issues relating to the intersectional spaces between communities, though there are many spaces of intersection still in need of critical attention. Brown's 1997 case study, for example, is a specific analysis of the potential for activists in working within the spatial interactions between the home, state, and civil society, between public and private. In doing so he questions the history of Western political thought that separates these spheres and challenges contemporary theorists to move beyond static theorizings that are "out of step" (85) with the changing forms of concrete politics today.

41. West notes, for example, that "the very idea of 'not fitting in' the US discourse of positively valued whiteness and negatively debased blackness meant one was subject to exclusion and marginalization by whites and blacks. For Malcom X, in a racist society, this was a form of social death" (1993b, 148). See also: Kaye/Kantrowitz 1992, Brettschneider 1996b, Abelman and Lie 1995, Gooding-Williams 1993, and Redd's early articulation "Something Latino Was Up With Us," in Smith 1983, 52–56.

42. See, for example, Steinberg 1989, Collins 1991, Brown 1995. Analysis of such occupation is also the explicit mission of academic journals such as *Race, Gender, and Class*, and others such as *Bridges: A Journal for Jewish Feminists and Our Friends*.

43. Some excellent reading may be found in Anzaldua 1990, Anzaldua and Moraga 1982, Moraga 1983, Asian Women United of California 1989, Brettschneider 1996a, 1996b.

44. See Sandel 1984 for a critique of the "unencumbered self."

45. Habermas discusses how Liberal thinkers by the nineteenth century, such as Mill and Tocqueville, "were forced almost to deny the principle of the public sphere of civil society even as they celebrated it" (1989, 130). He writes that by this stage in the development of the bourgeois public sphere, it "became an arena of competing interests fought out in the coarser forms of violent conflict. . . . Laws . . . corresponded more or less overtly to the compromise between competing private interests" (1989, 132).

46. Gregory's article on African American communities and the intersecting public spheres in Corona, Elmhurst, and Jackson Heights, Queens, New York, discusses Black social clubs in historical context since the 1930s and how the informal networks of voluntary associations also have served as a base for anti-racist political activities since that time. He writes that contrary to the view of these groups as without substance, from the 1930s to the 1970s "Corona's voluntary associations formed a fluid, heterogeneous and, from the vantage point of white society, largely invisible network of constituencies or publics, which could be and often were, mobilized for political activities" (1994,155). See also Brown's 1997 analysis, which seeks to complicate the political/apolitical interpretation of the role of volunteers in AIDS organizations.

47. For some examples of Liberal writings on neutrality in this vein, see Kymlicka 1989, and Rawls 1988. Habermas's account provides an historical context for such a perspective in the course of Liberalism's claim to neutrality. We can see this notion situated in the bourgeois ideal of the newly created eighteenth-century

public sphere: "the constitutional state predicated on civil rights pretended, on the basis of an effective public sphere, to be an organization of public power ensuring the latter's subordination to the needs of a private sphere itself taken to be neutralized as regards power and emancipated from domination" (1989, 84). Even with Habermas's stylized rendering, however, we see that not even he claims that this Liberal norm ever matched the reality. See also MacKinnon's critique of the misogyny involved in Liberalism's claim to neutrality (1987, 15).

48. See, for example, Dworkin 1989.

49. For a Liberal view of the individual, see Gauthier 1987. See also Taylor's 1979 critique of the atomistic view.

50. See Brettschneider 1996a.

51. Weiss (1995, 172) "Feminism and Communitarianism: Comparing Critiques of Liberalism" in Weiss and Friedman 1995, 161–86.

52. Friedman 1993 is a good example of a theorist bringing together insights of communitarianism with a diversity-based perspective.

53. Communitarianism is a term applied to those from across an ideological spectrum of conservative to socialist who rely on and/or argue for the individual as socially embedded. It should not be surprising that some on the left will fall under this label with some on the right. Historically, Liberalism's invention of the separative individual was a direct counter to conservatism's group-oriented view. In contrast to Liberalism, socialists, communists, left-wing anarchists, many radical ecologists, and others on the left have historically attempted explicitly to reclaim the terrain of community and social ties without the hierarchical and xenophobic tendencies that often propel conservative perspectives.

54. See, for example, Walzer 1992.

55. See Lorde's 1984 critique for example.

56. An example of an exception is Walzer 1983—note, for example, his argument for open immigration policies.

57. For example, MacIntyre (see "Is Patriotism a Virtue" from his Lindley Lecture reprinted in Daly 1994, 307–18) says that we "must exempt at least some fundamental structures of [a] community's life from criticism" (313). We can compare this to Benhabib's conception, which envisions that "presuppositions of the moral conversation can be challenged within the conversation itself"; although she will not open the possibility that "pragmatic rules necessary to keep the moral conversation going" can be suspended entirely, she does at least always leave room for them to be bracketed so that they may be challenged. (See Benhabib 1990, 340.) In contrast to MacIntyre's conservative communitarian view, an example of an exception on this point may be found in Ackelsberg 1986, writing as a feminist in the anarchist-communitarian tradition.

58. See for example MacIntyre 1981, Habermas 1989, Barber 1984, Sandel 1982.

59. Honig 1993, Kymlicka 1989, Gutmann 1985, Rosenblum 1987, 78–81, Hirsh 1986, Young 1990, Fraser 1997, 1991, Herzog 1986.

60. See Madison's *Federalist Paper* 10 (1961).

61. Ollman 1993 provides an excellent source for how to engage in this mode of analysis. See also Part 3 Dialectics and the Dialectical method, pages 94–137

in Selsam and Martel 1984, and Buber's rendition of this dialectic in *The Way of Response* (1966) and in *I and Thou (1970)*. For a feminist example see Daly 1978.

62. What is interesting is that for Habermas 1989 (whose book was originally published in the German in 1962), the problem set up in contrast to the "public" is that of the "mass." Among the generation of writers represented by Young and Fraser, "community" appears to replace "mass" as the fear-inspiring antithesis of the stylized ideal of a "public."

Although both Young and Fraser focus critique on Habermas, by distinguishing Arendt from Habermas, Villa 1992 offers a more multilayered analysis of similarities and differences between public sphere theory and postmodernism.

63. The insistence on agonism curried from the ancient Greek concept is interesting given the historical differences between the Greek conception of the public sphere and the modern bourgeois one. In the Greek sense, Habermas notes, "[t]he conduct of the citizens was agonistic merely in the sportive competition with each other that was a mock war against the external enemy and not in dispute with his own government" (1989 52). The contemporary insistence on agonism is situated not within this ancient historical framework, however, but within the Liberal framework. In insisting on agonism in the modern sense, postmoderns tend to reify, rather than dismantle, the fundamentally competitive economic relations of capitalism. See also Honig 1993; Phelan 1994; Mouffe 1992 78; and Anzaldua 1987 for other analyses relying on or at least more supportive of an agonistic worldview. For related critiques of the inadequacy of postmodern political visions when only attending to agonism and the like, see for example Gutiérrez 1993, 66; West 1993b, 10; Hartsock 1983; and Brown 1997.

64. As an alternative, Coombe and Stoller 1994 draw a picture of an "anxious" public sphere. Their characterization of the "transnational and intercultural relationships that characterize contemporary black public spheres" in particular where "Songhay men from Niger sell goods marked with Malcolm's X in the center of the African American cultural community" in New York City's Harlem is able to hold multilayered complexities of the politics of "place" without glorifying this anxiousness, or theorizing its necessity for the Black public sphere to be a public sphere.

65. Brown 1997 devotes much of his analysis of the geographical elements of gay-formed AIDS organizations in Canada to demonstrating the point that an agonistic approach is at times significantly ineffective. The failure of ACT UP in a city such as Vancouver, for example, highlights the need for theorists to stay based in the concrete conditions activists actually face when assessing the necessity of agonistic relations for a public sphere to be a place where people can struggle toward democratic ideals.

66. For example, Dyson 1993, Morrison 1992, and hooks and West 1991 are wonderful examples of African American scholars grounding their work and activism deep within a communal context, and affirm quite clearly that community is not about homogeneity.

67. We cannot excuse such dichotomizing on the basis of theorists' tendencies to identify essences to conceptual terms and treat them idealistically (and

therefore neatly), rather than actually (and therefore more complexly or more messily). Fraser's 1997 work is itself a critique of idealist theory in the face of actually existing democracies and their problems.

68. This is Brown's critique of Mouffe, that she "has ironically essentialized the spaces" she discusses as constituting new democratic public spheres. "There is a theoretical lesson to be learned about the effects of political spaces on citizens' struggles. Poststructuralism's quest for new locations of political engagement should not blind us to changes in the ways that 'old' and 'new' locations relate to each other and in turn resituate citizenship. Here, the geographic context of these sites becomes crucial to political theory's often all too abstract spatial categories" (1997, 82, 83).

69. Habermas's 1989 account of the bourgeois public sphere is the story of a space generated in a democratic impulse and then its demise over time. See Gregory 1994 for a well-done account of the politicization of a particular Black public space and its subsequent turn to a bureaucratic space that depoliticized racial inequalities. We will need a more fluid, historically grounded definition of publics if as theorists we are to be able to see and make critical sense of such dynamics.

70. Phelan writes: "Foucault provides us with historical examples that should lead us to question the automatic liberatory power of any struggle and instead to ask for further examination and self-criticism. He does not, however, leave us with any categories or frameworks for understanding historical change. In his zeal to address unique situations in their specificity, he declines to suggest any general process or means by which current forms of power may be addressed collectively. Although he hints at the possibility of 'new forms of right' based on reciprocity and re-creation or evasion of power/knowledge regimes, he does not go far enough to provide a positive vision. For this we must turn elsewhere" (1994, 20).

71. Dean's 1996 characterization of the histories of the three communities that she studies would also benefit from a more dialectical view of history. See also Brettschneider 1996a, 1996b for a different use of history when looking at communities and social movements.

72. For a critique of the dangers of a postmodern tendency to laud decentralization and fragmentation without a sufficient historical grounding, see West 1993b, 10.

NOTES TO CHAPTER 7

1. Gibbons, "Keynote Address," *N.Y.U. Law Review* 56: 260 (1981), cited in Torricella 1991, 1096.

2. Cited in Torricella 1991, 1094.

3. See Guinier 1994, 2 for her version.

4. Cited in Guinier 1994, 16.

5. This idea seems to be the basic thrust of, for example, democratic theorist Robert Dahl's articulation of pluralism, even with the fine-tuning from the early *Who Governs* (1961) to his more recent works. See, for example, Dahl (1982 or

1989). For a critical review of some changes in early pluralism, see Manley 1983. The theoretical work is supported by the many empirical studies conducted to see if this theory continued to bear itself out in practice. See, for example, Salisbury, Heinze, and Laumann 1987; Browne 1990; Cigler and Loomis 1986.

6. For example, legal scholar and professor of law at the University of Chicago Law School Michael W. McConnell now finds that "[o]ur Constitution is therefore a multicultural constitution" (1991, 132).

7. See for example Madison's distinction among the various interests he identifies as different classes in *Federalist Paper* 10 (1961, 79); John Adams's 1776 response to his wife Abigail Adams's plea to enfranchise women in the new code of laws (Scott and Scott 1982, 55); and the Constitution of the United States.

8. Thanks to Jane Litman for providing me with her files from her activities with small feminist groups. One of the main (hand-typed) documents she gave me turned out to be, as I discovered after much research, the text of the *Consensus Education Packet* published in 1979 by the Institute for Nonviolence Education, Research, and Training. INVERT is a local Maine group started in 1977 and still active today. These documents found their way to activists and small groups around the country in the early 1980s. Thanks also to Larry Dansinger from INVERT for his assistance placing and dating the document.

9. In addition to Wheeler and Chinn 1984 and Institute for Nonviolence Education, Research, and Training 1979, see also Evans and Boyte 1992, and Weiss and Friedman 1995. Attention to such issues did not always mean that the projects were successful. Some early critiques can be found in Koedt, Levine, and Rapone 1973.

10. Iris Young, for example, also suggests empowering groups with a veto option when there are policy proposals on the table that directly affect the particular group (1989, 259). In a more detailed analysis, Robert Dahl (1956, 92) references a contemporary revival of Calhoun's notion of concurrent majorities in his exploration of the potential benefits and drawbacks of such ideas. Dahl is critical of both Calhoun and Madison with regard to the practical promise of their propositions. But he does take seriously notions such as a concurrent majority as one method to measure intensity on political issues in the context of equality and diversity.

11. Johnson Reagon 1983, Brettschneider 1996a, Martin and Mohanty 1986, and Ackelsberg in Brettschneider 1996b.

12. As an early Liberal explanation, see Hobbes's discussion in chapter xvii on the common-wealth in *Leviathan* (1968, 225–27). Here he painstakingly delineates the difference between men and bees in order to answer why men cannot cooperate and work for any common benefit like bees can. He elaborates on six distinct points of difference, each basically amounting to the fact that instead of cooperation, men's nature leads them to envy, hatred, distraction, control over others, and civil war.

13. An historical counter to what came to be the social Darwinist argument that men are by nature selfish may be seen in Kropotkin 1955.

14. Sedgewick (1990) discusses how minorities must work through assump-

tions of the fundamental links between their groups and others or the citizenry as a whole. Her analysis of the potential of majoritizing strategies for minorities adds another layer also to the exploration of alternatives to majoritarian democracy echoed in West's (1993b) suggestion that Blacks are not a "problem people" but "fellow American citizens with problems" or Gutmann's argument (in her introduction to Taylor 1994) for the inclusion of minorities in the curriculum not only because they have been excluded, but because canonical thinkers simply could not have said everything there is to say on the matter at hand. See also Mohr 1994.

15. Toba Spitzer (1996) works on such an assumption in her article "Of Haiti and Horseradish" (in Brettschneider 1996b), which is in certain respects an updated version of Marx's vision expressed in the *Communist Manifesto,* where he states that the "free development of each is a precondition for the free development of all."

16. The Talmud usually refers to the collection of teachings, discussions, and commentaries from the Babylonian rabbis that was codified during the fifth century of the Christian Common Era.

17. Phillips (1993, 146), who is generally a critic of Liberalism, even calls for a proactive rather than a laissez-faire pluralism.

18. See, for example, Phillips 1993 and Young 1990. Although Posner 1996 does not use the term consociationalism, U.S. readers will find her critique of the Canadian example interesting (in Brettschneider 1996b).

19. Lijphart 1977. See Tamir 1993, 155–58 for interesting commentary.

20. Palanithurai 1991. Thanks also to S. Vandeveer.

21. Dahl's 1956 conception of polyarchy may be viewed as the informal version of this elite form of consociationalism operating in the United States. Radical democrats would demand a far more conscious and critical implementation of any form of corporated representation.

22. Though even in our time the battle for the vote remains an issue. "Fourteen percent of Black men in the United States are currently or permanently barred from voting either because they are in prison or because they have been convicted of a felony" (Butterfield 1997, p. A12).

23. Young's analysis of group-based oppression recognizes difference within groups, but such difference seems to get lost in her discussion of concrete corporated solutions—of public funding and veto power, for example. See critique by Phillips 1993, 116, on this point.

24. See for example Brettschneider 1996a and Weeks 1990, 94.

25. Some examples on this point are Allison 1994, Brettschneider 1996a, 1996b, Brewer 1993, Cross 1991, Espiritu 1992, Grosz 1993, Omi and Winant 1994, Phillips 1995, Skerry 1995, Swain 1993, Wei 1993, and Williams 1988.

26. Phelan 1989, 170, and Ackelsberg 1996 in Brettschneider 1996b.

27. For a discussion on such issues see, for example, Berman 1992, Gates 1994, and Matsuda et al. 1993.

References

Abelmann, Nancy, and John Lie. 1995. *Blue Dreams: Korean Americans and the Los Angeles Race Riots.* Cambridge: Harvard University Press.

Ackelsberg, Martha. 1983. "Sisters or Comrades? The Politics of Friends and Families." In *Families, Politics, and Public Policy: A Feminist Dialogue on Women and the State,* edited by Irene Diamond and Mary Lyndon Shanley. New York: Longman.

———. 1984. "Women's Collaborative Activities and City Life: Politics and Policy." In *Political Women: Current Roles in State and Local Government,* edited by Janet A. Flammang. Beverly Hills, Calif.: Sage Publications.

———. 1986. "Spirituality, Community, and Politics: B'not Esh and the Feminist Reconstruction of Judaism." *Journal of Feminist Studies in Religion* 2, 2 (Fall):109–20.

———. 1988. "Communities, Resistance, and Women's Activism: Some Implications for a Democratic Polity." In *Women and the Politics of Empowerment,* edited by Ann Bookman and Sandra Morgen. Philadelphia: Temple University Press.

———. 1996. "Toward a Multicultural Politics: A Jewish Feminist Perspective." In *The Narrow Bridge: Jewish Views on Multiculturalism,* edited by Marla Brettschneider, 89–104. New Brunswick, N.J.: Rutgers University Press.

Acuña, Rodolfo. 1972. *Occupied America: The Chicano's Struggle Toward Liberation.* San Francisco: Canfield Press.

Aeurbach, Judy, Linda Blum, Vicki Smith, and Christine Williams. 1985. "Commentary on Gilligan's 'In a Different Voice.'" *Feminist Studies* 11, 1 (Spring): 149–61.

Alarcón, Norma. 1990. "The Theoretical Subject(s) of *This Bridge Called My Back* and Anglo-American Feminism." In *Making Face, Making Soul: Haciendo Caras: Creative and Critical Perspectives by Women of Color,* edited by Gloria Anzaldua, 356–69. San Francisco: Aunt Lute.

Allen, Paula Gunn. 1986. *The Sacred Hoop: Recovering the Feminine in American Indian Traditions.* Boston: Beacon Press.

Allen, Theodore. 1994. *Invention of the White Race.* New York: Verso.

Allison, Dorothy. 1994. *Skin: Talking About Sex, Class and Literature.* Ithaca, N.Y.: Firebrand Books.

Almaguer, Thomas. 1987. "Ideological Distortions in Recent Chicano Historiography: The Internal Model and Chicano Historical Interpretation." *Aztlán* 18 (Spring): 7–27.

Altbach, Phillip, and Seymour Martin Lipset, eds. 1969. *Students in Revolt.* Boston: Beacon Press.

Amar, Akhil R. 1991. "The Bill of Rights as a Constitution." *Yale Law Journal* 100, 5 (March): 1131–1210.

Anderson, Terry H. 1995. *The Movement and the Sixties.* New York: Oxford University Press.

Anzaldua, Gloria. 1987. *Borderlands/La Frontera.* San Francisco: Spinsters/Aunt Lute.

———, ed. 1990. *Making Face, Making Soul: Haciendo Caras: Creative and Critical Perspectives by Feminists of Color.* San Francisco: Aunt Lute.

Anzaldua, Gloria, and Moraga, Cherrie, eds. 1982. *This Bridge Called My Back: Writings of Radical Women of Color.* New York: Kitchen Table, Women of Color Press.

Appadurai, Arjun. 1993. "Disjuncture and Difference in the Global Cultural Economy." In *The Phantom Public Sphere,* edited by Bruce Robbins, 269–95. Minneapolis: University of Minnesota Press.

Appadurai, Arjun, Lauren Berlant, Carol A. Breckenridge, and Manthia Diawara. 1994. "Editorial Comment: On Thinking the Black Public Sphere." *Public Culture* 7, 1 (Fall): xi–xiv.

Arendt, Hannah. 1958. *The Human Condition.* Chicago: University of Chicago Press.

Arnup, Katherine. 1995. *Lesbian Parenting: Living with Pride and Prejudice.* Charlottetown, P.E.I., Canada: Gynergy Books.

Asian Women United of California, eds. 1989. *Making Waves: An Anthology of Writings by and about Asian American Women.* Boston: Beacon Press.

Asante, Molefi K. 1988. *Afrocentricity.* Trenton, N.J.: Africa World Press.

Aufderheide, Patricia, ed. 1992. *Beyond P.C.: Toward a Politics of Understanding.* Saint Paul, Minn.: Graywolf Press.

Austin, Regina. 1994. "'A Nation of Thieves': Consumption, Commerce, and the Black Public Sphere." *Public Culture* 7 ,1 (Fall): 225–48.

Baker, Houston A., Jr. 1994. "Critical Memory and the Black Public Sphere." *Public Culture* 7, 1 (Fall): 3–33.

Baldwin, James. 1963. *The Fire Next Time.* New York: Dial Press.

Barber, Benjamin R. 1984. *Strong Democracy: Participatory Politics for a New Age.* Berkeley: University of California Press.

Barringer, Herbert, Robert Gardner, and Michael Levin. 1995. *Asian and Pacific Islanders in the United States.* New York: Russell Sage Foundation.

Beck, Evelyn Torton. 1984. *Nice Jewish Girls.* Trumansburg, N.Y.: Crossing Press.

Belenky, Mary Field, Blythe McVicker Clinchy, Nancy Rule Goldberger, and Jill Matuck Tarule. 1986. *Women's Ways of Knowing.* New York: Basic Books.

Bell, Derrick. 1987. *And We Are Not Saved: The Elusive Quest for Racial Justice.* New York: Basic Books.

———. 1992. *Faces at the Bottom of the Well: The Permanence of Racism.* New York: Basic Books.

Bell, Roger. 1984. *Last among Equals: Hawaiian Statehood and American Politics.* Honolulu: University of Hawaii Press.

Benhabib, Seyla. 1987. "The Generalized and the Concrete Other: The Kohlberg-Gilligan Controversy and Feminist Theory." In *Feminism as Critique*, edited by Seyla Benhabib and Drucilla Cornell. Minneapolis: University of Minnesota Press.

———. 1990. "Afterword: Communicative Ethics and Contemporary Controversies in Practical Philosophy." In *The Communicative Ethics Controversy*, edited by Seyla Benhabib and Fred Dallmayr. Cambridge, Mass.: MIT Press.

Benhabib, Seyla, Judith Butler, Drucilla Cornell, and Nancy Fraser. 1994. *Feminist Contentions: A Philosophical Exchange*. New York: Routledge.

Benjamin, Jessica. 1988. *The Bonds of Love*. New York: Pantheon Books.

Bennet, Jane. 1998. "Ethics and Enchantment." Paper presented to the Feminist Political Theory Conference, Los Angeles, March.

Bentley, A. F. 1908. *The Process of Government*. Evanston: Principia Press of Illinois.

Berlin, Isaiah. 1969. *Four Essays on Liberty*. New York: Oxford University Press.

Berns, Walter. 1992. "On Madison and Majoritarianism: A Response to Professor Amar." *Harvard Journal of Law and Public Policy* 15, 1 (Winter): 113–18.

Bernstein, Richard. 1994. *Dictatorship of Virtue: Multiculturalism, Diversity and the American Future*. New York: Knopf.

Berman, Marshall. 1989. "Why Modernism Still Matters." *Tikkun* 4, 1: 11.

Berman, Paul, ed. 1992. *Debating P.C.: The Controversy over Political Correctness on College Campuses*. New York: Laurell/Dell Publishers.

Bethel, Lorraine. 1979. "What Chou Mean WE, White Girl?" In *Conditions Five: The Black Women's Issue*, edited by Lorraine Bethel and Barbara Smith, 86–92. Brooklyn: Conditions.

Beuf, Ann H. 1977. *Red Children in White America*. Philadelphia: University of Pennsylvania Press.

Bhabha, Homi. 1990. "The Third Space: Interview with Homi Bhabha." In *Identity: Community, Culture, Difference*, edited by Jonathan Rutherford. London: Lawrence and Wishart.

Bickford, Susan. 1996. *The Dissonance of Democracy: Listening, Conflict, and Citizenship*. Ithaca: Cornell University Press.

Bloomfield, Richard J., ed. 1985. *Puerto Rico: The Search for a National Policy*. Boulder, Colo.: Westview Press.

Boswell, John. 1994. *Same Sex Unions in Premodern Europe*. New York: Villard Books.

Boxer, Marilyn J, and Jean H. Quataert. 1987. *Connecting Spheres: Women in the Western World, 1500 to the Present*. New York: Oxford University Press.

Boyarin, Jonathan, and Daniel Boyarin, eds. 1997. *Jews and Other Differences: The New Jewish Cultural Studies*. Minneapolis: University of Minnesota Press.

Branch, Taylor. 1988. *Parting the Waters: America in the King Years 1954–63*. New York: Simon and Schuster.

Brettschneider, Marla. 1996a. *Cornerstones of Peace: Jewish Identity Politics and Democratic Theory*. New Brunswick, N.J.: Rutgers University Press.

———, ed. 1996b. *The Narrow Bridge: Jewish Views on Multiculturalism*. New Brunswick, N.J.: Rutgers University Press.

————. 1997. "Jewish Feminist Dialectics in the Poetry of Marcia Falk and Melanie Kaye/Kantrowitz." Paper presented for the Society for the Study of Women in Philosophy at the American Philosophical Association Annual Meeting, Philadelphia, December.

————. 2001. "Racing Queer Studies and Queering Race Studies in a Jewish Context." In *Traversing Racialized Landscapes*, edited by Bat-Ami Bar On and Lisa Tessman. Walnut Creek, Calif.: Altamira Press. Forthcoming.

Brewer, Rose. 1993. *Theorizing Black Feminisms*. New York: Routledge, Chapman and Hall.

Brobeck, Stephen. 1990. *The Modern Consumer Movement*. Boston: G.K. Hall and Co.

Brodkin, Karen. 1998. *How Jews Became White Folks and What That Says About Race in America*. New Brunswick, N.J.: Rutgers University Press.

Brown, Michael P. 1997. *Replacing Citizenship: AIDS Activism & Radical Democracy*. New York: Guilford Press.

Brown, Wendy. 1995. *States of Injury: Power and Freedom in Late Modernity*. Princeton: Princeton University Press.

Browne, W. P. 1990. "Organized Interests and Their Issue Niches: Search for Pluralism in a Policy Domain." *Journal of Politics* 52, 2 (May): 477–509.

Buber, Martin. 1949. *Paths in Utopia*. New York: Macmillan Publishing.

————. 1966. *The Way of Response*. New York: Schocken Books.

————. 1970. *I and Thou*. New York: Scribner.

Buker, Eloise. 1999. *Talking Feminist Politics: Conversations on Law, Science, and the Postmodern*. Lanham, Md.: Rowman & Littlefield.

Burke, Edmund. 1969. *Reflections on the Revolution in France*. New York: Penguin.

Butler, Judith. 1990. *Gender Trouble: Feminism and the Subversion of Identity*. New York: Routledge, Chapman and Hall.

Butler, Judith, and Joan W. Scott, eds. 1992. *Feminists Theorize the Political*. New York: Routledge.

Butterfield, Fox. 1997. "Many Black Men Barred from Voting." *New York Times*, 30 January, A12.

Calhoun, Craig. 1997. *Habermas and the Public Sphere*. Cambridge, Mass.: MIT Press.

Calhoun, John C. 1943. *A Disquisition on Government*. New York: P. Smith.

Califia, Pat. 1997. *Sex Changes: The Politics of Transgenderism*. San Francisco: Cleis Press.

Cannon, Katie. 1988. *Black Womanist Ethics*. Atlanta: Scholars Press.

Carson, Clayborne. 1981. *In Struggle: SNCC and the Black Awakening of the 1960s*. Cambridge: Harvard University Press.

Caute, David. 1978. *The Great Fear: The Anti-Communist Purge under Truman and Eisenhower*. New York: Simon and Schuster.

Chafe, William. 1977. *Women and Equality: Changing Patterns in American Culture*. New York: Oxford University Press.

Choderow, Nancy. 1978. *The Reproduction of Mothering: Psychoanalysis and the Sociology of Gender*. Berkeley and Los Angeles: University of California Press.

Christian, Barbara. 1990. "The Race for Theory." In *Making Face Making Soul*, edited by Gloria Anzaldua. San Francisco: Aunt Lute.

Cigler, Allan J., and Burdett A. Loomis. 1983. *Interest Group Politics*. Washington, D.C.: Congressional Quarterly.

————. 1986. *Interest Group Politics*. Washington, D.C.: Congressional Quarterly.

Collins, Patricia Hill. 1990. *Black Feminist Thought*. New York: Routledge.

————. 1991. *Black Feminist Thought: Knowledge, Consciousness, and the Politics of Empowerment*. New York: Routledge, Chapman and Hall.

Collins, Patricia Hill, Lionel A. Maldonado, Dana Y. Takagi, Barrie Thorne, Lynn Weber, and Howard Winant. 1995. "Symposium: On West and Fenstermaker's 'Doing Difference.' " *Gender and Society* 9, 4 (August): 491–506.

Combahee River Collective. 1983. "The Combahee River Collective Statement." In *Home Girls: A Black Feminist Anthology*, edited by Barbara Smith, 272–82. New York: Kitchen Table: Women of Color Press.

Cordasco, Francesco, and Eugene Bucchioni. 1973. *The Puerto Rican Experience: A Sociological Sourcebook*. Totowa, N.J.: Rowman and Littlefield.

Coombe, Rosemary, and Paul Stoller. 1994. "X Marks the Spot: The Ambiguities of African Trading in the Commerce of the Black Public Sphere." *Public Culture* 7, 1 (Fall): 249–74.

Cordova, Teresa, et al., eds. 1983. *Chicana Voices: Intersections of Class, Race, and Gender*. Albuquerque: University of New Mexico Press.

Coupland, Douglas. 1991. *Generation X: Tales for an Accelerated Culture*. New York: St. Martin's Press.

Cross, William E., Jr. 1991. *Shades of Black: Diversity in African-American Identity*. Philadelphia: Temple University Press.

Crow Dog, Mary. 1991. *Lakota Woman*. New York: HarperCollins.

Cruikshank, Margaret. 1992. *The Gay and Lesbian Liberation Movement*. New York: Routledge.

Curtis, L. Perry. 1971. *Apes and Angels: The Irishman in Victorian Caricature*. Washington, D.C.: Smithsonian Institution.

Dahl, Robert. 1956. *A Preface to Democratic Theory*. Chicago: University of Chicago Press.

————. 1961. *Who Governs?* New Haven: Yale University Press.

————. 1982. *Dilemmas of Pluralist Democracy*. New Haven: Yale University Press.

————. 1989. *Democracy and its Critics*. New Haven: Yale University Press.

Daly, Markate, ed. 1994. *Communitarianism: A New Public Ethics*. Belmont, Calif.: Wadsworth.

Daly, Mary. 1978. *Gyn/Ecology: The Metaethics of Radical Feminism*. Boston: Beacon Press.

Davis, Angela. 1981. *Women, Race, and Class*. New York: Random House.

Dean, Jodi. 1996. *Solidarity of Strangers: Feminism after Identity Politics*. Berkeley: University of California Press.

Dekro, Jeffrey. 1996. "Facilitating Multicultural Progress: Community Economic Development and the American Jewish Community." In *The Narrow*

Bridge: Jewish Views on Multiculturalism, edited by Marla Brettschneider, 247–266. New Brunswick, N.J.: Rutgers University Press.

Del Castillo, Adelaida R. 1980. "Mexican Women in Organization." In *Mexican Women in the United States: Struggles Past and Present*, edited by Magdalena Mora and Adelaida R. Del Castillo, 7–16. Los Angeles: Chicano Studies Research Center Publications, University of California.

Delgado, Richard, and Jean Stefancic, eds. 1997. *Critical White Studies: Looking Behind the Mirror*. Philadelphia: Temple University Press.

Deutsch, Sarah. 1987. *No Separate Refuge: Culture, Class, and Gender on an Anglo-Hispanic Frontier in the American Southwest, 1880–1940*. New York: Oxford University Press.

Dietz, Mary. 1985. "Citizenship with a Feminist Face: The Problem with Maternal Thinking." *Political Theory* 13, 1 (February): 19–37.

diLeonardo, Micaela. 1984. *The Varieties of Ethnic Experience: Kinship, Class and Gender among California Italian-Americans*. Ithaca, N.Y.: Cornell University Press.

Disch, Lisa Jane. 1994. *Hannah Arendt and the Limits of Philosophy*. Ithaca, N.Y.: Cornell University Press.

Di Stefano, Christine. 1990. "Dilemmas of Difference: Feminism, Modernity, and Postmodernism." In *Feminism/Postmodernism*, edited by Linda Nicholson, 63–82. New York: Routledge.

Duberman, Martin. 1993. *Stonewall*. New York: Dutton.

Du Bois, W.E.B. 1903. *The Souls of Black Folk*. Chicago: McClurg.

———. 1935. *Black Reconstruction: An Essay Toward a History of the Part Which Black Folk Played in the Attempt to Reconstruct Democracy in America, 1860–1880*. New York: Harcourt, Brace, and Company.

Dworkin, Ronald. 1989. "Liberal Community." *California Law Review* 77: 479–504.

Dyson, Michael Eric. 1993. *Reflecting Black: African American Cultural Criticism*. Minneapolis: University of Minnesota Press.

———. 1995. *Making Malcolm: The Myth and Meaning of Malcolm X*. New York: Oxford University Press.

Edgerton, Robert B. 1964. "Pokot Intersexuality: An East African Example of the Resolution of Sexual Incongruity." *American Anthropologist* 66, 1: 1288–99.

Edwards, J. Michelle. 1990. "All-Women's Musical Communities: Fostering Creativity and Leadership." In *Bridges of Power: Women's Multicultural Alliances*, edited by Lisa Albrecht and Rose M. Brewer. Philadelphia and Santa Cruz: New Society Publishers, in cooperation with the National Women's Studies Association.

Eisenstein, Hester. 1996. "Equalizing Privacy and Specifying Equality." In *Revisioning the Political: Feminist Reconstructions of Traditional Concepts in Western Political Theory*, edited by Nancy J. Hirschmann and Christine Di Stefano, 181–92. Boulder, Colo.: Westview Press.

Eisgruber, Christopher L. 1997. "Democracy, Majoritarianism, and Racial Equality: A Response to Professor Karlan." *Vanderbilt Law Review* (March 1): 347–60.

Ellison, Ralph. 1947. *Invisible Man*. New York: Random House.

Elshtain, Jean Bethke. 1981. *Public Man, Private Woman: Women in Social and Political Thought*. Princeton: Princeton University Press.

Espiritu, Yen Le. 1992. *Asian American Panethnicity: Bridging Institutions and Identities*. Philadelphia: Temple University Press.

Evans, Sara M., and Harry C. Boyte. 1992. *Free Spaces: The Sources of Democratic Change in America*. 2d ed. Chicago: University of Chicago Press.

Evans, Sarah. 1979. *Personal Politics: The Roots of Women's Liberation in the Civil Rights Movement and the New Left*. New York: Alfred A. Knopf.

Eynon, Bret. 1989. "Community in Motion: The Free Speech Movement, Civil Rights and the Roots of the New Left." *Oral History Review* (Spring): 39–69.

Faderman, Lillian. 1991. *Odd Girls and Twilight Lovers: A History of Lesbian Life in Twentieth Century America*. New York: Penguin.

Falk, Marcia. 1996. *Book of Blessings*. San Francisco: Harper San Francisco.

Fanon, Franz. 1967. *Black Skin, White Masks*. New York: Grove Press.

Fauré, Christine. 1991. *Democracy without Women: Feminism and the Rise of Liberal Individualism in France*. Translated by Claudia Gorbman and John Berks. Bloomington: Indiana University Press.

Fausto-Sterling, Ann. 1993. "The Five Sexes: Why Male and Female Are Not Enough." *The Sciences* 33 (March/April): 20–25.

Feinberg, Leslie. 1998. *Transliberation: Beyond Pink or Blue*. Boston: Beacon Press.

Feldman, Lawrence. 1976. *Consumer Protection*. New York: West.

Feldman, Stephen M. 1997. *Please Don't Wish Me a Merry Christmas: A Critical History of the Separation of Church and State*. New York and London: New York University Press.

Ferguson, Ann, Jaquelyn N. Zita, and Kathryn Pyne Addelson. 1982. "On 'Compulsory Heterosexuality and Lesbian Existence': Defining the Issues." In *Feminist Theory: A Critique of Ideology*, edited by Nannerl O. Keohane, Michelle Z. Rosaldo, and Barbara C. Gelpi. Chicago: University of Chicago Press.

Fisher, Sue. 1993. "Gender, Power, Resistance: Is Care the Remedy?" In *Negotiating at the Margins: The Gendered Discourse of Power and Resistance*, edited by Sue Fisher and Kathy Davis, 87–122. New Brunswick, N.J.: Rutgers University Press.

Fisher, Sue, and Kathy Davis. 1993. *Negotiating at the Margins: The Gendered Discourses of Power and Resistance*. New Brunswick, N.J.: Rutgers University Press.

Flanagan, Owen J. 1982. "Virtue, Sex and Gender: Some Philosophical Reflections on the Moral Psychology Debate." *Ethics* 92, 3 (April): 499–512.

Flax, Jane. 1993. *Disputed Subjects*. New York: Routledge, Chapman and Hall.

Frankenberg, Ruth. 1993. *White Women, Race Matters: The Social Construction of Whiteness*. Minneapolis: University of Minnesota Press.

Fraser, Nancy. 1986. "Toward a Discourse Ethic of Solidarity." *Praxis International* 5, 4 (January): 425–29.

———. 1989. *Unruly Practices: Power, Discourse and Gender in Contemporary Social Theory*. Minneapolis: University of Minnesota Press.

———. 1997. *Justice Interruptus: Critical Reflections on the 'Postsocialist' Condition*. New York: Routledge.

Freeman, Jo. 1975. *The Politics of Women's Liberation*. New York: Longman.

Friedan, Betty. 1963. *The Feminine Mystique*. New York: Norton.

Friedman, Marilyn. 1993. *What Are Friends For? Feminist Perspectives on Personal Relationships and Moral Theory*. Ithaca, N.Y.: Cornell University Press.

Freie, John F. 1998. *Counterfeit Community: The Exploitation of Our Longings for Connectedness*. Lanham, Md: Rowman and Littlefield.

Frye, Marilyn. 1988. "Lesbian 'Sex.' " *Sinister Wisdom* (Summer/Fall): 35.

Fuss, Diana. 1989. *Essentially Speaking: Feminism, Nature, and Difference*. New York: Routledge.

Gates, Henry Louis. 1994. *Speaking of Race, Speaking of Sex: Hate Speech, Civil Rights and Civil Liberties*. New York: New York University Press.

Gauthier, David. 1986. *Morals by Agreement*. New York: Oxford University Press.

Gesensway, Deborah, and Mindy Roseman. 1987. *Beyond Words: Images from America's Concentration Camps*. Ithaca, N.Y.: Cornell University Press.

Gilkes, Townsend. 1988. "Building in Many Places: Multiple Commitments and Ideologies in Black Women's Community Work." In *Women and the Politics of Empowerment*, edited by Ann Bookman and Sandra Morgen. Philadelphia: Temple University Press.

Gilligan, Carol. 1982. *In a Different Voice: Psychological Theory and Women's Development*. Cambridge: Harvard University Press.

Glazer, Nathan. 1997. *We Are All Multiculturalists Now*. Cambridge: Harvard University Press.

Gold, Nora. 1996. "Voices from the Field: Multiculturalism as Experienced in Jewish Social Service Agencies." In *The Narrow Bridge: Jewish Views on Multiculturalism*, edited by Marla Brettschneider, 236–46. New Brunswick, N.J.: Rutgers University Press.

Gooding-Williams, Robert, ed. 1993. *Reading Rodney King/Reading Urban Uprising*. New York: Routledge.

Goodman, Paul. 1956. *Growing Up Absurd*. New York: Vintage Books.

Gould, Carol. 1988. *Rethinking Democracy: Freedom and Social Cooperation in Politics, Economy and Society*. Cambridge, England: Cambridge University Press.

Gould, Rebecca. 1995. "Lesbian Identity Development in Young Jewish Women." Bachelor's thesis: Hampshire College Division III.

Grant, Judith. 1993. *Fundamental Feminism: Contesting the Core Concepts of Feminist Theory*. New York: Routledge, Chapman and Hall.

Green, Arthur. 1995. *Judaism for the Post-Modern Era*. Cincinnati: Hebrew Union College–Jewish Institute of Religion.

Green, Phillip. 1992. "A Few Kind Words for Liberalism." *The Nation* (September 28): 309 ff.

Green, T. H. 1986. *Lectures on the Principles of Political Obligation*. New York: Cambridge University Press.

Greenberg, Jessica. 1998. "Placing Jewish Women into the Intersectionality of Race, Class, and Gender," edited by Marla Brettschneider. *Race, Gender, and Class: American Jewish Perspectives* 6, 4: 41–60.

Gregory, Steven. 1994. "Race, Identity and Political Activism: The Shifting Contours of the African American Public Sphere." *Public Culture* 7, 1 (Fall): 147–64.

Grimshaw, Jean. 1986. *Philosophy and Feminist Thinking.* Minneapolis: University of Minnesota Press.

Grosz, Elizabeth. 1993. *Feminism and the Politics of Difference.* Boulder, Colo.: Westview Press.

Guillaumin, Colette. 1995. *Racism, Sexism, Power, and Ideology.* New York: Routledge.

Guinier, Lani. 1994. *The Tyranny of the Majority.* New York: Free Press.

Gutiérrez, Ramón. 1993. "Community, Patriarchy and Individualism: The Politics of Chicano History and the Dream of Equality." *American Quarterly* 45, 1 (March): 44–72.

Gutman, Herbert George. 1976. *The Black Family in Slavery and Freedom: 1750–1925.* New York: Vintage Books.

Gutmann, Amy. 1985. "Communitarian Critics of Liberalism." *Philosophy and Public Affairs* 14, 3: 308–22.

———. 1994. "Introduction." In *Multiculturalism and "The Politics of Recognition,"* edited by Amy Gutman, 3–24. Princeton, N. J.: Princeton University Press.

Habermas, Jurgen. 1989. *The Structural Transformation of the Public Sphere: An Inquiry into a Category of Bourgeois Society.* Cambridge, Mass.: MIT Press.

Hall, Stuart. 1990. "Cultural Identity and Diaspora." In *Identity: Community, Culture, Difference,* edited by Jonathan Rutherford, 222–37. London: Lawrence and Wishart.

Hansberry, Lorraine. 1959. *A Raisin in the Sun.* New York: Random House.

Haraway, Donna. 1991. *Simians, Cyborgs and Women: The Reinvention of Nature.* New York: Routledge, Chapman and Hall.

Harding, Sandra. 1986. *The Science Question in Feminism.* Ithaca, N.Y.: Cornell University Press.

———. 1991. *Whose Science? Whose Knowledge? Thinking from Women's Lives.* Ithaca, N.Y.: Cornell University Press.

Hareven, Tamara. 1982. *Family Time and Industrial Time. The Relationship between the Family and Work in a New England Industrial Community.* Cambridge, Mass.: University Press of America.

Hartsock, Nancy. 1983. *Money, Sex, and Power: Toward a Feminist Historical Materialism.* New York: Longman Press.

———. 1990. "Foucault on Power: A Theory for Women?" In *Feminism/Postmodernism,* edited by Linda Nicholson. New York: Routledge.

Harzig, Christiane. 1989. "The Role of German Women in the German-American Working-Class Movement in Late Nineteenth-Century New York." *Journal of American Ethnic History* 8 (Spring): 87–107.

Hatamiya, Leslie T. 1993. *Righting a Wrong: Japanese Americans and the Passage of the Civil Liberties Act of 1988.* Stanford: Stanford University Press.

Hawes, Joseph M. 1991. *The Children's Rights Movement: A History of Advocacy and Protection.* Boston: Twayne.

Hawkesworth, Mary. 1997. "Theorizing Equality Work: Reflections on the Institutional Foundations for Democratic Citizenship." Paper presented at the American Political Science Association Meeting, Washington, D.C., August 28–31. Copyright by the APSA.

Held, David. 1996. *Models of Democracy.* Cambridge, England: Polity.

Hertzberg, Arthur. 1968. *The French Enlightenment and the Jews: The Origins of Modern Anti-Semitism.* New York: Schocken Books.

———. 1989. *The Jews in America: Four Centuries of an Uneasy Encounter.* New York: Simon and Schuster.

Herzog, Don. 1986. "Some Questions for Republicans." *Political Theory* 14, 3 (August): 473–93.

Heshel, Susannah. 1983. *On Being a Jewish Feminist.* New York: Schocken Books.

Hewitt, Nancy. 1992. "Compounding Differences." *Feminist Studies* 18, 2 (Summer): 313–26.

Hine, Darlene Clark, Elsa Barkley Brown, and Rosalyn Terborg-Penn, eds. 1993. *Black Women in America: An Historical Encyclopedia.* Bloomington: Indiana University Press.

Hirsch, H. N. 1986. "The Threnody of Liberalism: Constitutional Liberty and the Renewal of Community." *Political Theory* 14: 423–49.

Hirschman, Albert O. 1977. *The Passions and the Interests.* Princeton: Princeton University Press.

Hirschmann, Nancy J. 1992. *Rethinking Obligation: A Feminist Method for Political Theory.* Ithaca, N.Y.: Cornell University Press.

Hirschmann, Nancy J. 1996. "Revisioning Freedom: Relationship, Context, and the Politics of Empowerment." In *Revisioning the Political: Feminist Reconstructions of Traditional Concepts in Western Political Theory,* edited by Nancy J. Hirschmann and Christine Di Stefano, 51–74. Boulder, Colo.: Westview Press.

Hirschmann, Nancy J., and Christine Di Stefano, eds. 1996. *Revisioning the Political: Feminist Reconstructions of Traditional Concepts in Western Political Theory.* Boulder, Colo.: Westview Press.

Hitler, Adolf. 1971. *Mein Kampf.* Translated by Ralph Manheim. Boston: Houghton Mifflin.

Hobbes, Thomas. 1968. *Leviathan.* Edited with an introduction by C. B. Macpherson. New York: Penguin.

Holmes, Stephen. 1990. "The Secret History of Self-Interest." In *Beyond Self-Interest,* edited by Jane Mansbridge, 267–86. Chicago: University of Chicago Press.

Hong Kingston, Maxine. 1976. *The Woman Warrior: Memoirs of a Girlhood among the Ghosts.* New York: Knopf.

Honig, Bonnie. 1993. *Political Theory and the Displacement of Politics.* Ithaca, N.Y.: Cornell University Press.

Honneth, Axel. 1992. "Integrity and Disrespect: Principles of a Conception of a Morality Based on the Theory of Recognition." *Political Theory* 20, 2 (May): 187–201.

————. 1996. *The Struggle for Recognition: The Moral Grammar of Social Conflicts.* Translated by Joel Anderson. Cambridge: MIT Press.

hooks, bell. 1981. *Ain't I a Woman: Black Women and Feminism.* Boston: South End Press.

————. 1984. *Feminist Theory: From Margin to Center.* Boston: South End Press.

————. 1989. *Talking Back: Thinking Feminist, Thinking Black.* Boston: South End Press.

————. 1990. *Yearning: Race, Gender, and Cultural Politics.* Boston: South End Press.

————. 1992. *Black Looks: Race and Representation.* Boston: South End Press.

hooks, bell, and Cornel West. 1991. *Breaking Bread: Insurgent Black Intellectual Life.* Boston: South End Press.

Horne, Gerald. 1986. *Black and Red: W.E.B. DuBois and the Afro-American Response to the Cold War, 1944–1963.* Albany: State University of New York Press.

————. 1995. *Fire This Time: The Watts Uprising and the 1960s.* Charlottesville: University Press of Virginia.

Hoover, J. Edgar. 1958. *Masters of Deceit: The Story of Communism in America and How to Fight it.* New York: Holt.

Hoxie, Frederick E. 1984. *A Final Promise: The Campaign to Assimilate the Indians, 1880–1920.* Cambridge: Cambridge University Press.

Hyman, Paula. 1980. "Immigrant Women and Consumer Protest: The New York City Kosher Meat Boycott of 1902." *American Jewish History* 71: 91–105.

Institute for Nonviolence Education, Research, and Training (INVERT). 1979. "Consensus Education Packet." Newport, Maine: Institute for Nonviolence Education, Research, and Training.

Jacobs, Paul, and Saul Landau. 1966. *The New Radicals: A Report with Documents.* New York: Vantage Books.

Jaimes, M. Annette, ed. 1992. *The State of Native America: Genocide, Colonization and Resistance.* Boston: South End Press.

James, Susan. 1992. "The Good-Enough Citizen: Female Citizenship and Independence" In *Beyond Equality and Difference: Citizenship, Feminist Politics and Female Subjectivity,* edited by Gisela Bock and Susan James. London and New York: Routledge.

Johnson Reagon, Berenice. 1983. "Coalition Politics: Turning the Century." In *Home Girls: A Black Feminist Anthology,* edited by Barbara Smith, 356–69. New York: Kitchen Table: Women of Color Press.

Jordan, June. 1994. *Technical Difficulties: African-American Notes on the State of the Union.* New York: Vintage Books.

Joseph, Gloria I., and Jill Lewis. 1981. *Common Differences: Conflicts in Black and White Feminist Perspectives.* New York: Anchor Books.

Journalist, M. 1970. *A Year Is Eight Months.* Garden City, N.Y.: Doubleday.

Kaufman-Osborn, Timothy. 1997. *Creatures of Prometheus: Gender and the Politics of Technology.* Lanham, Md.: Rowman & Littlefield.

Kaye/Kantrowitz, Melanie. 1992. *The Issue Is Power: Essays on Women, Jews, Violence and Resistance.* San Francisco: Aunt Lute.

Kaye/Kantrowitz, Melanie, and Irena Klepfisz. 1986. *The Tribe of Dina*. Montpelier, Vt.: Sinister Wisdom.

Keane, John. 1988. *Democracy and Civil Society*. New York: Verso.

Kelley, Robin. 1994. *Race Rebels: Culture, Politics, and the Black Working Class*. New York: Free Press.

Kepnes, Steven, ed. 1996. *Interpreting Judaism in a Postmodern Age*. New York: New York University Press.

Keppel, Ben. 1995. *The Work of Democracy: Ralph Bunche, Kenneth B. Clark, Lorraine Hansberry, and the Cultural Politics of Race*. Cambridge: Harvard University Press.

Kifner, John. 1998. "Protesters Blame Police for 'Chaos' at Rally." *New York Times*, 21 October, A27 ff.

Koedt, Anne, Ellen Levine, and Anita Rapone, eds. 1973. *Radical Feminism*. New York: Quadrangle Books.

Krasniewicz, Louise. 1992. *Nuclear Summer: The Clash of Communities at the Seneca Women's Peace Encampment*. Ithaca, N.Y.: Cornell University Press.

Kraver, Jeraldine. 1999. "Restocking the Melting Pot: Americanization as Cultural Imperialism," edited by Marla Brettschneider. *Race, Gender, and Class: American Jewish Perspectives* 6, 4: 61–75.

Kristol, Irving. 1983. *Reflections of a Neoconservative: Looking Back, Looking Ahead*. New York: Basic Books.

Kropotkin, Petr. 1955. *Mutual Aid: A Factor of Evolution*. Boston: Extending Horizon.

Kushner, Tony. 1993a. *Angels in America: A Gay Fantasia on National Themes (Part I: Millenium Approaches)*. New York: Theatre Communications Group.

———. 1993b. *Angels in America: A Gay Fantasia on National Themes (Part II: Perestroika)*. New York: Theatre Communications Group.

Kymlicka, Will. 1989. "Liberal Individualism and Liberal Neutrality." *Ethics* 99: 883–905.

———. 1995. *Multicultural Citizenship: A Liberal Theory of Minority Rights*. Oxford, England: Oxford University Press.

Landes, Joan. 1980. *Women and the Public Space in the Age of the French Revolution*. Ithaca, N.Y.: Cornell University Press.

Lange, Linda. 1998. "Burnt Offerings to Rationality: A Feminist Reading of the Construction of Indigenous Peoples in Enrique Dusserl's Theory of Modernity." Keynote address at the IAPH: 8th Symposium of the International Association of Women Philosophers/Lessons from the Gynaeceum: Women Philosophizing—Past, Present, Future. Boston, August 6–10.

Laswell, Harold D. 1936. *Politics: Who Gets What, When, How?* New York: McGraw Hill.

Lerner, Gerda. 1997. *Why History Matters: Life and Thought*. New York and Oxford: Oxford University Press.

Levitt, Laura. 1997. *Jews and Feminism: The Ambivalent Search for Home*. New York: Routledge.

Lichter, S. Robert, and Stanley Rothman. 1982. *Roots of Radicalism: Jews, Christians and the New Left.* New York: Oxford University Press.

Lijphart, Arend. 1977. *Democracy in Plural Societies.* New Haven: Yale University Press.

Lorde, Audre. 1984. *Sister Outsider: Essays and Speeches.* Trumansburg, N.Y.: Crossing Press.

Lugones, Maria C., and Elizabeth Spelman. 1983. "Have We Got a Theory for You! Feminist Theory, Cultural Imperialism and the Demand for 'the Woman's Voice.' " *Women's Studies International Forum* 6, 6 (November/December): 573–81.

Lukes, Steven, ed. 1986. *Power.* New York: New York University Press.

MacIntyre, Alasdair. 1981. *After Virtue.* Notre Dame: University of Notre Dame Press.

———. 1994. "Is Patriotism a Virtue." In *Communitarianism: A New Public Ethics,* edited by Markate Daly, 307–18. Belmont, Calif.: Wadsworth.

MacKinnon, Catherine. 1987. *Feminism Unmodified: Discourses on Life and Law.* Cambridge: Harvard University Press.

Macpherson, C. B. 1962. *The Political Theory of Possessive Individualism: Hobbes to Locke.* New York: Oxford University Press.

Madison, James, Alexander Hamilton, and John Jay. 1961. *The Federalist Papers.* New York: Penguin.

Manley, John F. 1983. "Neo-Pluralism: A Class Analysis of Pluralism I and Pluralism II." *American Political Science Review* 77, 2 (June): 368–83.

Mansbridge, Jane, ed. 1990. *Beyond Self-Interest.* Chicago: University of Chicago Press.

Marcus, Eric. 1992. *Making History: The Struggle for Gay and Lesbian Equal Rights, 1945–1990: An Oral History.* New York: HarperCollins.

Marso, Lori Jo. 1999. *(Un)Manly Citizens: Jean-Jacques Rousseau's and Germaine de Staël's Subversive Women.* Baltimore, Md.: Johns Hopkins University Press.

Martin, Biddy, and Chanrda Talpade Mohanty. 1986. "Feminist Politics: What's Home Got to Do With It?" In *Feminist Studies/Critical Studies,* edited by Teresa De Lauretis. Bloomington: University of Indiana Press.

Martin, Jane Roland. 1994. "Methodological Essentialism, False Difference, and Other Dangerous Traps." *Signs* (Spring): 630–56.

Marx, Karl. 1975. *Early Writings.* New York: Vintage Books.

Massumi, Brian. 1997. "Which Came First? The Individual or Society? Which Is the Chicken and Which Is the Egg? The Political Economy of Belonging and the Logic of Relation." In *Anybody,* edited by Cynthia C. Davidson, 175–88. Cambridge, Mass.: MIT Press.

Matsuda, Mari, Charles R. Lawrence III, Richard Delgado, and Kimberle Williams Crenshaw. 1993. *Words That Wound: Critical Race Theory, Assaultive Speech, and the First Amendment.* Boulder, Colo.: Westview Press.

May, Larry. 1987. *The Morality of Groups: Collective Responsibility, Group-Based Harm and Corporate Rights.* Notre Dame: University of Notre Dame Press.

McAllister, Pam. 1988. *You Can't Kill the Spirit.* Philadelphia and Santa Cruz, Calif.: New Society Publishers.

McClaren, Peter. 1997. *Revolutionary Multiculturalism: Pedagogies of Dissent for the New Millennium.* Boulder, Colo.: Westview Press.

McConnell, Michael W. 1991. "Multiculturalism, Majoritarianism, and Educational Choice: What Does our Constitutional Tradition Have to Say?" *University of Chicago Legal Forum* 123–51.

McDonnell, Evelyn. 1994. "Queer Punk Meets Womyn's Music." *Ms.* (November/December):78–82.

Michaels, Walter Benn. 1995. *Our America: Nativism, Modernism, and Pluralism.* Durham, N.C.: Duke University Press.

Milkman, Ruth. 1985. *Women, Work, and Protest: A Century of U.S. Women's Labor History.* London and New York: Routledge.

Mill, John Stuart. 1984. *On Liberty.* New York: Penguin.

Miller, Douglas T., and Marion Nowak. 1977. *The Fifties: The Way We Really Were.* Garden City, N.Y.: Doubleday.

Minow, Martha. 1990. *Making All the Difference: Inclusion, Exclusion, and American Law.* Cambridge: Harvard University Press.

Mohr, Richard D. 1994. *A More Perfect Union: Why Straight America Must Stand Up for Gay Rights.* Boston: Beacon Press.

Montefiore, Alan, ed. 1975. *Neutrality and Impartiality, the University and Political Commitment.* New York: Cambridge University Press.

Moraga, Cherrie. 1983. *Loving in the War Years: Lo que nunca paso por sus labios.* Boston: South End Press.

Morgan, Edward. 1991. *The 60s Experience: Hard Lessons about Modern America.* Philadelphia: Temple University Press.

Morrison, Toni. 1992. *Rac-ing Justice, En-Gender-ing Power.* New York: Pantheon.

Mouffe, Chantalle. 1992. "Feminism, Citizenship and Radical Democratic Politics." In *Feminists Theorize the Political,* edited by Judith Butler and Joan Scott. New York and London: Routledge.

Mullings, Leith. 1997. *On Our Own Terms: Race, Class, and Gender in the Lives of African American Women.* New York: Routledge.

Nader, Ralph. 1965. *Unsafe at Any Speed.* New York: Grosman.

Nagata, Donna K. 1993. *Legacy of Injustice: Exploring the Cross-Generational Impact of the Japanese American Internment.* New York: Plenum Press.

Narayan, Uma. 1997a. *Dislocating Cultures: Identities, Traditions, and Third World Feminism.* New York and London: Routledge.

———. 1997b. "Toward a Feminist Vision of Citizenship: Rethinking Implications of Dignity, Political Participation, and Nationality." In *Reconstructing Political Theory: Feminist Perspectives,* edited by Uma Narayan and Mary Lyndon Shanley, 48–67. University Park: Pennsylvania State University Press.

———. 1989. "The Project of Feminist Epistemology: Perspectives from a Nonwestern Feminist." In *Gender/Body/Knowledge/Feminist Reconstructions of Being and Knowing,* edited by Alison M. Jaggar and Susan R. Bordo, 256–73. New Brunswick, N.J.: Rutgers University Press.

————. 1998. "Rethinking 'Culture': Gender Essentialism, Cultural Essentialism, and Cultural Relativism." Keynote address, Society for Women in Philosophy Conference Eastern Division, University of New Hampshire, Durham, March 27–29.

Nicholson, Linda, ed. 1990. *Feminism/Postmodernism*. New York: Routledge.

Nicholson, Linda, and Steven Seidman. 1995. *Social Postmodernism: Beyond Identity Politics*. New York: Cambridge University Press.

Nishimoto, Richard S. 1995. *Inside an American Concentration Camp: Japanese American Resistance at Poston, Arizona*. Tucson: University of Arizona Press.

Nozick, Robert. 1974. *Anarchy, State and Utopia*. New York: Basic.

Okihiro, Gary Y. 1996. *Whispered Silences: Japanese Americans and World War II*. Seattle: University of Washington Press.

Okin, Susan Moller, ed. 1999. *Is Multiculturalism Bad for Women?* Princeton: Princeton University Press.

Ollman, Bertell. 1993. *Dialectical Investigations*. New York: Routledge.

Omi, Michael, and Howard Winant. 1994. *Racial Formation in the United States from the 1960s to the 1990s*. New York: Routledge.

Pakaluk, Michael. 1991. *Other Selves: Philosophers on Friendship*. Indianapolis, Ind.: Hackett.

Palanithurai, G. 1991. "Cultural Diversity Uneven Development and Consociational Democracy: Integrative Progress of Quebec in Canada and Tamil Nadu in India." *Indian Journal of Political Science* 52, 2 (April–June): 262–78.

Pateman, Carole. 1979. *The Problem of Political Obligation: A Critique of Liberal Theory*. New York: Wiley.

————. 1989. *The Disorder of Women: Democracy, Feminism, and Political Theory*. Stanford, Calif.: Stanford University Press.

————. 1992. "Equality, Difference, Subordination: The Politics of Motherhood and Women's Citizenship." In *Beyond Equality and Difference: Citizenship, Feminist Politics and Female Subjectivity*, edited by Gisela Bock and Susan James. London: Routledge.

Peltier, Leonard. 1989. "War against the American Nation." In *It Did Happen Here: Recollections and Political Repression in America*, edited by Bud Schultz and Ruth Schultz, 213–29. Berkeley: University of California Press.

Phelan, Shane. 1989. *Identity Politics: Lesbian Feminism and the Limits of Community*. Philadelphia: Temple University Press.

————. 1994. *Getting Specific: Postmodern Lesbian Politics*. Minneapolis: University of Minnesota Press.

Phillips, Anne. 1993. *Democracy and Difference*. University Park: Pennsylvania State University Press.

————. 1995. *The Politics of Presence: Democracy and Group Representation*. New York: Oxford University Press.

Plaskow, Judith. 1991. *Standing Again at Sinai: Judaism from a Feminist Perspective*. San Francisco: Harper San Francisco.

Plato. 1945. *The Republic of Plato*. Translated with introduction and notes by Francis MacDonald Cornford. New York: Oxford.

Pomper, Gerald M. 1992. *Passions and Interests.* Lawrence: University Press of Kansas.

Posner, Rebecca. 1996. "Ashkenazi, Sephardi, Quebecois: Jewish Politics in Multicultural Canada." In *The Narrow Bridge: Jewish Views on Multiculturalism,* edited by Marla Brettschneider, 73–88. New Brunswick, N.J.: Rutgers University Press.

Prell, Riv-Ellen. 1989. *Prayer and Community: The Havurah in American Judaism.* Detroit: Wayne State University Press.

Rawls, John. 1971. *A Theory of Justice.* Cambridge: Belknap Press.

———. 1988. "The Priority of Right and Ideas of the Good." *Philosophy and Public Affairs* 17: 251–76.

Raymond, Janice. 1986. *A Passion for Friends: Toward a Philosophy of Female Affection.* Boston: Beacon Press.

Redd, Spring. 1983. "Something Latino Was Up with Us." In *Home Girls: A Black Feminist Anthology,* edited by Barbara Smith, 52–56. New York: Kitchen Table: Women of Color Press.

Reed, Ishmael, ed. 1997. *Multi-America: Essays on Cultural Wars and Cultural Peace.* New York: Penguin.

Reed, John. 1960. *Ten Days That Shook the World.* Edited by Bertram D. Wolfe. New York: Vintage Books.

———. 1967. *Ten Days That Shook the World.* With an introduction by John Howard Lawson. New York: International Publishers.

Rich, Adrienne. 1980. "Compulsory Heterosexuality and Lesbian Existence." *Signs* 5, 4 (Summer): 631–60.

———. 1986. *Of Woman Born.* Tenth anniversary ed. New York: Norton.

Riley, Denise. 1988. *"Am I That Name?" Feminism and the Category of "Women" in History.* Basingstoke and London: Macmillan.

Robbins, Bruce, ed. 1993. *The Phantom Public Sphere.* Minneapolis: University of Minnesota Press.

Roediger, David. 1994. *Towards the Abolition of Whiteness.* New York: Verso.

Roelofs, H. Mark. 1992. *The Poverty of American Politics: A Theoretical Interpretation.* Philadelphia: Temple University Press.

Rogin, Michael 1996. *Black Face, White Noise: Jewish Immigrants in the Hollywood Melting Pot.* Berkeley: University of California Press.

Rosenblum, Nancy. 1987. *Another Liberalism: Romanticism and the Reconstruction of Liberal Thought.* Cambridge: Harvard University Press.

Rosenthal, Rob. 1993. "Skidding/Coping/Escaping: Constraint, Agency, and Gender in the Lives of Homeless 'Skidders.' " In *Negotiating at the Margins: The Gendered Discourses of Power and Resistance,* edited by Sue Fisher and Kathy Davis, 205–32. New Brunswick, N.J.: Rutgers University Press.

Roof, Judith, and Robyn Wiegman. 1995. *Who Can Speak? Authority and Critical Identity.* Champaign: University of Illinois Press.

Rothman, Stanley, and Robert Lichter. 1982. *The Roots of Radicalism: Jews, Christians, and the New Left.* New York: Oxford University Press.

Rousseau, Jean-Jacques. 1973. *The Social Contract and Discourses*. Translated by G.D.H. Cole. London: Everyman's Library.

Ruddick, Sara. 1989. *Maternal Thinking: Toward a Politics of Peace*. Boston: Beacon Press.

Salinger, Jerome D. 1964. *A Catcher in the Rye*. New York: Bantam Books.

Salisbury, Robert H., John P. Heinze, and Edward O. Laumann. 1987. "Who Works with Whom? Interest Group Alliances and Opposition." *American Political Science Review* 81, 4 (December): 1217–34.

Sandel, Michael. 1982. *Liberalism and the Limits of Justice*. Cambridge: Cambridge University Press.

———. 1984. "The Procedural Republic and the Unencumbered Self." *Political Theory* 12, 2 (February): 81–96.

Sanders, Steve. 1998. "The 'X' Factor: Gay/Lesbian Politics and the Youth Vote." Paper presented at the American Political Science Association Annual Meeting, Boston, September 3–6.

Saragoza, Alex M. 1987. "The Significance of Recent Chicano-Related Historical Writings: An Appraisal." *Ethnic Affairs* (Fall): 24–62.

Saucedo, Dominic. 1996. "Chicanismo, DuBois and Double Consciousness." *Latino Studies Journal* 7, 3 (Fall): 90–101.

Schattschneider, E. E. 1960. *The Semi-Sovereign People*. Hinsdale, Ill.: Dryden Press.

Schlesinger, Arthur M. 1992. *The Disuniting of America: Reflections on a Multicultural Society*. New York and London: Norton.

Schultz, Bud, and Ruth Schultz, eds. 1989. *It Did Happen Here: Recollections of Political Repression in America*. Berkeley: University of California Press.

Scott, Anne Firor, and Andrew Mackay Scott. 1982. *One Half the People: The Fight for Woman Suffrage*. Chicago: University of Illinois Press.

Scott, James C. 1985. *Weapons of the Weak: Of the Everyday Forms of Peasant Resistance*. New Haven: Yale University Press.

Scott, Joan. 1992. "Experience." In *Feminists Theorize the Political*, edited by Judith Butler and Joan Scott, 22–40. New York: Routledge.

Sedgewick, Eve Kosofsky. 1990. *Epistemology of the Closet*. Berkeley: University of California Press.

Seidman, Steven. 1997. *Difference Troubles: Queering Social Theory and Sexual Politics*. New York: Cambridge University Press.

Seif, Hinda. 1999. "A 'Most Amazing Borsht': Multiple Identities in a Jewish Bisexual Community," edited by Marla Brettschneider. *Race, Gender and Class: American Jewish Perspectives* 6, 4: 88–109.

Selsam, Howard, and Harry Martel, eds. 1984. *Reader in Marxist Philosophy from the Writings of Marx, Engels, and Lenin*. New York: International.

Shokeid, Moshe. 1995. *A Gay Synagogue in New York*. New York: Columbia University Press.

Simke, Suzanne. 1989. "A Historiography of Immigrant Women in Nineteenth and Early Twentieth Centuries." *Ethnic Forum* 9, 1–2: 122–45.

Sinclair, Upton. 1965. *The Jungle*. Norwalk, Conn.: Heritage Press.

Skerry, Peter. 1995. *Mexican Americans: The Ambivalent Minority.* Cambridge: Harvard University Press.

Smelser, Neil. 1968. *Essays in Sociological Explanation.* Englewood Cliffs, N.J.: Prentice-Hall.

Smith, Barbara, ed. 1983. *Home Girls: A Black Feminist Anthology.* New York: Kitchen Table: Women of Color Press.

Smith, Raymond. 1998. "'Out' in Numbers: Political Participation in Lesbian-Gay-Bisexual Pride Marches." Paper presented at the American Political Science Association Annual Meeting, Boston, September 3–6.

Spelman, Elizabeth V. 1988. *Inessential Woman: Problems of Exclusion in Feminist Thought.* Boston: Beacon Press.

Sphere Collective. 1995. *The Black Public Sphere.* Chicago: University of Chicago Press

Spitzer, Toba. 1996. "Of Haitana Horseradish." In *The Narrow Bridge: Jewish Views on Multiculturalism,* edited by Marla Brettschneider, 149–60. New Brunswick, N.J.: Rutgers University Press.

Squires, Gregory, D. 1992. *From Redlining to Reinvestment: Community Responses to Urban Disinvestment.* Philadelphia: Temple University Press.

Stack, Carol. 1974. *All Our Kin: Strategies for Survival in a Black Community.* New York: Harper and Row.

Stahl Weinberg, Sidney. 1989. "Longing to Learn: The Education of Jewish Immigrant Women in New York City, 1900–1934." *Journal of Ethnic American History* (Spring): 108–25.

———. 1992. "The Treatment of Women in Immigrant History: A Call for Change." *Journal of American Ethnic History* (Summer): 25–46.

Steinberg, Stephen. 1989. *The Ethnic Myth: Race, Ethnicity and Class in America.* Boston: Beacon Press.

Svonkin, Stuart. 1997. *Jews against Prejudice: American Jews and the Fight for Civil Liberties.* New York: Columbia University Press.

Swain, Carol M. 1993. *Black Faces, Black Interests.* Cambridge: Harvard University Press.

Tamir, Yael. 1993. *Liberal Nationalism.* Princeton: Princeton University Press.

Tate, Claudia, ed. 1983. *Black Women Writers at Work.* New York: Continuum Publishing.

Taylor, Charles. 1979. "Atomism." In *Powers, Possessions and Freedom,* edited by Alkis Kontos, 39–61. Toronto: University of Toronto Press.

———. 1994. *Multiculturalism and "The Politics of Recognition."* Edited by Amy Gutmann. Princeton: Princeton University Press.

Tocqueville, Alexis de. 1994. *Democracy in America.* New York: Knopf.

Torricella, Roberto A., Jr. 1991. "Bablu Aye Is Not Pleased: Majoritarianism and the Erosion of Free Exercise." *University of Miami Law Review* 45, 5: 1061–1107.

Trebilcot, Joyce, ed. 1983. *Mothering: Essays in Feminist Theory.* Tototowa, N.J.: Rowman and Allanheld.

Tronto, Joan. 1993. *Moral Boundaries: A Political Argument for an Ethic of Care.* New York: Routledge, Chapman and Hall.

Truman, David. 1951. *The Governmental Process: Political Interests and Public Opinion*. New York: Knopf.

Tucker, Robert C., ed. 1978. *The Marx-Engels Reader*. 2d ed. New York and London: Norton.

Turner, Frederick Jackson. 1893. "The Significance of the Frontier in American History." Extracted from *Annual Report of the American Historical Association* 18: 197–227.

Vaid, Urvashi. 1996. *Virtual Equality: The Mainstreaming of Gay and Lesbian Liberation*. New York: Anchor/Doubleday.

Valdez, Theresa Arago'n de. 1980. "Organizing as a Political Tool for the Chicana." *Frontiers: A Journal of Women's Studies* 5: 7–13.

Vecchio, Diane C. 1989. "Italian Women in Industry: The Shoeworkers of Endicott, New York, 1914–1935." *Journal of American Ethnic History* 8 (Spring): 60–86.

Villa, Dana R. 1992. "Postmodernism and the Public Sphere." *American Political Science Review* 86, 3 (September): 712–21.

Viorst, Milton. 1979. *Fire in the Streets: America in the 1960s*. New York: Simon and Schuster.

Wagenheim, Kal, and Olga Jimenez de Wagenheim, eds. 1996. *The Puerto Ricans: A Documentary History*. Princeton: Markus Wiener Publishers.

Walch, Timothy, ed. 1994. *Immigrant America: European Ethnicity in the United States*. New York and London: Garland Publishing.

Walker, Alice. 1983. *In Search of Our Mothers' Gardens*. New York: Harcourt Brace Jovanovich.

Walzer, Michael. 1970. *Obligations: Essays on Disobedience, War and Citizenship*. Cambridge: Harvard University Press.

———. 1983. *Spheres of Justice*. New York: Basic Books.

———. 1996. "What Does it Mean to Be An 'American'?" In *The Narrow Bridge: Jewish Views on Multiculturalism*, edited by Marla Brettschneider, 267–86. New Brunswick, NJ: Rutgers University Press.

Waskow, Arthur. 1978. *God-Wrestling*. New York: Schocken Books.

———. 1983. *These Holy Sparks: The Rebirth of the Jewish People*. San Francisco: Harper and Row.

Weeks, Jeffrey. 1990. "The Value of Difference." In *Identity: Community, Culture and Difference*, edited by Jonathan Rutherford. London: Lawrence and Wishart.

Wei, William. 1993. *The Asian American Movement*. Philadelphia: Temple University Press.

Weisen Cook, Blanch. 1977. "Female Support Networks and Political Activism: Lilian Wald, Crystal Eastman, Emma Goldman." *Chrysalis* 3: 43–61.

Weiss, Andrea, and Greta Schiller. 1988. *Before Stonewall: The Making of a Gay and Lesbian Community*. Tallahassee, Fla · Naiad Press.

Weiss, Penny A. 1995. "Feminism and Communitarianism: Comparing Critiques of Liberalism." In *Feminism and Community*, edited by Penny A. Weiss and Marilyn Friedman, 161–86. Philadelphia: Temple University Press.

Weiss, Penny A., and Marilyn Friedman, eds. 1995. *Feminism and Community*. Philadelphia: Temple University Press.

West, Candace, and Sarah Fenstermaker. 1995a. "Doing Difference." *Gender and Society* 9 (February): 8–37.

———. 1995b. "Reply: (Re)Doing Difference." *Gender and Society* 9, 4 (August): 506–13.

West, Cornel. 1993a. *Beyond Eurocentrism and Multiculturalism*. Monroe, Maine: Common Courage Press.

———. 1993b. *Race Matters*. Boston: Beacon Press.

West, Guida, and Rhoda Lois Blumberg. 1990. *Women and Social Protest*. New York: Oxford University Press.

Wheeler, Charlene Eldridge, and Peggy L. Chinn. 1984. *Peace and Power: A Handbook of Feminist Process*. Buffalo, N.Y.: Margaretdaughters.

Wiarda, Howard J. 1997. *Corporatism and Comparative Politics: The Other Great "Ism."* Armonk, N.Y.: M.E. Sharpe.

Williams, Patricia. 1991. *The Alchemy of Race and Rights*. Cambridge: Harvard University Press.

Williams, Walter L. 1988. *The Spirit and the Flesh: Sexual Diversity in American Indian Culture*. Boston: Beacon Press.

X, Malcolm. 1989. *Malcolm X: The Last Speeches*. New York: Pathfinder.

Yanagisako, Sylvia. 1985. *Transforming the Past: Tradition and Kinship among Japanese Americans*. Stanford: Stanford University Press.

Young, Iris Marion. 1987. "Impartiality and the Civic Public: Some Implications of Feminist Critiques of Moral and Political Theory." In *Feminism as Critique*, edited by Seyla Benhabib and Drucilla Cornell. Minneapolis: University of Minnesota Press.

———. 1989. "Polity and Group Difference: A Critique of the Ideal of Universal Citizenship." *Ethics* 99 (January): 250–74.

———. 1990. *Justice and the Politics of Difference*. Princeton: Princeton University Press.

Zack, Naomi. 1995. *American Mixed Race: The Culture of Microdiversity*. Lanham, Md.: Rowman and Littlefield.

Zangwill, Israel. 1975. *The Melting Pot: A Drama in Four Acts*. New York: Arno Press.

Zavella, Patricia. 1987. *Women's Work and Chicano Families: Cannery Workers of the Santa Clara Valley*. Ithaca, N.Y.: Cornell University Press.

Zeman, Zbynek A. B. 1969. *Prague Spring*. New York: Hill and Wang.

Zerubavel, Yael. 1995. *Recovered Roots: Collective Memory and the Making of Israeli National Tradition*. Chicago: University of Chicago Press.

Zinn, Howard. 1990. *A People's History of the United States*. New York: Harper-Collins.

Zunz, Olivier. 1982. *The Changing Face of Inequality: Urbanization, Industrial Development, and Immigrants in Detroit, 1880–1920*. Chicago: University of Chicago Press.

Index